Communities of Practice in World Politics

By defining international communities of practice (CoPs) as domains of knowledge, this book investigates the adoption of new international practices via *collective learning*—that is, the redefinition of what is acceptable and feasible. Explaining how inclusive practices at the World Bank became institutionalized, it shows that while changes in presidents can influence practices of international organizations, shifts in collective thinking are even more important to understand world ordering.

Collective learning happens at the boundaries between CoPs when practitioners interact with others inside or outside the formal walls of an organization—through processes of boundary encounters, boundary brokering, and the use of epistemic boundary objects. Since the 1980s, despite stability in their technocratic political rationality, World Bank employees arranged in CoPs collectively learned that program ownership and consultation in policymaking were more effective than top-down practices. However, while learning that more democratic practices rendered their projects and policies more effective, Bank employees did not fully challenge colonial epistemic hierarchies in North South relations. This CoP framework draws from, combines, and extends various strands of cutting-edge IR scholarship (i.e., practice-oriented and constructivist IR), management theory (communities of practice), organizational studies (narratives and day-to-day procedures), as well as development and critical studies (feminist and decoloniality approaches).

This book will be of interest not only to scholars and students interested in IR theory, international organizations, development practices, and social theory but also to development workers and anyone interested in global governance.

Maïka Sondarjee is an associate professor at the School of International Development and Global Studies at the University of Ottawa. Her research addresses communities of practice, the coloniality of power in global governance, the marginalization of feminist and Global South research in IR, as well as inclusive development at the World Bank. She has published in outlets such as *International Studies Quarterly, Third World Quarterly, Millenium, Global Society, International Journal, International Studies Perspectives,* and *Global Studies Quarterly.*

Global Governance

Series Editor: John J. Kirton

University of Toronto, Canada

Global governance is growing rapidly to meet the compounding challenges of a globalized 21st-century world. Many issues once dealt with largely at the local, national or regional level are now going global, in the economic, social and political-security domains. In response, new and renewed intergovernmental institutions are arising and adapting, multilevel governance is expanding, and sub-national actors are playing a greater role, creating complex combinations and private-partnerships to this end.

This series focuses on the new dynamics of global governance in the 21st century by:

- Addressing the changes in the structure, operation and impact of individual intergovernmental institutions, above all their innovative responses to the growing global challenges they confront.
- Exploring how they affect, are affected by and relate to non-state actors of global relevance and reach.
- Examining the processes of cooperation, competition and convergence among international institutions and the many global governance gaps where global challenges such as terrorism, transnational crime and energy do not confront powerful international institutions devoted to their control.
- Dealing with how global institutions govern the links among key issues such as climate change and health.

In all cases, the series focuses on the central questions of how global governance institutions and processes generate the effective, legitimate, accountable results required to govern today's interconnected, complex, uncertain and crisis-ridden world.

Communities of Practice in World Politics
Collective Learning, Contestation and Coloniality at the World Bank
Maïka Sondarjee

For more information about this series, please visit: www.routledge.com/Global-Governance/book-series/ASHSER1420

Communities of Practice in World Politics

Collective Learning, Contestation and Coloniality at the World Bank

Maïka Sondarjee

Routledge
Taylor & Francis Group
LONDON AND NEW YORK

First published 2025
by Routledge
4 Park Square, Milton Park, Abingdon, Oxon OX14 4RN

and by Routledge
605 Third Avenue, New York, NY 10158

Routledge is an imprint of the Taylor & Francis Group, an informa business

British Library Cataloguing-in-Publication Data
A catalogue record for this book is available from the British Library

ISBN: 978-1-032-78922-4 (hbk)
ISBN: 978-1-032-86804-2 (pbk)
ISBN: 978-1-003-52927-9 (ebk)

DOI: 10.4324/9781003529279

Typeset in Times New Roman
by Apex CoVantage, LLC

Contents

Acronyms

Bank	World Bank
CoPs	Communities of Practice
IMF	International Monetary Fund
IR	International Relations
NGO	Non-governmental organization
OHP	Oral History Project
PEAP	Poverty Eradication Action Plan
PFP	Policy framework paper
PRSP	Poverty reduction strategy paper
UK	United Kingdom
UN	United Nations
UNDP	United Nations Development Program
US	United States
WDR	World Development Report

Figures

Acknowledgments

"If you are relatively untalented, as I am, you can make up a good deal of the difference simply by giving more time to your chosen endeavor than others do and sticking with it through the difficult patches."[1] The writing of the following pages was a long journey, but thankfully not a lonely one. My first and most sincere thanks go to my doctoral advisor, mentor, and friend, Emanuel Adler. An intellectual inspiration and an indefectible supporter, Manolo's consideration of my work and my ideas was invaluable. With kindness, availability, and thought-provoking advice, he helped me sharpen my thinking and provided an example of what I wish to become as a scholar. A great deal of appreciation also goes to Steven Bernstein, Jacqueline Best, Niklas Bremberg, Christian Bueger, Jérémie Cornut, Matthew Hoffmann, Maren Hofius, Markus Kornprobst, Deepak Nair, Vincent Pouliot, Christian Reus-Smit, Ole Jacob Sending, Jean-Philippe Thérien, and Wendy Wong for their constructive criticisms on various drafts of this research. Thanks also to Dominique Caouette for his unconditional academic and personal support over the past 15 years and to Kari Polanyi-Levitt for her intellectual inspiration and friendship along this journey. I am also thankful to everyone who agreed to speak to me for this book. From World Bank vice presidents to managing directors, staff in country teams, and NGO workers, they gave me their time and invaluable insights on development policies and practices. Their intricate knowledge of the world they live in led to the following pages. I hope to have merited their trust.

Thanks also to the participants of the 2018 workshop on cognitive evolution at the Vienna School of Public Policy (Vienna), the participants of the 2020 workshop Practice Theory in International Relations (Reykjavik), as well as the organizers of the workshop on New Voices in International Practice Research (Copenhagen) and of the workshop on practices of inclusion in global governance (Berlin) for inviting me to participate in their communities of practice. Thanks to the journal editors who let me reproduce parts of my work published in their journals (*Third World Quarterly*, *Global Society,* and *Global Studies Quarterly*) and the editors of the volume *Cognitive Evolution and World Ordering: Opening New Vistas* (CUP). Thanks to all the participants of the Special Issue on Communities of Practice I co-edited in 2024 at *Global Studies Quarterly*, which advances this important theoretical agenda. A special thanks to my co-editors Niklas and Emanuel, who gracefully finished the copyediting while I was on maternal leave.

Writing a book is not a small affair, intellectually and personally. My gratitude also goes to colleagues and friends who walked with me along the way, whose comments and encouragement enabled me to keep going with this research. Among others, and probably with many omissions: Zak Black, Adam Casey, Alice Chessé, Lucas Dolan, Kirstyn Hevey, Dan Hutton Ferris, Lennart Maschmeyer, Christian Pépin, Simon Pratt, Lou Pingeot, Alain Savard, Tayla Smith, and Jason Vanden-Beukel. Chris LaRoche, especially, was a tremendous help during this entire writing period. Thanks to my amazing research assistants, Clothilde Parent-Chartier, Ghadir Salame and Janyck Beaulieu, who helped me finish parts of this book.

Last but not least, thanks to my family for their support on this journey. They did not always understand where this was going, but they never let me down. The reproductive work of my mother and my grandmothers has been especially significant in enabling me to write the following pages. In particular, thanks to my partner, Jonathan Durand Folco, for inspiring me intellectually on a daily basis and for pushing me to new boundaries and challenges—the last of which being called Aïna Sondarjee Folco.

Note

1 Giddens and Pierson, *Conversation with Anthony Giddens*, 39.

Speeches

Clausen, Alden. "Progress and Innovation." Address to the Board of Governors at the Annual Meetings of the World Bank and IMF, Washington, DC, September 27, 1983, 16–18.

Conable, Barber. "To the Board of Governors." Address to the Board of Governors at the Annual Meetings of the World Bank and IMF, Washington, DC, September 30, 1986, 32–36.

Conable, Barber. "To the Board of Governors." Address to the Board of Governors at the Annual Meetings of the World Bank and IMF, Berlin, September 27, 1988, 68.

Preston, Lewis. "Opening Remarks." Address to the Board of Governors at the Annual Meetings of the World Bank and IMF, Washington, DC, October 15, 1991, 8.

Stern, Nicholas. "A Strategy for Development." Speech at People's University, Beijing, June 2001, 19; Interview 20, July 17, 2017.

Wolfensohn, James. "New Directions and New Partnerships." Address to the Board of Governors at the Annual Meetings of the World Bank and IMF, Washington, DC, October 10, 1995, 8.

Wolfensohn, James. "The Challenge of Inclusion." Address to the Board of Governors at the Annual Meetings of the World Bank and IMF, Washington, DC, September 23, 1997, 6.

Wolfensohn, James. "The Other Crisis." Address to the Board of Governors at the Annual Meetings of the World Bank and IMF, Washington, DC, October 6, 1998, 116.

Wolfensohn, James. "A Proposal for a Comprehensive Development Framework." Address to the Board of Governors at the Annual Meetings of the World Bank and IMF, Washington, DC, January 21, 1999.

Wolfensohn, James. "Scaling Up the Fight Against Poverty." Opening Remarks at the Shanghai Conference on Scaling Up Poverty Reduction, Shanghai, May 26, 2004.

Wolfensohn, James. "Securing the 21st Century, Protecting the Planet." Address to the Board of Governors at the Annual Meetings of the World Bank and IMF, Washington, DC, October 3, 2004.

Wolfowitz, Paul. "Charting a Way Ahead – The Results Agenda." Address to the Board of Governors at the Annual Meetings of the World Bank and IMF, Washington, DC, September 24, 2005, 3.

Wolfowitz, Paul. "Improving Governance and Fighting Corruption." Keynote Speech, International Conference on Improving Governance and Fighting Corruption, Brussels, March 14, 2007, 2.

Zoellick, Robert. "Opening Remarks." Address to the Board of Governors at the Annual Meetings of the World Bank and IMF, Washington, DC, October 22, 2007, 2.

Zoellick, Robert. "The World Bank Group Beyond the Crisis." Address to the Board of Governors at the Annual Meetings of the World Bank and IMF, Istanbul, October 6–7, 2009.

Zoellick, Robert. "From Hubris to Humility." Speech at Georgetown University, 2010, 18.

1 Introduction

The principles by which international actors are arranged is one of the most fundamental questions in the field of International Relations (IR): "What makes the world hang together?"[1] More than 40 years ago, Kenneth Waltz's answer to that question became famous: international systems are decentralized and anarchic in comparison to centralized and hierarchical domestic systems. The anarchic character of the international realm became one of Western IR scholars' most widely shared assumptions, implying that units are "functionally undifferentiated."[2] Recent theoretical developments instead theorize world politics as relations of super- and subordination hierarchies,[3] a core–periphery order,[4] patterns of authority relationships beyond states,[5] or relations of authority, domination, and resistance.[6] In short, for an increasing number of IR scholars, hierarchical structuring principles "produce the boundaries that define who and what belongs where in world politics."[7]

However, a great deal of world politics can be explained by what exists between anarchy and formally layered hierarchies, that is, structures of authority, inequality, and rules produced and reproduced through practices. International practices, as meaningful actions based on collectively shared background knowledge, do not float around. Social practices are circumscribed by domains of knowledge and enacted by practitioners organized in these "communities of practices." Building on Étienne Wenger's[8] work in management theory and Emanuel Adler's[9] concept of cognitive evolution in IR, international communities of practice (CoPs) are domains of knowledge in which practitioners are bounded by like-mindedness, engagement in joint meaningful actions, and share a repertoire of tools, concepts, and actions. More than a mere group of people acting collectively, CoPs are the "*social fabric of relations in action.*"[10] As such, they make the world hang together.

CoPs are intersubjective social structures that constitute the normative and epistemic ground for action, but they are also agents made up of real people who make things happen in the world.[11] As domains of knowledge, CoPs are the perfect concept to study world ordering through collective learning, or the redefinition of consensual knowledge about reality. Collective learning happens when community members are confronted with contestation or different ways of doing things at the boundaries with other communities. In other words, practitioners constantly modify their shared understandings about how the world works and what we should do about it by interacting with people who have other ways of doing things. In those

DOI: 10.4324/9781003529279-1

liminal spaces where differences interact, individuals arranged in social groups within a domain of knowledge negotiate meaning and confront different cognitive and normative understandings of their practices. While the literature on contestation in global governance has focused on individual norm entrepreneurs and normative changes,[12] the cognitive learning process studied in this book does not happen only through individuals' agency but as a social phenomenon when a community gradually alters its practice due to the evolution of collectively shared assumptions.

Furthermore, while principal-agent approaches to organizations have pointed at external demands for change, organizational sociologists have distinguished between external and internal factors to theorize endogenous incremental change and problematize the black box of organizations.[13] They have analytically separated culture (from within) and rational pressure (from outside). However, in management sociologies, *boundary spaces* are recognized as spaces where change is likely: this is where differences collapse to create newness.[14] If one agrees with both organizational sociologists about endogenous change and with boundary theorists about change due to interactions of differences, there may be something more to say about international organizations (IOs) when we deconstruct what happens inside of them in various interacting fields of knowledge.

The contribution of a collective learning approach in the CoP literature is to examine sites where learning occurs most: boundaries between communities, which can be endogenous to an organization or transcend its formal walls. For example, a trans-organization working group on intellectual property can interact with the World Health Organization's Bolivian country team in a way that promotes change for both communities. This book is interested in those in-between spaces where knowledge is transformed. If borders are lines, boundaries are liminal spaces where differences interact.[15] Exploring both in the case of Norway and Russia after the invasion of Ukraine in 2022, Nina Græger examines practitioners' engagement in formal and informal boundary-crossing practices at international borders in times of conflict.[16] In short, identities are formed and transformed during social interactions at the boundaries.[17] I define three processes of interaction in those meso spaces: boundary encounters, the use of boundary objects, and boundary brokering, which are all mediated through contestation and epistemic power struggles regarding who can define new tools, concepts, or procedures.

Epistemic power, or the authority to validate, confirm, or formulate new knowledge,[18] should be understood as the power to establish valid epistemes and voices. It often acts as a reproductive mechanism of existing modes of thought,[19] and, in the case of development practices, contributes to the reproduction of a colonial or white gaze.[20] While looking at all forms of meaning contestation, this book also acknowledges the racial and colonial underpinnings of interactions to complement research on multilateral practices that avoid mentioning race or colonial legacy.[21] Following Junru Bian,[22] Stephen Pampinella,[23] and Deepak Nair,[24] for example, I believe that international practices need to be analyzed through the lenses of coloniality of power and racial hierarchies. By doing so, I integrate for the first-time research on epistemic violence and coloniality of power by Global South scholars into the IR literatures on international practices and CoPs. If the most fundamental international hierarchies were arguably established through colonization, colonial/racialized processes still affect the attribution of epistemic validity. I posit that day-to-day international practices exemplify these processes. This book looks at an attempt to dismantle (at least partly) formal epistemic hierarchies to integrate new actors into multilateral policymaking.

The World Bank Since 1980

Following the large infrastructure projects it undertook in the 1950s and 1960s, the Bank[25] focused on macroeconomic issues and poverty in the 1970s and on structural adjustment in the 1980s. The structural adjustment programs, based on macroeconomic stability and technocratic solutions to development, were also (though not always) top-down and often one-size-fits-all neoliberal policy packages based on the expertise of Bank economists. Since the mid-1990s, the authority of Bank employees has eroded because of the perceived failures of the structural adjustment strategy and dissatisfaction with Bank employees' condescension, which prompted them to explore ways to include dissenting voices in their practice. The Bank asked borrowing governments to participate in developing structural adjustment plans, mobilized non-governmental organizations (NGOs) to advise on social issues, and consulted populations for data collection and project implementation.

All the staff and senior officials at the Bank interviewed for this research agreed that the 1980s failed to trigger long-term development or growth. As a former vice president explained, "No matter how you look at it, from a development perspective, it was a failure."[26] While many observers have written about the "failure of conditionality,"[27] this former Bank leader noted that, due to the increasing criticisms in the 1980s and 1990s, the organization "could not do business as usual."[28] Bank employees were neither deaf nor blind to criticisms to other organizations' successful practices, waiting for a superior to instruct them to change their practices. Change happened in multiple settings, and CoPs around and within the Bank were paving the way for new practices to emerge.

From the late 1980s to the 2010s, many Bank employees shifted from believing that expertise from outside the aid-targeted community was the only credible source with which to build development programs and policies (expert-led practices) to recognizing the knowledge and ownership within aid-targeted communities (inclusive practices). This is not to suggest that recipients' priorities were entirely disregarded in the 1980s, that consultation never occurred, or that variations between contexts did not exist.[29] The Bank's policymaking has always been a complex matrix of feedback between "top-down" central prescriptions and more dynamic, even "inclusive" negotiations with policymakers in recipient countries. What is new in the period under consideration is the degree to which the Bank explicitly grapples with problems of participation. Large-scale consultations, government ownership, and participatory methodologies were mainstreamed. Furthermore, while service-oriented NGOs have been a part of the Bank's practices since the 1970s, advocacy NGOs and civil society groups from the Global South have historically been excluded from it.

This shift does not imply that borrowing governments were suddenly "in the driving seat" of externally funded policies, as many Bank leaders hoped. Furthermore, given that the Bank was lending approximately $20 billion annually in that period, inclusive practices represented a tiny portion of the Bank's portfolio. For those reasons, this research does not suggest to a paradigm shift influencing all the communities and departments within the Bank. However, despite well-founded criticisms about the extent to which power was transferred between the Bank and borrowing countries,[30] the data from this research demonstrates that the adoption of inclusive practices was a meaningful change to Bank practitioners and many aid-targeted populations. A discussion paper registering the opinions of dozens of civil society organizations and NGOs in the 2000s noted that, while the content of the Bank's policies remained broadly consistent over time, there had been "significant breaks with the past" regarding policy formulation.[31] While it did not trigger a major shift like the one from infrastructure to macroeconomic policy in the 1970s, inclusive practices changed how World Bank employees collectively understood policymaking practices. In less than ten years, social development professionals went from outcast to making participatory development a requirement in many instances.[32]

Most importantly, learning about procedural practices of inclusion improved the effectiveness of Bank policies (even if they seldom changed the policies themselves). As one country manager explained, when her team began to sit down and consult with targeted populations to talk about poverty, they started to redefine terms and measurement criteria; this taught her "simple things like how much a mother can spend on batteries. And you'll see in the report, they look at things like batteries. Something I might not have thought of, but it measures poverty!"[33] In sub-Saharan Africa, a series of participatory poverty assessments were implemented in the late 1990s in Zambia, Mali, Ghana, and Nigeria, which identified new variables to define poverty. For example, consulted populations listed geographical isolation and lack of access to water as concerns, which led the Bank to identify new priorities.[34] Redefining poverty in such a way is a challenging change, and it took decades of learning about new concepts, routines, and tools that rendered Bank projects and policies more effective.

This inclusion of a larger number of stakeholders in Bank policymaking practices expanded the mandate of the Bank but complicated its power over projects and policies. As one Bank manager stated in the World Bank's *Participation Sourcebook*, through participation, Bank teams often lose " 'control' of the project."[35] It is unclear why the Bank or member states would adopt practices that complicate their control over their projects, cost much more money, take more time, and have uncertain effects on effectiveness. First, participatory projects, the delegation of control to borrowing governments, and consultation with NGOs all create unknown outcomes. Greater inclusion reduces the control by managers (and member states) over the elaboration and the outcomes of projects and policies. Second, the inclusion of more stakeholders requires additional resources from top-down policymaking. On average, participatory projects cost 10–15 percent more than non-participatory ones, with the most expensive element being the salary of employees with expertise in participation.[36] Third, consulting with other stakeholders may change the planned course of events, causing delays in the completion of projects or the adoption of policies. An internal World Bank evaluation in 1994 uncovered that employees' supervision of regular projects took only two-thirds of the time required for a participatory project.[37]

To this day, the value of consulting with NGOs or communities is still very much debated.[38] Some scholars argued that authoritarian regimes that rule without input from their populations had triggered economic growth more effectively than democratic governments.[39] Teresa Kramarz also argues that partnerships between the World Bank and private actors have generally not fulfilled their promises.[40] One senior Bank official interviewed for this research still disagrees with the new focus on consulting with NGOs, stating that the Bank's mandate is to work with governments and that including all stakeholders is a "poor substitute for democratic functions."[41] According to her, the Bank's role is to strengthen civil societies' capacity to lobby governments rather than to replace governments, which should be the ones consulting with their populations.

Another puzzle at the center of this book is that the Bank has indeed been criticized for its lack of responsiveness and accountability, but why were *these* criticisms heard while *others* were not? For example, the Bank has been condemned since the 1980s for promoting macroeconomic neoliberal prescriptions, but the organization still supports liberalization, privatization, and macroeconomic stability. In short, external (or internal) contestation of an organization's ways of doing is important but insufficient for practices to evolve. In this case, bank employees learned that inclusive practices were more effective because other communities set inspiring examples; they learned in the boundary spaces with other CoPs. Moreover, as will be explored in the conclusion, new proposed practices were easily translatable through the Bank's political rationality because it fits how the Bank defined effectiveness.

Because this book is aimed at theory-building in the CoP literature, the chosen case study is an ideal type of practice change. While most observers remain critical as to the extent to which this move toward greater inclusion triggered *substantive* changes in the macroeconomic policies promoted at the Bank, there is no doubt that there were *procedural* changes since the 1980s (how they design those policies). Accordingly, this book focuses on changes in the procedures of policy formulation (which changed in many ways) instead of changes to the content of the economic prescriptions (which arguably remained similar). As will be explored in the conclusion, the fact that the Bank is considered more effective today (regarding both social acceptability and measurable outcomes), despite supporting the same macroeconomic policies, underscores the importance of viewing change and stability as part of the same process. While the case of inclusive practices at the Bank is not understudied *per se*, it remains a significant one in international development. The emergence and institutionalization of inclusive practices are one of the most significant new sets of practices in global governance, having affected how development institutions deal with borrowing governments and NGOs and determining which stakeholders deserve a seat at the table. As a knowledge institution, the World Bank still has a tremendous impact not only in countries where they manage projects but on development thinking as a whole. Chapter 3 will explore to what extent the Bank has changed.

In short, Bank employees collectively recognized that inclusive practices were more effective of projects and policies. But how? Bank employees, arranged in various domains of knowledge, collectively learned that inclusive practices were more effective than top-down expert-led ones; they redefined the appropriate means to reach their goals. Bank employees adopted inclusive mechanisms, concepts, and tools that they considered more "effective" than those from a top-down, expert-led mentality. Effectiveness here refers to producing the intended result or doing the right/adequate thing to obtain a desired outcome. If it does not address the goals themselves or the core precepts of the development project, which are arguably very similar today to those of the 1980s, Bank various communities of practice redesigned what was needed *to accomplish these stated goals*.

To claim that inclusive practices are "more effective" would be trivial; other authors have already argued that such practices were adopted to respond to previous failures.[42] Additionally, criteria for effectiveness evolve over time. This book thus explores how Bank staff *changed their perceptions* of which practices were effective in achieving their goals. The following pages do not answer the question of "why inclusive practices were adopted" (because they were more effective), but "how Bank employees learned that inclusive practices were more effective than expert-led top-down ones." The answer is that Bank employees changed their perceptions by interacting with other CoPs. As a result, they redefined their understanding of what they should do and how they should act to achieve specific goals. Like Jacqueline Best's 2014 study on "governing failure," this case focuses on techniques that increase chances of success and, like Susan Park and Antje Vetterlein,[43] how policy failures can lead to change. This book starts with the same intention of understanding the emergence of new practices in IOs. However, it complements these studies by not focusing on *why* the Bank adopted inclusive practices (because of previous failures or to expand their mandate) but by examining at the process of *how* the organization came to interpret inclusive practices as more effective, and how coloniality of power mediated this process. A collective learning approach is based on the cognitive processes leading the Bank's CoPs to collectively learn that inclusive practices are a productive tool to increase effectiveness and minimize failure, that is, to achieve their goals. While not every failure leads to change, the processes detailed in the following chapters amounted to a point where communities inside the Bank could no longer do business as usual.

Studying CoP to explain world ordering

Rationalist explanations of IOs' practices (and thus world orders) focus on state preferences. Many still argue, for example, that states utilize IOs to manage their interactions. Even if they can create norms or use persuasion, IOs mostly do so to enable states to achieve preferred ends.[44] Rationalist scholars studying the Bank often see the organization as an extended arm of the United States.[45] States can indeed influence the Bank's political orientations, push organizations to perform better, appoint presidents, or advance certain "high politics" foreign policy goals, such as when the United States prevented the Bank from lending to Vietnam in the 1960s, or when France advocated for more lending to French-speaking West Africa.[46] Based on rationalist premises, principal-agent theories acknowledge more autonomy to IOs but still attribute significant shifts in them to states' interests.[47] Change for rationalists is thus exogenous, rare, and mostly discrete in time.

In response to this overreliance on external factors, organizational sociologists in IR have explained the emergence of new practices as a matter of organizational culture: embedded ideologies, norms, and routines that govern the expectations and behaviors of bureaucrats.[48] These approaches, like the one developed in this book, focus on how individuals working within organizations interpret and negotiate the meaning of their mandates, instructions, and guidelines through their organizational culture.[49] They have developed a much-needed explanation of organizations' adaptation to their environment. The most-cited work in this trend remains Michael Barnett and Martha Finnemore, who explain IOs' institutional autonomy via the delegation of powers from states to international bureaucrats.[50]

Most organizational sociologists distinguish between two levels of analysis. After acknowledging the *external* influence of member states on IOs actions and policies, they explain how the *internal* bureaucratic culture produces changes in routines and actions. The internal examination at bureaucratic culture leads to an understanding of microchanges, however, due to the stability of culture, it leads many organizational sociologists to emphasize the development of pathologies[51] or to argue that change in IOs is elusive.[52] Despite the analytical usefulness of separating the two levels of analysis, the interactions of Bank employees with external actors are crucial to understanding changes in internal practices. This is why this book looks at the interactions between CoPs within and outside an IO.

Norm-oriented frameworks argue that the Bank adopted inclusive practices because norm entrepreneurs advocated for new standards of behavior that were more conducive to "doing the right thing." Early norm approaches, still best epitomized by the norm life cycle,[53] the spiral model,[54] or the boomerang effect,[55] assumed a linear and unidirectional process of norm emergence, travel, and internalization. While these early norm scholars were criticized for focusing on static norms,[56] critical norm literature has developed more complex frameworks of translation and contestation to explain the evolution of normative structures.[57] Antje Wiener's norm contestedness theory rightly focuses on contestation as a meta-organizing principle instead of a time-bounded event. However, she focuses on *individual* norm entrepreneurs contesting *normative structures* (not collectively held cognitive knowledge).[58] Similarly, Martha Finnemore points to the influence of Bank presidents (notably Robert McNamara) as leading advocates of normative change at the Bank in the 1970s.[59] Focusing on individual entrepreneurs cannot explain why new practices emerge simultaneously at a smaller scale in multiple sectors and locations.

Ontologies based on individual entrepreneurs would dismiss the fact that inclusive practices emerged as early as the mid-1980s in many different Bank country teams (e.g., Bolivia, Philippines, Uganda), with many different advocates (e.g.,

Michael Cernea, Robert Chambers, Deepa Narayan), and even before the Bank's ninth President James Wolfensohn, considered the main advocate for inclusive practices, was appointed Bank president in 1995. While the approach developed in this book underlines the influence of powerful managers as boundary *brokers*, it focuses on the social embeddedness of all individual actors in boundary *brokering*, even the most powerful ones. In short, when individuals enact a practice, they can never separate themselves from intersubjectively held cognitive assumptions, yet they can enact creativity through collectively held knowledge.[60]

This book is more inclined to agree with recent research on normativity in practice. Critical constructivist or pragmatist norm research has redefined norms as "rarely consistent, singular social things," viewing them instead as "entangled, often internally inconsistent arrays of practices and standards, undergoing ongoing revision and contestation by the people enacting them."[61] For normativity-in-practice scholars, norms are also always "in use." Practice-oriented scholars like Simon Pratt attempt to de-reify norms by analyzing the embodiment of normativity in action or "normative configurations,"[62] and others like Sebastian Schmidt study how intersubjective creativity in action can lead to transformation in notions of appropriate behavior.[63] Like them, this book sees change in world politics through the interconnections between normativity and action,[64] and between normativity and power.[65]

This book thus confirms and extends many of the insights of scholars of IOs and NGOs in IR, development studies, and institutional change. While acknowledging that the Bank's member states impact broad policy orientations, it focuses on processes of collective learning that happen in parallel to such a causal impact. Moreover, while studying the impact of individual norm entrepreneurs on practices can be analytically useful, it investigates learning as a collective process to emphasize the interaction between our individual consciousness and our participation in collectivities. Additionally, in a collective learning framework, contestation (normative or otherwise) is not merely a phase in a process[66] or individually and discursively triggered.[67] The data collected for this research instead shows that contestation is a social, generative, multidirectional, and continuous process. Like institutional change scholars,[68] this book asserts that practices are never adopted once and for all; they are continuously contested and evolving.

This book primarily aims to contribute to the literature in IR about international practices as meaningful patterns of action. Over the past ten years, scholars in IR, especially constructivist ones,[69] have studied meaningful patterns of actions as essential processes in world politics. Practice-oriented scholars have studied diplomacy, piracy, security, deterrence, media publishing, European Union practices, regionalism, international negotiations, peacekeeping, sovereignty, and international intervention, among other subjects. Some scholars have focused on hierarchies in fields of action,[70] on how individual practitioners build on their background knowledge to act,[71] and on different types of practices, such as interstitial actions.[72] It must be noted that before practice-oriented literature was dubbed the "practice turn" in IR, feminist scholars were already studying the everyday practices that sustain international relations, such as militarization,[73] sexual,[74] nuclear,[75] or academic practices.[76] Lauren Wilcox, for example, explores how Judith Butler's work on competent performance has been surprisingly overlooked by practice researchers in IR.[77]

While individualistic frameworks have traditionally dominated IR, practice-oriented scholars have emphasized collective background knowledge, shared tools and mechanisms, and mutual recognition of competence.[78] While all praxeologies are about social relations, more robust pragmatist relational understandings of practices have solidified around the concept of communities of practice (CoPs). With such a social ontology, CoP scholars have deepened our understandings of, for example, diplomacy, international security, military attachés, and European CoPs. For example, Christian Bueger[79] analyzed pirates' grand narrative as collectively held beliefs; Niklas Bremberg[80] presented the European Union as a security community-building institution; Thomas Kwasi Tieku and Afua Boatemaa Yakohene look at informality in shared practices at the African Union[81]; Maren Hofius[82] analyzed communities' shared (and differentiated) sense of belonging; and I studied feminist scholars in IR as a CoP rather than members of a shared theoretical paradigm.[83] Federica Bicchi[84] defined CoPs as bonding through a shared sense of timing, placing, and humor. Strangely, while development scholars have studied policymaking and project-development practices for decades, the World Bank and development practices, in general, are an understudied case in the practice-oriented literature in IR, which has heavily focused on diplomatic and security practices. This book seeks to open new empirical doors for IR scholars interested in contributing to the CoP literature and exploring collective learning.

Practice-oriented scholars in IR examine how meaningful patterns of actions structure social orders. They define social orders as sets of practices and CoPs; social orders are made of interactions, negotiations, and political agreements, all nexus of practices.[85] These dynamics occur in the interstices of hierarchies and what gives order to perceived anarchy. For practice-oriented scholars, global governance consists of such social orders: "landscapes,"[86] "constellations,"[87] "collections,"[88] or "fields"[89] of practices and CoPs (or domains of knowledge). International practices (and the social configurations they are embedded in) are the social fabric of world politics; they make the world hand together. Intersubjective understandings enacted in actions give order to the social world and sustain global governance, that is, what is structuring the international. Though largely overlooked, this structuring process is mediated through colonial epistemic inequalities, which easily appear in day-to-day practices.

A focus on international CoPs aims to explain *social ordering* processes instead of looking at substantive social orders. The focus is, therefore, on how and why specific configurations of meaningful performances organize world politics and how these configurations—and the collective meanings associated with them—evolve over time. All CoP theorists believe that like-mindedness and shared endeavors are the rule and not the exception in world politics and that practical interactions structure social ordering. However, a focus on collective learning enables an understanding of the intricacies of meaning-making in those domains of knowledge and how those interactions are soaked in coloniality of power. This book illustrates how the coloniality of epistemic power functions.

From a Bourdieusian standpoint, Vincent Pouliot defines international pecking orders as overlapping fields of meaningful practices organized hierarchically through conflict.[90] In his work on cognitive evolution and social ordering, Emanuel Adler adds to this theorization of the "hardware" of global governance a vision of its software, that is, sites of negotiation of meaning and competence.[91] By agreeing that interactions rather than "decisions" structure the world, they both understand social ordering through practices. Vertical hierarchies between actors (the hardware, as conceptualized by Bourdieusian scholars) act in conjunction with horizontal systems of rules and knowledge (software, best represented by CoPs scholars). Vertical and horizontal systems of power and rules are not mutually exclusive but interact with each other like a computer's software and hardware. One does not preclude the other. Looking at day-to-day interactions structured in CoPs does not mean that hierarchies or power differentials cease to exist but that negotiation in action is the basis of social order(ing). Similarly, formal hierarchies between multilateral actors (e.g., the World Bank) and aid-targeted groups (e.g., Global South NGOs) act in conjunction with informal systems of authority, inequality, and rules, including epistemic power.

A theory of collective learning through CoPs

A theory of collective learning through CoPs in IOs looks at how embodied activities lead to the "acquisition, maintenance, and transformation of knowledge through processes of social interaction."[92] To achieve this, this book focuses on CoPs and the boundaries between them as sites where differences interact, leading to the transformation of collectively held perception of reality. In those non-geographical areas, practitioners with different background knowledge interact and negotiate knowledge. A framework of collective learning at the boundaries, that is, the modification of collectively held cognitive assumptions, will enable a processual/relational understanding of practice change in communities and of coloniality of power through inclusive practices. There is no linearity or chronology between the different collective learning processes detailed in the next pages (encounters between communities, boundary brokering, and the use of epistemic boundary objects).

It is noteworthy that a collective learning framework cannot predict why one outcome occurred and *not others*. The goal of IR theory should not be a prediction of matters in global governance but an explanation. Ultimately, prediction in open systems is almost impossible.[93] Stating that the emergence and institutionalization of inclusive practices were primarily due to collective learning processes thus does not mean that this is the only possible outcome or that collective learning is the only *explanan*. Observers cannot predict change in practice, as they happen in a creative, contingent process.[94] A theoretical framework of collective learning thus explains *how* an outcome happened rather than *why* this outcome happened.

If practitioners in various CoPs learned that inclusive practices increased the effectiveness of projects and policies, it would be too bold to argue that learning was the only factor for the adoption of new practices. The emergence of inclusive practices cannot be explained solely by the processes described in this book; various factors were necessary, such as the composition of borrowing countries' governments and central banks and increasing capacity in those countries. Environmental factors, normative changes, and rational decisions by member states also influenced the change's direction, timing, and extent. Nonetheless, the approach developed in this book points to crucial processes of social change that are sometimes downplayed in IR theory or considered self-explanatory: "Of course, people learn! But isn't this outcome caused by this other more important variable [read: rational decision, a new leader, or a new norm]?" However, this is how day-to-day practices work, according to most people interviewed for this research: you do your job day after day, you encounter difficulties, and, often, you fail to resolve them. You then try something else and fail again. Eventually, you find a way to make your practice more effective, or you drop existing practices altogether.

In that sense, a collective learning framework complements previous bodies of literature by focusing on the intricacies of *how* practice change happens. Collective learning processes led Bank employees in many communities to perceive inclusive practices as more effective than purely expert-led ones. While inclusive practices were not objectively or intrinsically more effective, they came to be *considered* more effective than solely expert-based policymaking and other potential practices. This new perception was more readily accepted because inclusive practices fit into the Bank's overall ethos and existing sets of practices without challenging its ontological security. Alternative practices, such as redistributing its funds to civil society organizations or changing macroeconomic prescriptions, would have profoundly changed the power distribution in the organization or might not have fit the neoliberal/technocratic political rationality.[95] In short, policymaking practices changed while other alternative outcomes did not play out (e.g., changing the substance of the programs but not the procedures, focusing only on low-income countries, or hiring consultants rather than decentralizing). Furthermore, the emergence and institutionalization of inclusive practices were due (at least in part) to collective learning.

A reconstructed ethnography

The most appropriate methodology to study the learning processes of meaningful actions would have been ethnography or participant observation. However, due to the historical component of this research, conducting ethnographic work was impossible. Furthermore, highly institutionalized organizations such as the Bank are very opaque to outsiders. A *post hoc* practice tracing was a more viable option. Through in-depth interviews and archival work, I reconstructed how practitioners interpret and explain the changes in their knowledge, practices, and narratives. This reconstructed ethnography assumes that giving weight to what people say about what they do is crucial to understanding how they give meaning to their practice.

Semi-structured interviews were thus used as a proxy for participant observation. I analyzed interviews from two sources. First, I conducted and analyzed 41 interviews with various people at the World Bank, United Nations, various think tanks, and NGOs. Of the 41 firsthand interviews, 22 were with Bank staff and officials and 19 with employees from other IOs or NGOs; 21 were with men and 20 with women. Second, I analyzed and coded 80 publicly available semi-directed interviews with Bank officials and member state representatives, conducted since 1980 by Bank archivists for the Oral History Project (OHP). Because they were mostly recorded in the early years of the historical period chosen for this case and the representation of women in positions of leadership at the time was weak, 76 interviewees are men and only four are women; 78 are senior Bank employees and two are executive directors from member states (from the United States and Great Britain). The following table shows the number of interviewees (firsthand and OHP) working at the Bank in each year of this historical period (e.g., someone having worked from 1982 to 2010 counts as one for each year during that period). Because OHP interviews were conducted with senior Bank officials, the number of interviews from earlier periods is higher, which enabled better triangulation of older data, of which interviewees might have a weaker memory.

Because I studied decentralized practice changes, I interviewed a variety of people, from senior economists and vice presidents to NGO specialists, participation experts, and sector specialists in country teams. I also consciously prioritized internal sources of evidence. A sociological study of an organization, especially one that studies changes in the policymaking process (rather than the substance or impact of a policy), requires an internal look at the origins of this change. Shedding light

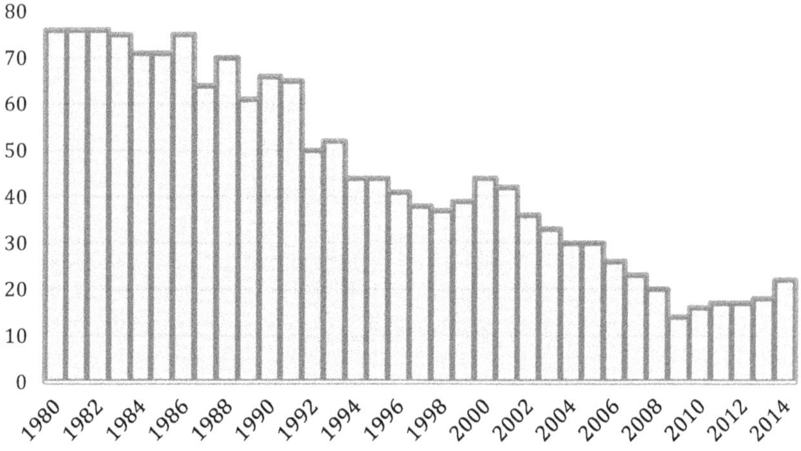

Figure 1.1 Interviewees' Employment at the World Bank by Year

on the intricacies of what happens within an organization can illuminate issues of human agency and intentionality, helping us to understand the mechanisms through which new practices emerge. It should be noted that this methodological position does not lead to an overly optimistic position, as even Bank employees are prone to self-criticism.[96]

I also conducted an interpretative archival analysis of over 75 documents to strengthen the historical and contextual background of the reconstructed ethnography. Archives can offer a great deal about how change is visible in the wording and framing of issues and in documents like meeting minutes, internal reports, and biographies. This meticulous reading of the written traces of a practice strengthened the tracing of practices. I analyzed archival documents in five categories:

- Official internal and external reports, such as those on poverty produced by country teams. I coded the World Development Report from 1980 and 2014, classifying each reference to terms relating to inclusion, empowerment, participation, NGO, and civil society.
- Working papers, discussion papers, meeting proceedings, reviews, and memos published internally.
- Practical guides, how-to manuals, learning modules, and sourcebooks used in practice.
- Blog posts and online documents produced by various Bank teams.
- Biographies and memoirs by senior officials, such as presidents and chief economists.

I also analyzed the Bank's public discourses to determine the shift in organizational narrative. I inductively coded and interpretively analyzed close to 50 public speeches and policy addresses by Bank presidents and senior officials. I examined the speeches of Presidents Alden W. Clausen, Barber B. Conable, Lewis T. Preston, James Wolfensohn, Paul Wolfowitz, Robert Zoellick, as well as Chief Economist Joseph Stiglitz and Vice President Nicholas Stern. This discourse analysis was conducted through inductive coding and classification with the qualitative analysis software MAXQDA.

Interviews, archival work, and discourse analysis enabled me to elaborate a double-layer hermeneutic, in which I interpreted how informants interpreted their own practices. Because I studied how practitioners give meaning to the emergence of new practices, it was necessary to analyze the impact of a set of practices and how their enactors interpreted their meaningfulness, significance, and unfolding over time. Corroborating what was said or written with interviews, speeches, reports, and biographical accounts led to a particularly novel story of how practices changed at the World Bank since the 1980s. The empirical application of a processual and relational theoretical framework contributes to the literature on cognitive evolution and CoPs through its exploration of how to methodologically apply concepts such as communities, boundaries, and relations in motion. By showing how configurations of CoPs interact in social learning, this book offers a way to study constellations of communities in IOs that may guide other researchers empirically.

Plan of the book

The next chapter develops a meta-theoretical apparatus to explain collective learning in CoP by developing a relational and processual ontology based on intersubjectivity between community members, social practices, and narratives. It lays the ground for a relational/processual analysis of world ordering. Chapter 3 presents the nuts and bolts of a theoretical framework of collective learning at the boundaries of CoPs and lays out three processes of collective learning: boundary encounters, boundary brokering, and the use of epistemic boundary objects.

To address potential skeptics about the extent of the practice change at the Bank, Chapter 4 presents the case of inclusive practices and details what happened in the organization between 1980 and 2014 regarding ownership of development policies by borrowing governments, public participation of countries' populations, and communications with civil society actors. The period extends from the adoption of the first structural adjustment programs in 1980 to the end of the Highly-Indebted Poor Countries initiative and the PRSP in 2014. This chapter offers parts of the comprehensive history of the Bank, which others have contributed to equal depth but in other spheres.[97] Instead of presenting a complete story of the Bank, which would be impossible and not particularly useful for explanation purposes, it provides a selective history of the Bank from 1980 to 2014, especially regarding inclusive practices at the International Development Association. Readers interested in the application of the concept of CoPs may want to go straight to the next ones.

Chapters 5, 6, and 7 present empirical material on the emergence and institutionalization of inclusive practices at the World Bank from 1980 to 2014, with the help of the theoretical apparatus previously developed. These chapters each explore aspects of how collective learning processes influenced the institutionalization of inclusive practices: Chapter 5 puts emphasis on epistemic boundary objects and boundary encounters; Chapter 6 explores narratives, epistemic power, and boundary brokering; and Chapter 7 delves into contestation in practice. Chapter 8 explores how coloniality of power mediated the emergence and institutionalization of inclusive practices. This last substantive chapter goes beyond critiques of inclusive practices as being only rhetorical or "co-opted." Instead, one of the most interesting aspects of this case is that, through a genuine intent to render their projects more effective, racial stratifications still permeates how Bank employees include Global South populations.

Chapter 9 concludes the book by exploring its broader implications for development practices and critical theory more generally. It emphasizes the relationship between power and knowledge and the role of exclusions in development policymaking. It specifically explores how the Bank's neoliberal political rationality mediated the emergence of inclusive practices, often stabilizing existing predispositions instead of challenging them. In short, if new practices can be translated by practitioners, the technocratic mode of thinking will be upheld; if they can't, they can reach a tipping point of rupture or fade away.

Notes

1 (1998).
2 Waltz, *Theory of International Politics*, 93.
3 Lake, *Hierarchy in International Relations*; Zarakol, *Hierarchies in World Politics.*
4 Buzan and Lawson, *The Global Transformation.*
5 Zürn, *A Theory of Global Governance.*
6 Deitelhoff and Daase, "Rule and Resistance in Global Governance."
7 Zarakol, 7.
8 (1998).
9 (2019).
10 Adler, Bremberg, and Sondarjee, "Communities of Practice in World Politics," 2.
11 Adler and Pouliot, *International Practices*, 17.
12 Bural, "Parody as Norm Contestation"; Wiener, *Contestation and Constitution of Norms in Global International Relations*; Deitelhoff and Zimmermann, "Things We Lost in the Fire."
13 Barnett and Finnemore, *Rules for the World*; Weaver, *Hypocrisy Trap*; Xu and Weller, *Inside the World Bank*; Park and Vetterlein, *Owning Development*; Chwieroth, "Controlling Capital."
14 Abbott, "Things of Boundaries"; Wenger, *Communities of Practice*, 254; Hofius, *European Union Communities of Practice*; Glas and Martel, "Boundary Work"; Qiao-Franco, "An Emergent Community of Cyber Sovereignty."
15 Anzaldúa, *Borderlands.*
16 (2024).
17 Glas and Martel; Qiao-Franco; Hofius.
18 Adler and Bernstein, "Knowledge in Power."
19 Sondarjee, "Change and Stability at the World Bank."
20 Ndlovu-Gatsheni, *Epistemic Freedom in Africa*; Pailey, "De-centring the 'White Gaze' of Development."
21 Autesserre, *Peaceland*; Pouliot and Thérien, "The Politics of Inclusion"; Pouliot, *International Pecking Orders.*
22 (2022).
23 (2021).
24 (2020).
25 In this book, the Bank is used as a shortcut for the International Development Association, the agency of the World Bank that deals with low-income countries.
26 Interview 20, July 17, 2017.
27 Collier, "The Failure of Conditionality"; Collier, "Conditionality, Dependence and Coordination."
28 Collier, "The Failure of Conditionality"; Collier, "Conditionality, Dependence and Coordination."
29 Gibbon, "A Failed Agenda?"; Meulbroek, "Gillian Hart in Beijing."
30 Cornwall and Brock, "What Do Buzzwords Do for Development Policy?"; Ruckert, "The Forgotten Dimension of Social Reproduction"; Vestergaard and Wade, "Protecting Power."
31 Rowden and Irama, "Rethinking Participation," 41.
32 Bebbington, "Theorizing Participation and Institutional Change," 279.
33 Interview 35, November 9, 2017.
34 World Bank, "Taking Action for Poverty Reduction in Sub-Saharan."
35 World Bank, *The World Bank Participation Sourcebook.*
36 Hentschel, *Does Participation Cost the World Bank More?*; World Bank and Rietbergen-McCracken, *Participation in Practice*, 2.
37 Operations Policy Department, *The World Bank and Participation.*

38 Pattberg et al., *Public-Private Partnerships for Sustainable Development.*
39 Cling, Razafindrakoto, and Roubaud, *Les Nouvelles Stratégies Internationales de Lutte Contre La Pauvreté*, 197.
40 Kramarz, "Partnerships in Global Governance."
41 Interview 24, November 13, 2017.
42 Easterly, *The Tyranny of Experts*; Best, *Governing Failure.*
43 Vetterlein, "Lacking Ownership."
44 Abbott and Snidal, "Why States Act through Formal International Organizations"; Fang and Stone, "International Organizations as Policy Advisors."
45 Wade, "US Hegemony and the World Bank"; Andersen, Hansen, and Markussen, "US Politics and World Bank IDA-Lending"; Stones, *Controlling Institutions.*
46 Clegg, *Controlling the World Bank and IMF Shareholders, Stakeholders, and the Politics of Concessional Lending*, 44.
47 Hawkins et al., *Delegation and Agency in International Organizations*; Nielson, Tierney, and Weaver, "Bridging the Rationalist–Constructivist Divide."
48 Nelson, *The World Bank and Non-Governmental Organizations*; Miller-Adams, *The World Bank*; Weaver and Leiteritz, "'Our Poverty is a World Full of Dreams"; Weaver; Park and Vetterlein; Park, *World Bank Group Interactions with Environmentalists*; Vetterlein, "Seeing Like the World Bank on Poverty."
49 Weick, *Sensemaking in Organizations*; March, "How Decisions Happen in Organizations"; Miles and Snow, *Organizational Strategy, Structure, and Process.*
50 Barnett and Finnemore; see also Chwieroth, *Capital Ideas.*
51 Barnett and Finnemore.
52 Weaver, 7.
53 Finnemore and Sikkink, "International Norm Dynamics and Political Change."
54 Risse, Ropp, and Sikkink, *The Power of Human Rights International Norms and Domestic Change.*
55 Keck and Sikkink, "Transnational Advocacy Networks in International and Regional Politics."
56 For more on the limits of the norm literature, see Krook and True, "Rethinking the Life Cycles of International Norms"; Hoffmann, "Norms and Social Constructivism in International Relations."
57 Acharya, "How Ideas Spread"; Welsh, "Norm Contestation and the Responsibility to Protect"; Hofmann, *Ten Years R2P—What Doesn't Kill a Norm Only Makes It Stronger?*; Bural; Zimmermann, "More for Less"; Wiener; Gutterman and Lohaus, "What Is the 'Anti-Corruption' Norm in Global Politics?"; Deitelhoff and Zimmermann.
58 Wiener.
59 Finnemore, "Redefining Development at the World Bank," 199; see also Kraske, *Bankers with a Mission.*
60 Adler, *World Ordering*; Mead, *The Individual and the Social Self*; Joas, *G. H. Mead.*
61 Pratt, "From Norms to Normative Configurations," 1; Wiener and Puetter, "The Quality of Norms is What Actors Make of It."
62 Pratt.
63 Schmidt, "Foreign Military Presence and the Changing Practice of Sovereignty," 817.
64 Hofferberth and Weber, "Lost in Translation"; Gadinger, "The Normativity of International Practices."
65 Chessé and Sondarjee, "A Feminist Critique of International Practices."
66 Park and Vetterlein.
67 Wiener.
68 Streeck and Thelen, "Introduction."
69 McCourt, *The New Constructivism in International Relations Theory.*
70 Pouliot.
71 Cornut, "Diplomacy, Agency and the Logic of Improvisation."
72 Kuru, "Back at Home."

73 Sjoberg and Via, *Gender, War, and Militarism.*
74 Enloe, *Bananas, Beaches and Bases.*
75 Cohn, "Sex and Death in the Rational World of Defense Intellectuals."
76 Tickner, "On the Frontlines or Sidelines of Knowledge and Power"; Sondarjee, "We Are a Community of Practice, Not a Paradigm!"
77 Wilcox, Lauren, *Review of International Studies.*
78 Adler and Pouliot; Bueger and Gadinger, *International Practice Theory*; Drieschova, Bueger, and Hopf, *Conceptualizing International Practices.*
79 Bueger, "Practice, Pirates and Coast Guards."
80 Bremberg, "The European Union as Security Community-Building Institution."
81 Tieku, Thomas Kwasi and Afua Boatemaa Yakohene, *Global Studies Quarterly.*
82 Hofius.
83 Sondarjee.
84 Bicchi, "Communities of Practice and What They Can Do for International Relations."
85 Schatzki, "Introduction," 14.
86 Wenger-Trayner et al., *Learning in Landscapes of Practice.*
87 Wenger, 129.
88 Adler, *Communitarian International Relations*, 14.
89 Schatzki, 5.
90 Pouliot.
91 Adler, 154.
92 Contu and Willmott, "Re-Embedding Situatedness," 285.
93 Wendt, *Quantum Mind and Social Science.*
94 Schmidt, 820.
95 Sondarjee.
96 Stone and Wright, *The World Bank and Governance.*
97 Kapur, Lewis, and Webb, *The World Bank.*

References

Abbott, Andrew. "Things of Boundaries." *Social Research* 62, no. 4 (1995): 857–82.

Abbott, Kenneth W., and Duncan Snidal. "Why States Act through Formal International Organizations." *The Journal of Conflict Resolution* 42, no. 1 (1998): 3–32.

Acharya, Amitav. "How Ideas Spread: Whose Norms Matter? Norm Localization and Institutional Change in Asian Regionalism." *International Organization* 58, no. 2 (2004): 239–75.

Adler, Emanuel. *Communitarian International Relations. The Epistemic Foundations of International Relations.* London and New York: Routledge, 2005.

Adler, Emanuel. *World Ordering. A Social Theory of Cognitive Evolution.* Cambridge: Cambridge University Press, 2019.

Adler, Emanuel, and Steven Bernstein. "Knowledge in Power: The Epistemic Construction of Global Governance." In *Power in Global Governance*, 294–318. Cambridge: Cambridge University Press, 2005.

Adler, Emanuel, Niklas Bremberg, and Maïka Sondarjee. "Communities of Practice in World Politics: Advancing a Research Agenda." *Global Studies Quarterly* 4, no. 1 (2024): ksad070.

Adler, Emanuel, and Vincent Pouliot. *International Practices.* Edited by Emanuel Adler and Vincent Pouliot. New York: Cambridge University Press, 2011.

Andersen, Thomas Barnebeck, Henrik Hansen, and Thomas Markussen. "US Politics and World Bank IDA-Lending." *The Journal of Development Studies* 42, no. 5 (July 2006): 772–94.

Anzaldúa, Gloria. *Borderlands: The New Mestiza = La Frontera.* 3rd ed. San Francisco: Aunt Lute Books, 2007.

Autesserre, Séverine. *Peaceland: Conflict Resolution and the Everyday Politics Of International Intervention*. Cambridge: Cambridge University Press, 2014.
Barnett, Michael, and Martha Finnemore. *Rules for the World: International Organizations in Global Politics*. Ithaca and London: Cornell University Press, 2004.
Bebbington, Anthony. "Theorizing Participation and Institutional Change: Ethnography and Political Economy." In *Participation, from Tyranny to Transformation?: Exploring New Approaches to Participation in Development*, edited by Samuel Hickey and Giles Mohan, 278–83. London and New York, NY: ZED Books, Distributed Exclusively in the U.S. by Palgrave Macmillan, 2004.
Bennett, Andrew, and Jeffrey Checkel. *Process-Tracing: From Metaphor to Analytical Tool*. Cambridge: Cambridge University Press, 2015.
Best, Jacqueline. "Legitimacy Dilemmas: The IMF's Pursuit of Country Ownership." *Third World Quarterly* 28, no. 3 (April 2007): 469–88.
Best, Jacqueline. *Governing Failure: Provisional Expertise and the Transformation of Global Development Finance*. Cambridge and New York: Cambridge University Press, 2014.
Bian, Junru. "The Racialization of Expertise and Professional Non-Equivalence in the Humanitarian Workplace." *Journal of International Humanitarian Action* 7, no. 3 (December 2022): 1–14.
Bicchi, Federica. "Communities of Practice and What They Can Do for International Relations." *Review of International Studies* 48, no. 1 (2021): 24–43.
Bremberg, Niklas. "The European Union as Security Community-Building Institution: Venues, Networks and Co-Operative Security Practices." *JCMS: Journal of Common Market Studies* 53, no. 3 (May 2015): 674–92.
Bueger, Christian. "Practice, Pirates and Coast Guards: The Grand Narrative of Somali Piracy." *Third World Quarterly* 34, no. 10 (2013): 1811–27.
Bueger, Christian, and Frank Gadinger. *International Practice Theory: New Perspectives*. Basingstoke: Palgrave Macmillan, 2014.
Bural, Erna. "Parody as Norm Contestation. Russian Normative Justifications in Georgia and Ukraine and Their Implications for Global Norms." *Global Society* 30, no. 1 (2016): 67–77.
Buzan, Barry, and George Lawson. *The Global Transformation: History, Modernity and the Making of International Relations*. Cambridge: Cambridge University Press, 2015. https://doi.org/10.1017/CBO9781139565073.
Chessé, Alice, and Maïka Sondarjee. "A Feminist Critique of International Practices." *International Studies Quarterly* 68, no. 2 (2024): 1–10.
Chwieroth, Jeffrey M. *Capital Ideas: The IMF and the Rise of Financial Liberalization*. Princeton, NJ: Princeton University Press, 2010.
Chwieroth, Jeffrey M. "Controlling Capital: The International Monetary Fund and Transformative Incremental Change from Within International Organisations." *New Political Economy* 19, no. 3 (2014): 445–69.
Civil Society Unit. *Consultations with Civil Society Organizations. General Guidelines for the World Bank Staff*. Washington, DC: World Bank Social Development Department, 2000.
Clegg, Liam. *Controlling the World Bank and IMF Shareholders*, Stakeholders, and the Politics of Concessional Lending. London, UK: Palgrave MacMillan, 2013.
Cling, Jean-Pierre, Mireille Razafindrakoto, and François Roubaud. *Les Nouvelles Stratégies Internationales de Lutte Contre La Pauvreté*. Paris: DIAL/Economica, 2002.
Cohn, Carol. "Sex and Death in the Rational World of Defense Intellectuals." *Signs* 12, no. 4 (1987): 687–718.
Collier, Paul. "The Failure of Conditionality." In *Perspectives on Aid and Development*, edited by Catherine Gwyn and Joan Nelson, 51–77. Washington, DC: Overseas Development Council, 1997.
Collier, Paul. "Conditionality, Dependence and Coordination." In *The World Bank: Structure and Policies, Digitally Printed 1. Paperback Version*, 299–348. Cambridge: Global Economic Institutions, Cambridge University Press, 2006.

Contu, Alessia, and Hugh Willmott. "Re-Embedding Situatedness: The Importance of Power Relations in Learning Theory." *Organization Science* 14, no. 3 (June 2003): 283–96.
Cornut, Jérémie. "Diplomacy, Agency and the Logic of Improvisation and Virtuosity in Practice." *European Journal of International Relations* 24, no. 3 (2018): 712–36.
Cornwall, Andrea, and Karen Brock. "What Do Buzzwords Do for Development Policy? A Critical Look at 'Participation', 'Empowerment' and 'Poverty Reduction.'" *Third World Quarterly* 26, no. 7 (October 2005): 1043–60.
Danaher, Kevin, ed. *50 Years Is Enough: The Case against the World Bank and the International Monetary Fund*. Boston, MA: South End Press, 1994.
Deitelhoff, Nicole, and Christopher Daase. "Rule and Resistance in Global Governance." *International Theory* 13, no. 1 (March 2021): 122–30.
Deitelhoff, Nicole, and Lisbeth Zimmermann. "Things We Lost in the Fire: How Different Types of Contestation Affect the Robustness of International Norms." *International Studies Review* 22 (2020): 51–76.
Dollar, David, and Jakob Svensson. "What Explains the Success or Failure of Structural Adjustment Programs?" *Policy Research Working Paper*. Washington, DC: The World Bank, 1998.
Drabek, A. G. "Development Alternatives: The Challenge of NGOs." *World Development* 15 (1987): ix–xv.
Drieschova, Alena, Christian Bueger, and Ted Hopf, eds. *Conceptualizing International Practices: Directions for the Practice Turn in International Relations*. Cambridge, United Kingdom and New York, NY: Cambridge University Press, 2022.
Easterly, William. *The Tyranny of Experts: Economists, Dictators, and the Forgotten Rights of the Poor*. New York: Basic Books, Inc., 2014.
Enloe, Cynthia H. *Bananas, Beaches and Bases: Making Feminist Sense of International Politics*. 1st U.S. ed. Berkeley: University of California Press, 1990.
Fang, Songying, and Randall W. Stone. "International Organizations as Policy Advisors." *International Organization* 66, no. 4 (2012): 537–69.
Finnemore, Martha. "Redefining Development at the World Bank." In *International Development and the Social Sciences: Essays on the History and Politics of Knowledge*, edited by Frederick Cooper and Randall M. Packard. Berkeley: University of California Press, 1997.
Finnemore, Martha, and Kathryn Sikkink. "International Norm Dynamics and Political Change." *International Organization* 52, no. 4 (1998): 887–917.
Gadinger, Frank. "The Normativity of International Practices." In *Conceptualizing International Practices: Directions for the Practice Turn in International Relations*, edited by Alena Drieschova, Christian Bueger, and Ted Hopf, 100–21. Cambridge, United Kingdom and New York, NY: Cambridge University Press, 2022.
Gibbon, Peter. "A Failed Agenda? African Agriculture Under Structural Adjustment with Special Reference to Kenya and Ghana." *The Journal of Peasant Studies* 20, no. 1 (October 1992): 50–96. https://doi.org/10.1080/03066159208438501.
Giddens, Anthony, and Christopher Pierson. *Conversation with Anthony Giddens. Making Sense of Modernity*. Cambridge: Polity Press, 1998.
Glas, Aarie. "Habits of Peace: Long-Term Regional Cooperation in Southeast Asia." *European Journal of International Relations* 23, no. 4 (2017): 833–56.
Glas, Aarie, and Stéphanie Martel. "Boundary Work, Overlapping Identities, and Liminality in Communities of Practice: Diplomacy within and Beyond ASEAN." *Global Studies Quarterly* 4, no. 1 (January 27, 2024): ksad072. https://doi.org/10.1093/isagsq/ksad072.
Græger, Nina. " 'High Politics' and Everyday Practices at the Border: Emerging Communities of Practice in the High North." *Global Studies Quarterly* 4, no. 1 (January 27, 2024): ksad075. https://doi.org/10.1093/isagsq/ksad075.
Gutterman, Ellen, and Mathis Lohaus. "What is the 'Anti-Corruption' Norm in Global Politics? Norm Robustness and Contestation in the Transnational Governance of Corruption." In *Corruption and Norms. Why Informal Rules Matter*, edited by Ina Kubbe and Annika Engelbert. London: Palgrave MacMillan, 2018.

Hawkins, Darren G., David Lake, Daniel L. Nielson, and Michael J. Tierney, eds. *Delegation and Agency in International Organizations*. Cambridge: Cambridge University Press, 2006.

Hentschel, Jesko. *Does Participation Cost the World Bank More? Emerging Evidence*. Washington, DC: The World Bank, 1994.

Hofferberth, Matthias, and Christian Weber. "Lost in Translation: A Critique of Constructivist Norm Research." *Journal of International Relations and Development* 18, no. 1 (January 2015): 75–103. https://doi.org/10.1057/jird.2014.1.

Hoffmann, Matthew J. "Norms and Social Constructivism in International Relations." In *The International Studies Encyclopedia*, edited by Robert Allen Denemark. Malden, MA: Wiley-Blackwell, 2010.

Hofius, Maren. *European Union Communities of Practice: Diplomacy and Boundary Work in Ukraine. Routledge Global Cooperation Series*. London and New York: Routledge, 2023.

Hofmann, Gregor. *Ten Years R2P – What Doesn't Kill a Norm Only Makes It Stronger? Contestation, Application and Institutionalization of International Atrocity Prevention and Response. PRIF Report*. Frankfurt: Peace Research Institute, 2015.

Joas, Hans. *G. H. Mead, a Contemporary Re-Examination of His Thought*. Cambridge [Cambridgeshire]: Polity Press, 1985.

Kapur, Devesh, John P. Lewis, and Richard Charles Webb. *The World Bank: Its First Half Century*. Washington, DC: Brookings Institution, 1997.

Keck, Margaret E., and Kathryn Sikkink. "Transnational Advocacy Networks in International and Regional Politics." *International Social Science Journal* 51, no. 159 (1999): 89–101.

Killick, Tony, Ramani Gunatilaka, and Ana Marr. *Aid and the Political Economy of Policy Change*. London and New York: Routledge, 1998.

Kramarz, Teresa. "Partnerships in Global Governance: The Growth of a Procedural Norm Without Substance?" In *Governing the Provision of Ecosystem Services*. Vol. 4, edited by Roldan Muradian and Laura Rival, 47–65. Dordrecht: Springer Netherlands, 2013.

Kraske, Jochen, ed. *Bankers with a Mission: The Presidents of the World Bank, 1946–91*. New York: Oxford University Press, 1996.

Krook, Mona Lena, and Jacqui True. "Rethinking the Life Cycles of International Norms: The United Nations and the Global Promotion of Gender Equality." *European Journal of International Relations* 18, no. 1 (March 2012): 103–27. https://doi.org/10.1177/1354066110380963.

Kuru, Deniz. "Back at Home: The Ambassadors Conference as an Interstitial Practice." *Global Affairs* 5, no. 4–5 (October 20, 2019): 295–313.

Lake, David A. *Hierarchy in International Relations. Cornell Studies in Political Economy*. Ithaca, NY: Cornell University Press, 2009.

March, James G. "How Decisions Happen in Organizations." *Human-Computer Interaction* 6 (1991): 95–117.

McCourt, David M. *The New Constructivism in International Relations Theory*. 1st ed. Bristol University Press, 2022. https://doi.org/10.2307/j.ctv293p48m.

McIntosh, Mary, Anni Poikolainen, Kimberly Hewitt, Tara Lubin, Kathlen Knoll, Elizabeth McGaha, and Jean D'Amico. *The Global Poll: Multinational Survey of Opinion Leaders 2002*. Washington, DC: Princeton Survey Research Associates for the World Bank, 2003.

Mead, George Herbert. *The Individual and the Social Self: Unpublished Work of George Herbert Mead*. Chicago: University of Chicago Press, 1982.

Meulbroek, Chris. "Gillian Hart in Beijing: Negotiating Capitalist Models at the World Bank–China Nexus." *Environment and Planning A: Economy and Space* (May 4, 2022). https://doi.org/10.1177/0308518X221099299.

Miles, Raymond E., and Charles C. Snow. *Organizational Strategy, Structure, and Process*. Stanford, CA: Stanford University Press, 2003.

Miller-Adams, Michelle. *The World Bank: New Agendas in a Changing World*. London: Routledge, 1999.
Nair, Deepak. "Sociability in International Politics: Golf and ASEAN's Cold War Diplomacy." *International Political Sociology* 14, no. 2 (June 1, 2020): 196–214. https://doi.org/10.1093/ips/olz024.
Narayan, Deepa. *The Contribution of People's Participation: 121 Rural Water Supply Project*. Washington, DC: World Bank, 1994.
Ndlovu-Gatsheni, Sabelo J. *Epistemic Freedom in Africa: Deprovincialization and Decolonization. Rethinking Development*. London and New York: Routledge, Taylor & Francis Group, 2018.
Nelson, Paul Jeffrey. *The World Bank and Non-Governmental Organizations: The Limits of Apolitical Development. Nachdr. International Political Economy Series*. Basingstoke: Macmillan Press [u.a.], 1999.
Nielson, Daniel L., Michael J. Tierney, and Catherine E. Weaver. "Bridging the Rationalist–Constructivist Divide: Re-Engineering the Culture of the World Bank." *Journal of International Relations and Development* 9, no. 2 (June 2006): 107–39.
Operations Evaluations Department. *Annual Review of Evaluation Results*. Washington, DC: World Bank, 1992.
Operations Policy Department. *The World Bank and Participation*. Washington, DC: The World Bank, 1994.
Pailey, Robtel Neajai. "De-centring the 'White Gaze' of Development." *Development and Change* 51, no. 3 (May 2020): 729–45.
Pampinella, Stephen. "'The Way of Progress and Civilization': Racial Hierarchy and US State Building in Haiti and the Dominican Republic (1915–1922)." *Journal of Global Security Studies* 6, no. 3 (March 1, 2021): 1–17.
Park, Susan. *World Bank Group Interactions with Environmentalists: Changing International Organisation Identities*. Manchester: Manches, 2010.
Park, Susan, and Antje Vetterlein. *Owning Development. Creating Policy Norms in the IMF and the World Bank*. Edited by Susan Park and Antje Vetterlein. Cambridge: Cambridge University Press, 2010.
Pattberg, Philipp, Frank Biermann, Sander Chan, and Aysem Mert, eds. *Public-Private Partnerships for Sustainable Development: Emergence, Influence and Legitimacy*. Northampton, MA: Edward Elgar, 2013.
Phillips, David A. *Reforming the World Bank: Twenty Years of Trial -- and Error*. New York: Cambridge University Press, 2009.
Pouliot, Vincent. "Practice Tracing." In *Process-Tracing. From Metaphor to Analytical Tool*, edited by Andrew Bennett and Jeffrey T. Checkel, 237–59. Cambridge: Cambridge University Press, 2015.
Pouliot, Vincent. *International Pecking Orders: The Politics and Practice of Multilateral Diplomacy*. New York: Cambridge University Press, 2016.
Pouliot, Vincent, and Jean-Philippe Thérien. "The Politics of Inclusion: Changing Patterns in the Governance of International Security." *Review of International Studies*, no. 41 (2015): 211–37.
Pratt, Simon Frankel. "From Norms to Normative Configurations: A Pragmatist and Relational Approach to Theorizing Normativity in IR." *International Theory* 12, no. 1 (March 2020): 59–82.
Qiao-Franco, Guangyu. "An Emergent Community of Cyber Sovereignty: The Reproduction of Boundaries?" *Global Studies Quarterly* 4, no. 1 (January 27, 2024): ksad077. https://doi.org/10.1093/isagsq/ksad077.
Risse, Thomas, Stephen C. Ropp, and Kathryn Sikkink. *The Power of Human Rights International Norms and Domestic Change*. Cambridge: Cambridge University Press, 1999.
Rowden, Rick, and Jane Ocaya Irama. *Rethinking Participation. Questions for Civil Society about the Limits of Participation in PRSPs. Discussion Paper*. Washington, DC: Action Aid, 2004.

Ruckert, Arne. "The Forgotten Dimension of Social Reproduction: The World Bank and the Poverty Reduction Strategy Paradigm." *Review of International Political Economy* 17, no. 5 (2010): 816–39.
Ruggie, John G. "What Makes the World Hang Together? Neo-Utilitarianism and the Social Constructivist Challenge." *International Organization* 52 (1998): 855–85.
Schatzki, Theodore Richard. "Introduction: Practice Theory." In *The Practice Turn in Contemporary Theory*, edited by Theodore R. Schatzki, Karin Knorr Cetina, and Eike Von Savigny, 10–23. London and New York: Routledge, 2001.
Schmidt, Sebastian. "Foreign Military Presence and the Changing Practice of Sovereignty: A Pragmatist Explanation of Norm Change." *American Political Science Review* 108, no. 4 (2014): 817–29.
Sjoberg, Laura, and Sandra Via, eds. *Gender, War, and Militarism: Feminist Perspectives. Praeger Security International*. Santa Barbara, CA: Praeger, 2010.
Sondarjee, Maïka. "Change and Stability at the World Bank: Inclusive Practices and Neoliberal Technocratic Rationality." *Third World Quarterly* 42, no. 2 (2021): 348–65.
Sondarjee, Maïka. "We Are a Community of Practice, Not a Paradigm! How to Meaningfully Integrate Gender and Feminist Approaches in IR Syllabi." *International Studies Perspectives* 23, no. 3 (2022): 229–48.
Stone, Diane, and Christopher Wright, eds. *The World Bank and Governance: A Decade of Reform and Reaction. Routledge/Warwick Studies in Globalisation 14*. London and New York: Routledge, 2007.
Stones, Rob. *Controlling Institutions: International Organizations and the Global Economy*. Cambridge: Cambridge University Press, 2011.
Streeck, Wolfgang, and Kathleen Ann Thelen. "Introduction: Institutional Change in Advanced Political Economies Wolfgang Streeck and Kathleen Thelen." In *Beyond Continuity: Institutional Change in Advanced Political Economies*, edited by Wolfgang Streeck and Kathleen Ann Thelen, 1–39. Oxford and New York: Oxford University Press, 2005.
Tickner, J. Ann. "On the Frontlines or Sidelines of Knowledge and Power: Feminist Practices of Responsible Scholarship." *International Studies Review* 8, no. 3 (2006): 283–395.
Vestergaard, Jakob, and Robert H. Wade. "Protecting Power: How Western States Retain the Dominant Voice in The World Bank's Governance." *World Development* 46 (2013): 153–64.
Vetterlein, Antje. "Lacking Ownership: The IMF and Social Development." In *Owning Development. Creating Policy Norms in the IMF and the World Bank*, edited by Susan Park and Antje Vetterlein. Cambridge: Cambridge University Press, 2010.
Vetterlein, Antje. "Seeing Like the World Bank on Poverty." *New Political Economy* 17, no. 1 (2012): 35–58.
Wade, Robert. "US Hegemony and the World Bank: The Fight Over People and Ideas." *Review of International Political Economy* 9, no. 2 (2002): 215–43.
Waltz, Kenneth N. *Theory of International Politics*. 1st ed. Boston, MA: McGraw-Hill, 1979.
Weaver, Catherine. *Hypocrisy Trap: The World Bank and the Poverty of Reform*. Princeton: Princeton University Press, 2008.
Weaver, Catherine, and Ralf J. Leiteritz. " 'Our Poverty is a World Full of Dreams:' Reforming the World Bank." *Global Governance* 11 (2005): 369–88.
Weick, Karl E. *Sensemaking in Organizations. Foundations for Organizational Science*. Thousand Oaks: Sage Publications, 1995.
Welsh, Jennifer. "Norm Contestation and the Responsibility to Protect." *Global Responsibility to Protect* 5, no. 4 (2013): 217–38.
Wendt, Alexander. *Quantum Mind and Social Science*. Cambridge: Cambridge University Press, 2015.
Wenger, Etienne. *Communities of Practice. Learning, Meaning, and Identity*. Cambridge: Cambridge University Press, 1998.
Wenger-Trayner, Etienne, Mark Fenton-O'Creevy, Steven Hutchison, and Beverly Wenger-Trayner, eds. *Learning in Landscapes of Practice: Boundaries, Identity, and Knowledgeability in Practice-Based Learning*. London and New York: Routledge, 2015.

Wiener, Antje. *Contestation and Constitution of Norms in Global International Relations*. Cambridge: Cambridge University Press, 2018. https://doi.org/10.1017/9781316718599.

Wiener, Antje, and Uwe Puetter. "The Quality of Norms is What Actors Make of It. Critical Constructivist Research on Norms." *Journal of International Law and International Relations* 5, no. 1 (2009): 1–16.

World Bank. *Taking Action for Poverty Reduction in Sub-Saharan Africa Report of an Africa Region Task Force*. Washington, DC: Word Bank, 1996a.

World Bank, ed. *The World Bank Participation Sourcebook*. Washington, DC: The World Bank, 1996b.

World Bank, and Jennifer Rietbergen-McCracken. *Participation in Practice: The Experience of the World Bank and Other Stakeholders. World Bank Discussion Paper, No. 333*. Washington, DC: The World Bank, 1996.

Xu, Yi-Chong, and Patrick Moray Weller. *Inside the World Bank: Exploding the Myth of the Monolithic Bank*. 1st ed. New York: Palgrave Macmillan, 2009.

Zarakol, Ayşe, ed. *Hierarchies in World Politics. Cambridge Studies in International Relations*. New York: Cambridge University Press, 2017.

Zimmermann, Lisbeth. "More for Less: The Interactive Translation of Global Norms in Postconflict Guatemala." *International Studies Quarterly* 61, no. 4 (December 1, 2017): 774–85. https://doi.org/10.1093/isq/sqx044.

Zürn, Michael. *A Theory of Global Governance: Authority, Legitimacy, and Contestation*. 1st ed. Oxford and New York, NY: Oxford University Press, 2018.

2 Relations, processes, and narratives in communities of practice

Nearly two decades after Patrick Jackson and Daniel Nexon defined for mainstream IR scholars "processual/relationalism,"[1] Alexander Wendt, Yaqing Qin, Emanuel Adler, and others have suggested fully-fledged theories of entities, relations, and practices as processes, respectively based on quantum physics,[2] Chinese philosophy,[3] and evolutionary constructivism.[4] If some have called it a "revolution,"[5] most research published in IR (as well as so-called IR paradigms) are still implicitly substantialists, maintaining that the primitive units of analysis are things, actors, or reified structures. In the field's mainstream, entities (states, capabilities, organizations, and norms) predate interaction, and if relations are studied, they are reduced to the interactions between already formed entities.

David McCourt might be right to argue that most practice and CoP-oriented research sit nicely under the label of a "new constructivism."[6] However, as he associates field theory, network, and actor-network approaches under this umbrella, practice approaches, a fortiori those focused on communities of practice (CoPs), have the potential to build on a more robust relational and processual ontology than the others. The concept of international CoPs (within and outside the so-called practice turn) enables a conceptualization of world ordering and not only of relationships or ties between already formed entities or actors.[7] Focusing on interactions instead of position in a network, CoP approaches look at performance and epistemic power and not at nodes and structural power. In short, they look at the software instead of the hardware of world politics. Before delving into collective learning processes in the next chapter, this one develops a processual/relational framework focused on the dynamic processes of performances in communities. It presents the armature for developing a theory of collective learning at the boundaries of CoPs. Even if relational approaches are challenging to operationalize methodologically because we tend to see the world as made of things instead of processes that collapse in thingness, the next chapter will aim to develop empirically applicable theoretical concepts.

Relationalism in IR

Substantialism relies on basic intuitions about the world. Humans' basic instinct sees a world made of things: trees, books, cars, people, treaties, borders, norms,

DOI: 10.4324/9781003529279-2

or interests. When one sees the Blue Danube, no one says, "look at that perpetual flowing of the water," but "look at how fast the river is flowing."[8] A similar way of thinking occurs when we think that "the wind is blowing," that "the US is signaling" or that "countries adopted an anti-slavery norm." However, the wind, states, and norms are not things; they are evolving processes that we conveniently reduce to static conditions. This procedure of reducing them to a stable state is an analytical tool preventing us from understanding the continually evolving character of the world.

Coming from American sociology, feminist sensibilities, or non-Western philosophies, relational scholars reject substantialism under-problematization of agency. It is self-explanatory that they see relations (i.e., configurations of ties or recurrent social interactions between individual or collective agents) as ontologically prior to entities and actions.[9] For relational scholars, society does not possess relations but *is* relations: "society is not a space 'containing' relations, or an arena where relations are played. It is rather the very tissue of relations."[10] They usually agree on one precept: no pre-given units or entities exist without the transactional context within which they are embedded. It would be unreasonable, for example, to define colonized populations without an understanding of colonial masters or enslaved African women without an understanding of white men and women enslavers, as well as enslaved African men.

Actors are immanent to each other; they are social beings only in interaction processes. This actor-context immanence is also context-oriented, which leads relational researchers to focus not on individual actors in isolation from their context but as part of a larger environment and in constant relationship with their surroundings.[11] Therefore, the owner of the means of production cannot be defined without the workers but also without defining capitalism as a system. As Yaqing Qin argues, if we conceive of the world as made of relatedness, we are forced to focus on the relationships between the actor and her context. Humans are part of an intersubjective whole, and these relations are crucial to understanding world politics. A classic example is Cynthia Enloe's[12] work on how diplomatic wives' unpaid labor contributes to promoting national interests and sustaining a hierarchical systemic order between the Global North and the Global South. Such an understanding of the role of women in diplomacy is silenced in mainstream IR research on diplomacy when diplomats (read, male diplomats) are considered in isolation from their personal relations and care work within the field.

Relationalism thus goes against scientific realists who argue that "our sense of self, as part of our humanity, is prior and primitive to our sociality," and for whom creativity requires that an actor separates herself from social structures.[13] This undersocialized conceptualization of agency[14] precludes the fact that from kindergarten to nursing homes, we are socialized in communities and always use that knowledge and know-how in our present and future actions. A logic of action based on practical consciousness, or what Theodore Schatzki[15] calls action intelligibility, is thus profoundly social. Because it refers to the appropriate rule-following in social life or a specific practice, practical consciousness implies *shared* skills and understandings.[16] Practical consciousness does not exist only in individuals' minds; communities of practitioners intersubjectively share it as collective knowledge and act as part of a collective doing. The evolution of practices is a collective process akin to, for example, language. Seldom is the name of a linguistic innovator remembered (e.g., who decided that "thou" would now be pronounced "you"?). Because words, expressions, and idioms evolve in a highly intersubjective process, finding individual norm promoters or contesters appears futile in understanding the evolution of language.

Sociality and relations are not the results of "conscious actions of pre-social individuals," but an "intermeshing of individuals."[17] Similarly, pragmatist philosopher George Herbert Mead argued that the mind cannot exist except with its social environment and that "an organized set or pattern of social relations and interactions . . . is necessarily presupposed by it and involved in its nature."[18] A robust relational ontology based on intersubjectivity means that no one can set themselves apart from existing bodies of knowledge acquired by and from other people. As Ernst and Peter Haas explain, learning does not happen in individual minds, but through the evolution of collectively held knowledge:

> You probably know that the earth is round and that it is in orbit around the sun. But how do you know this? . . . Obviously, it takes a brain in a living body, but it also takes a very complex social, cultural, and historical system, which has accumulated learning over time.[19]

African and Chinese relational philosophies

If IR scholars often describe relational ontologies as coming from American or French critical theorists and interactionists, the "relational turn" in IR has always been supported by the contributions of postcolonial scholars, most of whom had never adopted the field's individualist and substantialist biases. Most practice-oriented scholars have also ignored relational or collectivist approaches from the Global South (just as they have ignored feminist approaches).[20] This is surprising because Sub-Saharan African and Chinese philosophers have theorized the relational character of agency in communities for a long time. An example present in many African cultures is the Ubuntu philosophy, which refers to the "interconnectedness of all things,"[21] or the fact that "my humanness depends on your humanness."[22] Like many American relational sociologists and Chinese IR social theories, Thomas Kwasi Tieku asserts that many Africans who adopt an Ubuntu philosophy do not think they "have" relations with each other, but that they "are" relations.[23] Considering collectivist and relational aspects of IR and developing relational methodological tools to study world politics would make our understanding of world orders much deeper and broader.

While not all African philosophies build on relational ontologies, the Ubuntu philosophy's profound attachment to the community led many African scholars to develop approaches that perceive the individual only within a larger context of the whole community.[24] As Michael Onyebuchi Eze explains, African communitarianism does not preclude subjectivity, but individuals and the community both need each other to exist purposefully.[25] This idea does not mean that all members are equal or similar, nor that social structures predetermine us, but that we share a sense of unified purpose in communities. This robust relational ontology is what implicitly or explicitly predominates in CoPs (more so than other IR practice approaches).

Chinese relational philosophers also inspired the relational/processual turn in IR and the one developed in this book. For them, the social world is in a "universe of relatedness."[26] In a community, intersubjectivity means members' "properties and attributes are forged through the self's relations with significant others and with the relational totality she is embedded in."[27] Like Ubuntu approaches about humanness, existence in Chinese ontologies refers to coexistence, which means that "self-existence is simultaneously coexistence with others."[28] Moreover, this coexistence in Chinese thought refers not only to relations but also to a continuous process of becoming in relations. This mutual constitution with other community members, but also with the surrounding context, is at the core of a CoP approach to collective learning. Chinese society and Confucian philosophy tend to converge on the argument that humans are relational beings and, therefore, relations have preeminence to both units and societies:

> Interpersonal relations are of crucial importance (for Asians) not only historically in the formation of the human character but also contemporaneously in defining what it means to be human throughout the individual's lifetime. The life of the individual . . . derives its meaning only from the coexistence of other individuals. Without others, the very notion of individual identity loses meaning. In this sense, Asian conceptions of social existence are relation centered.[29]

A theory of collective learning in CoPs fully embraces what Qin calls a logic of relationality, in which actions are based mainly on relations and identities are forged in the process of relating and being related to other humans. Interestingly, the word "I" has many different translations in Chinese (and in Japanese), all reflecting the positionality of actors in a web of relations: for example, "I" can be in relation to a spouse or to a colleague. The self is always in relation to others, and these relationships take form only in a specific context. "I" is thus always in a certain setting and relationship to others.[30] The logic of relationality means that actors exist, act, and make judgments according to these relationships, and these relations are dynamic rather than fixed. This quick introduction to Ubuntu and Chinese relational philosophies seeks to address the silencing of these approaches in praxeologies in IR.

The exclusion of non-Western aspects of the relational turn in IR (and most CoP approaches) comes from the fact that knowledge produced by researchers in IR is indebted to the cultural community they come from.[31] Western scholars, adopting relational approaches or not, continue to prioritize, cite, and teach Western scholars to further develop the families they created. So, these scholarly families remain exclusionary of non-Western thought, in publications and in teaching.[32] The collective learning framework at the heart of this book is indebted to both Western and non-Western traditions of thought, as well as feminist activists and scholars.[33]

Relations in motion in processual/relationalism

Adhering to Chinese philosophical insights as formulated by Qin, the evolutionary constructivism as formulated by Adler and decolonial feminists like Gloria Anzaldúa, this book seeks to bring the relational turn further by conceiving the social world as made not only of relations but also of relations *in motion*. In comparison to many relational approaches in IR, including many networks, feminists, and postcolonial ones, processual/relational ontologies assume that both entities and relations are processes in constant evolution. If many IR scholars theorize the "relational turn" in IR as one family of theories alongside substantialist ones,[34] there are also differences between relational and relational/processual theories. The former, while looking at relations, does not necessarily look at constant fluctuations of relations in world ordering. In other words, as an emergent effect of a process, a social relation can be a reality (a "thing") existing between two or more agents.[35] However, not all relational sensibilities study the "unfolding, dynamic, and productive *processes* through which states, civilizations and individual emerges."[36]

One example of a relational approach not *necessarily* processual is how Bourdieu (or, rather, Bourdieusian applications in IR) adopts a relational sociology of fields made of hierarchical relations between actors or social classes.[37] There is no doubt that in Bourdieu's fields, "the real is the relational."[38] However, relations are not defined as evolving interactions but "*objective relations*, which exist independently of individual consciousness and will."[39] A field is "either a structure in formation or already formed and imposing itself on agents as recipients."[40] Anna Leander even argues that while the habitus allows for a range of choices and strategies, the rules entrenched in the habitus are ultimately inescapable.[41]

Similarly, like some early IR feminist scholars,[42] most network approaches favor relations over processes: actors (men/women) exist a priori, and they enter relations as such. Despite a trend of dynamic actor-network approaches,[43] networks in IR have primarily been defined as modes of organization among actors. To explain social ordering, network theories have put the focus on the coexistence of multiple (and potentially overlapping) smaller social orders.[44] Many focus on relations as "structural properties of networks" and how these networks have a long-lasting effect on actors' hierarchies or positions.[45] This is where CoP analysis jumps in to theorize the intricacies of *how* interactions shape social ordering. While some actor-network theories are also relational and processual by looking at the ongoing enactment of reality, network members do not necessarily engage in a joint enterprise, domain of knowledge, or shared practice. A robust processual/relational approach is not about changes in the position of things but about a collection of processes and relations leading to what entities *are* or *are becoming*.[46]

The theoretical innovation of a robust processual/relational ontology is to see relations, entities, practices, and knowledge as all in a *constant state of becoming*; that is, because actors or entities (substances) and relations are both in process.[47]

A process of becoming in a processual/relational ontology does not refer to changes in one specific thing but to changes in the general condition of things; it involves not only one event but also various events, and events exist "only in and through processes."[48]

The French philosopher Emanuel Renault argues that the distinctive aspect of processual ontologies is that a relation or substance's dawn or endpoint is nothing but moments of becoming.[49] This argument does not mean that relational and substantial properties are subordinated to processes, but that they are made of processes. Most things appear stable, but such seemingly persistent things are in fact dynamic organizations made of the continuous interaction of manifolds of processes.[50] In other words, entities are instantiations of processes or analytically separated moments during a process. This does not mean that relations are *prior* to actors or entities, but that relations and actors exist processually in simultaneity.

Social ordering through CoP

Practice-oriented scholars in IR have solidified a novel research program based on the ontological primacy of social practices, that is, "socially meaningful patterns of action, which, in being performed more or less competently, simultaneously embody, act out, and possibly reify background knowledge and discourse in and on the material world."[51] In other words, practices are routinized deeds individuals arranged in social configurations perform while constantly negotiating shared knowledge. Practices are the building blocks of the social world and are organized in domains of knowledge (or CoP). The ongoing enactment of practices by actors sustains or modifies social structures so that practices connect individuals and structures in a constant process of change.[52]

As demonstrated by Jean Lave and Etienne Wenger,[53] we practice in communities, as part of a "nexus of connections."[54] Despite injunctions to look at individual subjectivities to explain change,[55] domains of knowledge are the vehicles of practices where collective learning (and change) happens, and where to look to understand social ordering. Members bounded together by a CoP adopt new practices not only because someone tells them to do so vertically, triggered by a person of greater seniority, but also because they negotiate meaningful actions with their peers horizontally. Because communities enact practices through shared and collectively recognized criteria of competence, it gives a unique role to intersubjective relations, defined as structures of communicative relations between individuals who can take the perspective of the other into their own.[56] An intersubjective dialogue also means that individuals mutually relate to each other's beliefs, given a shared background of assumptions and practice.[57]

Enacted within communities, international practices make the world "hang together," where intersubjective understandings sustaining the international realm coalesce.[58] In other words, social orders are features of nexuses of practices and CoPs.[59] As "landscapes,"[60] "constellations,"[61] "collections,"[62] or "fields"[63] of practices and CoP, social orders are continually evolving arrangements of people and material entities rendered meaningful collectively by social practices. Thus, social orders are temporal processes reproduced (and challenged) collectively by practices; CoP and their practice thus "do" the social ordering of the world.[64] Sometimes overlapping, clusters of CoPs and practices are part of what interconnects organizations, states, non-governmental actors, normative structures, along with their social environment. An IO is a constellation of communities of practice.[65]

A processual ontology aimed at explaining social ordering inevitably leads to a conceptualization of change and stability as parts of the same process of fluctuations of practices enacted in communities instead of opposites waiting to be bridged. This is why many CoP scholars, as well as most practice scholars, prefer active (or processual) verbs such as ordering or structuring over their static counterparts of order or structure,[66] since "social orders" are often associated with social reproduction.[67] Change happens continuously, but as part of a meta-stability: "a continuous flow halted only temporarily when obstacles crop up and which can be divided into discrete unit acts only in retrospect."[68]

Since practices entail irregularities and unexpected elements, they are in "constant motion" despite routinization.[69] Scholars of social orders usually picture international practices and IOs as stable unless in times of great transformation.[70] As do historical institutionalists, norm-oriented constructivists have a path-dependent vision of the evolution of social orders, that is, how past norms, culture, and critical junctures shape the future. The ratchet effect, for example, understands the emergence of new norms and practices as an accumulation over time, whereas changing patterns of practice lock in and accumulate over time.[71] It makes sense that new norms must indeed have "pertinence, relevance, or significance" to targeted groups; therefore, policymakers shape new ideas in resonance with existing structures to make them acceptable (e.g., liberal environmentalism or sustainable development) or with their political rationality.[72] However, social structures do not simply evolve to accumulate new knowledge, rules, or norms that fit pre-existing ones. Social learning involves participants in a CoP discarding part of existing knowledge, slightly changing others, and bringing new understandings to the forefront.

Ontological narrative as discourse of becoming

Collective learning is mediated through the evolution of ontological narratives. "We live by stories; we also live in them."[73] Ontological narratives relate to what Rescher calls "spatiotemporal continuity"[74] (the process of creating the future with the materials of the past) and Adler's concept of immanence (the preservation of the past in the present, the present being creatively "pulled" forward by expectations of the future).[75] Wenger uses the example of traditional apprentices, who not only acquire new skills but are also exposed to possible futures.[76] Narratives refer to how actors mobilize a sense of who they are and where they come from, developing a sense of trajectory that expands their identity in time.[77] A becoming ontology that integrates the past, the present, and the future in a novel vision of temporality helps us understand how actors give a sense of their evolution and integrate their past, present, and future actions.

A modification in how an organization interprets its narrative can accelerate the pace of changes in practice and institutionalize such fluctuations in practices. When senior managers alter the organization's narrative (i.e., its verbalized purpose and justification for action), it enables employees to adopt new practices. If discourse is a mode of communication following certain norms and assigning meaning to the world, a narrative concerns a temporally defined discursive interpretation of oneself. An organization's narrative concerns shared beliefs about the evolution over time of its purpose and its goals. A shift in narrative is not sufficient to trigger a change in practices, but it is necessary to institutionalize any significant change.

If some scholars of literary art reduced narratives to their simplest expression: a "manner of speaking about events,"[78] philosophers of history conceptualized narratives as forms of representations: representational templates used to order the chaos of lived experience.[79] Narrative psychologists believe that people view themselves and others following narratives, as in stories of success and failure, of development and decline.[80] More recently, rationalist political scientists have represented narratives as a discursive "thing" that individuals and organizations can use strategically.[81] Methodologically, narrative inquiry assumes that people lead storied lives that they communicate in the narrative form.[82] Following Margaret Somers' conceptualization,[83] this book shifts from these representational, methodological, and instrumental views toward an *ontological* view of social narratives.

Narratives (stories and their telling) are far from being a pure representation of events, they are hermeneutic understandings of past, present, or future action. They are based on our interpretation of reality instead of a depiction of it. As "self-interpreting animals,"[84] individuals, communities, and collective actors believe in a particular narrative about themselves, which evolves over time. This narrative becomes a plausible explanation, rationalization, and justification meant to create order in a shifting, unpredictable, and confusing social world.[85] People (through individual narratives) and organizations (through collective or social narratives) use discourse to make sense of events by assembling and integrating them into stories that subsequently become part of their identity, and lead their practices.[86] Social narratives are thus a crucial concept to understanding the trajectories of practices. For example, solely analysing refugees actions is insufficient to understand them. How they define their journey, reconstruct their history, and where their expectations lead them are crucial stories to understanding their practice.

Because narratives provide "a moral compass" for practitioners to make practical judgments, they are often more tacit than verbalized.[87] It is difficult to distinguish between a narrative mode of thought and its discourse, and trying to do so would be a vain enterprise.[88] Researchers' goal is thus often to reconstruct a discourse that has yet to be previously verbalized. Bueger, for example, reconstructed the narrative of Somali pirates through publicly available interviews and found a discourse that was not verbalized apart from these interviews. He recognized that pirates organized themselves around a "grand narrative" of piracy as a legitimate practice of protecting borders against foreign intruders instead of viewing themselves as thieves.[89] The concept of narrative is not used to understand what people have "in their minds" but the becoming process of a collective actor – how their interpretation of their actions evolved. Narratives often resist contradictory information because they are entrenched in a community's identity and give them a sense of ontological security.

The relationship between narrative and practice is constitutive in that neither has ontological or temporal precedence over the other. Because they participate in meaning-making processes, narratives do not "cause" a given practice but give "reasons" for it.[90] While some scholars see narratives in an instrumental manner, as something promoted by a practice, ontological narratives are often not the stories used by actors strategically. Instead, they are normative and cognitive templates for making practical judgments or negotiating moral dilemmas. They help organizations adjust to new situations or explain past deeds. As the organizational sociologist Nancy Dixon argues, we interpret the world in light of an existing meaning structure (i.e., we often see what we expect to see); new narratives give actors new avenues to interpret their external environment and their own practice.[91]

Neither action nor narrative is prior to the other because a CoP's practice would be illegible without an associated narrative. While understandings of ourselves in the world "make practice possible," practices also largely "carry the understanding."[92] Narratives circumscribe changes in practice, enable new practices to emerge, and give intelligibility to routinized actions.

Narratives and practices are co-constituted in three main ways. First, formulating narratives about one's practices gives the world intelligibility, that is, what actions make sense to perform in each situation. Practices are the site where understanding is structured and intelligibility articulates; thus, narratives do not create practices or knowledge in a causal fashion; they dynamically enable a practice to unfold as it does.[93] Practices of non-proliferation, on the one hand, are what they are not only because of what states do but also because of what states say and believe about the effectiveness of performing non-proliferation. On the other hand, if states were only talking about non-proliferation but not acting accordingly *at all*, discourse would not lead to non-proliferation. The usefulness of narratives to understand an organization's action is pointing to *the reasons* rather than the of the *causes* for a practice. Second, the evolution of a narrative does not cause a given repertoire of practices in the traditional sense because practices are often already in motion when discourse shifts. A shift in narrative can lead to an acceleration, multiplication, scaling up, and institutionalization of existing practices, or the downgrading or termination of others. An evolving narrative opens possibilities for new practices to emerge and for existing ones to gain traction. Third, changes in practices can make a new discourse more coherent, acceptable, and resilient, reinforcing the discursive change. A leader or someone in an IO's CoP will only be successful in changing a narrative if a change in practices somehow follows. Conversely, if marginal practices become more frequent, they will strengthen or downgrade an IO's existing narrative. A narrative thus depends on action to become more legitimate and to be recognized as a CoP's ontological narrative. The relationship between narratives and practices is thus co-constitutive and self-reinforcing.

Conclusion

Although constantly evolving relations and interactions between communities make up the social world, these processes are seldom studied in IR. A processual and relational approach that examines CoPs can bring a new vocabulary to explain processes of becoming over time. By doing so, it furthers our understanding of world ordering. Individuals, institutions, and organizations are in a constant process of realignment of experience and competence, which presupposes that intersubjectivity plays a role in ordering things. Collective learning forms the basis for changes in and of practices in world politics, as much as (and sometimes more than) contestation or changes in shareholders' interests. Without such processes of cognitive evolution, we would stop *becoming* and simply *be.*

Notes

1 Jackson and Nexon, "Relations before States."
2 Wendt, *Quantum Mind and Social Science.*
3 Qin, *A Relational Theory of World Politics.*
4 Adler, *World Ordering.*
5 Kurki, "Relational Revolution and Relationality in IR."
6 McCourt, "Practice Theory and Relationalism as the New Constructivism."
7 Adler, Bremberg, and Sondarjee, "Communities of Practice in World Politics."
8 Elias, *What is Sociology?* 111.
9 Qin; Kurki; McCourt, *The New Constructivism in International Relations Theory.*
10 (Donati 2015, 87; see also Dladla 2017; Enloe 1990; Collins 2019).
11 Qin, 115.
12 (1990).
13 Archer, *Being Human*, 121.
14 Gronow, *From Habits to Social Structures.*
15 Schatzki, *Social Practices.*
16 Schatzki, "Introduction," 12.
17 Joas, *G. H. Mead*, 184.
18 Mead, *Mind, Self, and Society*, 223.
19 Haas and Haas, "Learning to Learn," 262.
20 Chessé and Sondarjee, "A Feminist Critique of International Practices"; Wilcox, "Practising Gender, Queering Theory."
21 Graham, "Expanding the Philosophical Base of Social Work," 144.
22 Tamale, *Decolonization and Afro-Feminism*, 21.
23 Tieku, "Collectivist Worldview: Its Challenge to International Relations," 36.
24 Cobbah, "African Values and the Human Rights Debate: An African Perspective"; Ramose, *African Philosophy through Ubuntu*; Tamale; Sow, "Mobiliser Les Femmes Dans l'Afrique Contemporaine"; Sarr, *Afrotopia.*
25 Eze, "What Is African Communitarianism?" 388.
26 Qin, 108; Zhao, "Rethinking Empire from a Chinese Concept."
27 Qin, 117.
28 Qin and Nordin, "Relationality and Rationality in Confucian and Western Traditions of Thought," 606; Zhao.
29 Ho, "Relational Orientation and Methodological Individualism," 82; Huang, Bedford, and Zhang, "The Relational Orientation Framework for Examining Culture in Chinese Societies."
30 Nisbett, *The Geography of Thought*, 158.

31 Qin and Nordin, 604.
32 Odoom and Andrews, "What/Who Is Still Missing in International Relations Scholarship?"; Tickner and Smith, *International Relations from the Global South*; Medie and Kang, "Power, Knowledge and the Politics of Gender in the Global South"; Fonseca, "Global IR and Western Dominance"; Sondarjee, "We Are a Community of Practice, Not a Paradigm!"
33 Chessé and Sondarjee.
34 (Kurki 2021; Nordin et al. 2019; McCourt 2022; Jackson and Nexon 1999).
35 Donati, "Manifesto for a Critical Realist Relational Sociology," 90.
36 Nordin et al., 572–73.
37 Bourdieu, *The Logic of Practice*; Renault, "Critical Theory and Processual Social Ontology," 22.
38 Bourdieu and Wacquant, *An Invitation to Reflexive Sociology*, 97.
39 Bourdieu and Wacquant, 97, emphasis added.
40 Bigo, "Pierre Bourdieu and International Relations," 239; King, "Thinking with Bourdieu Against Bourdieu."
41 Leander, "The Promises, Problems, and Potentials of a Bourdieu-Inspired Staging of International Relations," 299.
42 Tickner, "Hans Morgenthau's Principles of Political Realism"; Enloe, *Bananas, Beaches and Bases*.
43 Lapid and Kratochwil, *The Return of Culture and Identity in IR Theory*; Somers, "The Narrative Constitution of Identity."
44 Slaughter, *A New World Order*.
45 Hafner-Burton, Kahler, and Montgomery, "Network Analysis for International Relations," 559; Zarakol, *Hierarchies in World Politics*.
46 Adler, 47; Whitehead, *Process and Reality*.
47 Adler; Wendt.
48 Rescher, *Process Metaphysics*, 38.
49 Renault, 22.
50 Rescher, 51; Qin.
51 Adler and Pouliot, *International Practices*, 6.
52 Giddens, *The Constitution of Society*.
53 (1991).
54 Nicolini, *Practice Theory, Work, and Organization an Introduction*, 229.
55 Hopf, "Change in International Practices."
56 Joas, 13; Daanen and Sammut, "G. H. Mead and Knowing How to Act," 557.
57 Kögler, "Agency and the Other," 53.
58 Ruggie, "What Makes the World Hang Together?" 2–3.
59 Schatzki, 14.
60 Wenger-Trayner et al., *Learning in Landscapes of Practice*.
61 Wenger, *Communities of Practice. Learning*, 129.
62 Adler, *Communitarian International Relations*, 14.
63 Schatzki, 5.
64 Adler, Bremberg, and Sondarjee; Bueger, Hofius, and Edwards, "Global Ordering and the Interaction of Communities of Practice."
65 Brown and Duguid, "Organizational Learning and Communities of Practice"; Fox, "Communities of Practice, Foucault and Actor-Network Theory."
66 Bueger and Gadinger, "The Play of International Practice," 453.
67 Reckwitz, "Toward a Theory of Social Practices," 255; Schatzki, 13.
68 Joas and Knöbl, *Social Theory. Twenty Introductory Lectures*, 290.
69 Nicolini, 164; Schatzki, *The Site of the Social*, 101.
70 Cox and Sinclair, *Approaches to World Order*; Nexon, *The Struggle for Power in Early Modern Europe*; Phillips, *War, Religion and Empire*; Ikenberry, *After Victory*.

71 Pouliot and Thérien, "The Politics of Inclusion."
72 Sondarjee, "Change and Stability at the World Bank."
73 Nigerian storyteller Ben Okri, cited in King, *The Truth about Stories*, 153.
74 Rescher, 39.
75 Adler, 47.
76 Wenger.
77 Lave and Wenger, *Situated Learning*.
78 White, "The Value of Narrativity in the Representation of Reality."
79 Mink, "The Autonomy of Historical Understanding."
80 Sugiman, *Meaning in Action*.
81 Roselle, Miskimmon, and O'Loughlin, "Strategic Narrative."
82 Clandinin, "Narrative Inquiry"; Connelly and Clandinin, "Stories of Experience and Narrative Inquiry."
83 Somers.
84 Taylor, *Modern Social Imaginaries*, chapter 2.
85 Wagenaar, *Meaning in Action*, 215.
86 Somers and Gibson, "Reclaiming the Epistemological 'Other'," 38.
87 Bueger, "Practice, Pirates and Coast Guards," 1817.
88 Bruner, "The Narrative Construction of Reality," 5.
89 Bueger.
90 Bruner, 7.
91 Dixon, *The Organizational Learning Cycle*.
92 Taylor, 25.
93 Schatzki, 118.

References

Adler, Emanuel. *Communitarian International Relations. The Epistemic Foundations of International Relations*. London and New York: Routledge, 2005.
Adler, Emanuel. *World Ordering. A Social Theory of Cognitive Evolution*. Cambridge: Cambridge University Press, 2019.
Adler, Emanuel, Niklas Bremberg, and Maïka Sondarjee. "Communities of Practice in World Politics: Advancing a Research Agenda." *Global Studies Quarterly* 4, no. 1 (2024): ksad070.
Adler, Emanuel, and Vincent Pouliot. *International Practices*. Edited by Emanuel Adler and Vincent Pouliot. New York: Cambridge University Press, 2011.
Archer, Margaret S. *Being Human: The Problem of Agency*. Cambridge: Cambridge University Press, 2003.
Bergson, Henri. *Creative Evolution*. New York: The Modern Library, 1911.
Bigo, Didier. "Pierre Bourdieu and International Relations: Power of Practices, Practices of Power." *International Political Sociology* 5 (2011): 225–58.
Bourdieu, Pierre. *The Logic of Practice*. Translated by Richard Nice. Stanford, CA: Stanford University Press, 1990.
Bourdieu, Pierre, and Loic Wacquant. *An Invitation to Reflexive Sociology*. Chicago: The University of Chicago Press, 1992.
Brown, John Seely, and Paul Duguid. "Organizational Learning and Communities of Practice." *Organization Science* 2 (1991): 40–57.
Bruner, Jerome. "The Narrative Construction of Reality." *Critical Inquiry* 18, no. 1 (1991): 1–21.
Bueger, Christian. "Practice, Pirates and Coast Guards: The Grand Narrative of Somali Piracy." *Third World Quarterly* 34, no. 10 (2013): 1811–27.
Bueger, Christian, and Frank Gadinger. "The Play of International Practice." *International Studies Quarterly*, no. 59 (2015): 449–60.

Bueger, Christian, Maren Hofius, and Scott Edwards. "Global Ordering and the Interaction of Communities of Practice: A Framework for Analysis." *Global Studies Quarterly* 4, no. 1 (January 27, 2024): ksad079. https://doi.org/10.1093/isagsq/ksad079.

Chessé, Alice, and Maïka Sondarjee. "A Feminist Critique of International Practices." *International Studies Quarterly* 68, no. 2 (2024): 1–10.

Clandinin, D. Jean. "Narrative Inquiry: A Methodology for Studying Lived Experience." *Research Studies in Music Education*, no. 27 (2006): 11.

Cobbah, Josiah. "African Values and the Human Rights Debate: An African Perspective." *Human Rights Quarterly* (1987): 309–31.

Connelly, F. M., and D Jean Clandinin. "Stories of Experience and Narrative Inquiry." *Educational Researcher* 19, no. 5 (1990): 2–14.

Cox, Robert W., and Timothy J. Sinclair. *Approaches to World Order. Cambridge Studies in International Relations 40.* Cambridge and New York: Cambridge University Press, 1996.

Daanen, Paul, and Gordon Sammut. "G. H. Mead and Knowing How to Act: Practical Meaning, Routine Interaction, and the Theory of Interobjectivity." *Theory and Psychology* 22, no. 5 (2012): 556–71.

Daft, Richard L., and Karl E. Weick. "Toward a Model of Organizations as Interpretation Systems." *The Academy of Management Review* 9, no. 2 (April 19 84): 284.

Dixon, Nancy M. *The Organizational Learning Cycle: How We Can Learn Collectively*. 2nd ed. Brookfield, VT: Gower, 1999.

Donati, Pierpaolo. "Manifesto for a Critical Realist Relational Sociology." *International Review of Sociology – Revue Internationale de Sociologie* 25, no. 1 (2015): 86–109.

Elias, Norbert. *What is Sociology?* Translated by Stephen Mennell and Grace Morrissey. New York: Columbia University Press, 1978.

Enloe, Cynthia H. *Bananas, Beaches and Bases: Making Feminist Sense of International Politics.* 1st U.S. ed. Berkeley: University of California Press, 1990.

Eze, Michael Onyebuchi. "What is African Communitarianism? Against Consensus as a Regulative Ideal." *South African Journal of Philosophy* 27, no. 4 (January 2008): 386–99.

Fonseca, Melody. "Global IR and Western Dominance: Moving Forward or Eurocentric Entrapment?" *Millennium: Journal of International Studies* 48, no. 1 (September 2019): 45–59.

Fox, Stephen. "Communities of Practice, Foucault and Actor-Network Theory." *Journal of Management Studies* 37, no. 6 (September 2000): 853–68.

Giddens, Anthony. "Comments on the Theory of Structuration." *Journal for the Theory of Social Behaviour* 13, no. 1 (1983): 75–80.

Giddens, Anthony. *The Constitution of Society*. Cambridge: Polity Press with Blackwell Publishing, 1984.

Graham, Mekada. "Expanding the Philosophical Base of Social Work." In *Social Work: A Reader*, 142–48. London: Routledge, 2011.

Gronow, Antti. *From Habits to Social Structures: Pragmatism and Contemporary Social Theory. Studies in Sociology: Symbols, Theory and Society*. Vol. 7. Frankfurt am Main and New York: Peter Lang, 2011.

Haas, Peter M., and Ernst B. Haas. "Learning to Learn: Improving International Governance." *Global Governance* 1 (1995): 255.

Hafner-Burton, Emilie M., Miles Kahler, and Alexander H. Montgomery. "Network Analysis for International Relations." *International Organization* 63 (2009): 559–92.

Ho, D. Y. F. "Relational Orientation and Methodological Individualism." *Bulletin of the Hong Kong Psychological Society* 26–27 (1991): 81–95.

Hopf, Ted. "Change in International Practices." *European Journal of International Relations* (2017): 1–25.

Huang, Yi-Hui, Olwen Bedford, and Yin Zhang. "The Relational Orientation Framework for Examining Culture in Chinese Societies." *Culture & Psychology* 24, no. 4 (December 2018): 477–90.

Ikenberry, G. John. *After Victory*. Princeton: Princeton University Press, 2001.
Ish-Shalom, Piki, Markus Kornprobst, and Vincent Pouliot, eds. *Theorizing World Orders: Cognitive Evolution and Beyond*. Cambridge and New York: Cambridge University Press, 2021.
Jackson, Patrick Thaddeus, and Daniel H. Nexon. "Relations Before States: Substance, Process and the Study of World Politics." *European Journal of International Relations* 5, no. 3 (1999): 291–332.
Joas, Hans. *G. H. Mead, a Contemporary Re-Examination of His Thought*. Cambridge [Cambridgeshire]: Polity Press, 1985.
Joas, Hans, and Wolfgang Knöbl. *Social Theory. Twenty Introductory Lectures*. Cambridge: Cambridge University Press, 2009.
Kavalski, Emilian. *The Guanxi of Relational International Theory*. New York: Routledge, 2018.
King, Anthony. "Thinking with Bourdieu Against Bourdieu: A 'Practical' Critique of the Habitus." *Sociological Theory* 18, no. 3 (2000): 417–33.
King, Thomas. *The Truth about Stories*. Toronto: Anansi Press, 2003.
Kögler, Hans-Herbert. "Agency and the Other: On the Intersubjective Roots of Self-Identity." *New Ideas in Psychology*, no. 30 (2012): 47–64.
Kurki, Milja. "Relational Revolution and Relationality in IR: New Conversations." *Review of International Studies* (March 31, 2021): 1–16.
Lapid, Yosef, and Friedrich Kratochwil. *The Return of Culture and Identity in IR Theory*. Boulder, CO: Lynne Rienner Publishers, 1997.
Lave, Jean, and Etienne Wenger. *Situated Learning. Legitimate Peripheral Participation*. Cambridge: Cambridge University Press, 1991.
Leander, Anna. "The Promises, Problems, and Potentials of a Bourdieu-Inspired Staging of International Relations." *International Political Sociology* 5 (2011): 294–313.
McCourt, David. "Practice Theory and Relationalism as the New Constructivism." *International Studies Quarterly* 60, no. 3 (2016): 475–85.
McCourt, David M. *The New Constructivism in International Relations Theory*. 1st ed. Bristol University Press, 2022. https://doi.org/10.2307/j.ctv293p48m.
Mead, George Herbert. *Mind, Self, and Society: From the Standpoint of a Social Behaviorist. Works of George Herbert Mead, George Herbert Mead*. Vol. 1. Chicago: University of Chicago Press, 1934.
Medic, Peace A., and Alice J. Kang. "Power, Knowledge and the Politics of Gender in the Global South." *European Journal of Politics and Gender* 1, no. 1 (July 13, 2018): 37–53.
Mink, Louis O. "The Autonomy of Historical Understanding." In *Philosophical Analysis and History*, edited by William H. Dray and Harper & Row, 160–92. New York: Harper & Row, 1966.
Nexon, Daniel H. *The Struggle for Power in Early Modern Europe: Religious Conflict, Dynastic Empires, and International Change*. Princeton, NJ: Princeton University Press, 2009.
Nicolini, Davide. *Practice Theory, Work, and Organization an Introduction*. Oxford: Oxford University Press, 2012.
Nisbett, Richard E. *The Geography of Thought: How Asians and Westerners Think Differently . . . and Why. Nachdr*. New York: Free Press, 2004.
Nordin, Astrid H. M., Graham M. Smith, Raoul Bunskoek, Chiung-Chiu Huang, Yih-Jye (Jay) Hwang, Patrick Thaddeus Jackson, Emilian Kavalski, et al. "Towards Global Relational Theorizing: A Dialogue between Sinophone and Anglophone Scholarship on Relationalism." *Cambridge Review of International Affairs* 32, no. 5 (September 3, 2019): 570–81.
Odoom, Isaac, and Nathan Andrews. "What/Who is Still Missing in International Relations Scholarship? Situating Africa as an Agent in IR Theorising." *Third World Quarterly* 38, no. 1 (January 2, 2017): 42–60.

Phillips, Andrew. *War, Religion and Empire: The Transformation of International Orders. Cambridge Studies in International Relations 117*. Cambridge and New York: Cambridge University Press, 2011.
Pouliot, Vincent, and Jean-Philippe Thérien. "The Politics of Inclusion: Changing Patterns in the Governance of International Security." *Review of International Studies*, no. 41 (2015): 211–37.
Qin, Yaqing. *A Relational Theory of World Politics*. Cambridge: Cambridge University Press, 2018.
Qin, Yaqing, and Astrid H. M. Nordin. "Relationality and Rationality in Confucian and Western Traditions of Thought." *Cambridge Review of International Affairs* 32, no. 5 (September 3, 2019): 601–14.
Ramose, Mogobe B. *African Philosophy through Ubuntu*. Harare: Mond Books, 2005.
Reckwitz, Andreas. "Toward a Theory of Social Practices. A Development in Culturalist Theorizing." *European Journal of Social Theory* 5, no. 2 (2002): 243–63.
Renault, Emmanuel. "Critical Theory and Processual Social Ontology." *Journal of Social Ontology* 2, no. 1 (2016): 17–32.
Rescher, Nicholas. *Process Metaphysics: An Introduction to Process Philosophy*. Albany: State University of New York Press, 1996.
Roselle, Laura, Alister Miskimmon, and Ben O'Loughlin. "Strategic Narrative: A New Means to Understand Soft Power." *Media, War and Conflict* 7, no. 1 (2014): 70–84.
Ruggie, John G. "What Makes the World Hang Together? Neo-Utilitarianism and the Social Constructivist Challenge." *International Organization* 52 (1998): 855–85.
Sarr, Felwine. *Afrotopia*. Paris: Philippe Rey, 2016.
Schatzki, Theodore Richard. *Social Practices. A Wittgensteinian Approach to Human Activity and the Social*. Cambridge: Cambridge University Press, 1996.
Schatzki, Theodore Richard. "Introduction: Practice Theory." In *The Practice Turn in Contemporary Theory*, edited by Theodore R. Schatzki, Karin Knorr Cetina, and Eike Von Savigny, 10–23. London and New York: Routledge, 2001.
Schatzki, Theodore Richard. *The Site of the Social: A Philosophical Account of the Constitution of Social Life and Change*. University Park: The Pennsylvania State University Press, 2002.
Slaughter, Anne-Marie. *A New World Order*. Princeton: Princeton University Press, 2004.
Somers, Margaret R. "The Narrative Constitution of Identity: A Relational and Network Approach." *Theory and Society* 23, no. 5 (1994): 605–49.
Somers, Margaret R., and Gloria Gibson. "Reclaiming the Epistemological 'Other': Narrative and the Social Construction of Identity." In *Social Theory and the Politics of Identity*, edited by Craig Calhoun. Malden, MA: Blackwell Publishers, 2017.
Sondarjee, Maïka. "Change and Stability at the World Bank: Inclusive Practices and Neoliberal Technocratic Rationality." *Third World Quarterly* 42, no. 2 (2021): 348–65.
Sondarjee, Maïka. "We Are a Community of Practice, Not a Paradigm! How to Meaningfully Integrate Gender and Feminist Approaches in IR Syllabi." *International Studies Perspectives* 23, no. 3 (2022): 229–48.
Sow, Fatou. "Mobiliser Les Femmes Dans l'Afrique Contemporaine." In *Perspectives Féministes En Relations Internationales. Penser Le Monde Autrement*, edited by Maïka Sondarjee, 71–80. Montreal, Quebec: Presses de l'Université de Montréal, 2022.
Standfield, Catriona. "Gendering the Practice Turn in Diplomacy." *European Journal of International Relations*, 6, no.1: 140–165.
Sugiman, Toshio, ed. *Meaning in Action: Constructions, Narratives, and Representations*. Tokyo: Springer, 2008.
Tamale, Sylvia. *Decolonization and Afro-Feminism*. Ottawa: Daraja Press, 2020.
Taylor, Charles. *Modern Social Imaginaries*. Durham: Duke University Press, 2004.
Tickner, Arlene B., and Karen Smith, eds. *International Relations from the Global South: Worlds of Difference. Wording Beyond the West*. New York: Routledge, 2020.

Tickner, J. Ann. "Hans Morgenthau's Principles of Political Realism: A Feminist Reformulation." *Millennium – Journal of International Studies* 17, no. 3 (1988): 430–40.

Tieku, Thomas Kwasi. "Collectivist Worldview: Its Challenge to International Relations." In *Africa and International Relations in the 21st Century*, edited by Scarlett Cornelissen, Fantu Cheru, and Timothy M. Shaw, 36–50. New York: Palgrave MacMillan, 2012.

Tieku, Thomas Kwasi, and Afua Boatemaa Yakohene. "Exploring Communities of Practice from an Informality Perspective: Insights from the AU, ECOWAS, and UN in West African Mediation Theaters." *Global Studies Quarterly* 4, no. 1 (2024): 1–1.

Wagenaar, Hendrik. *Meaning in Action. Interpretation and Dialogue in Policy Analysis*. London and New York: Routledge, 2011.

Wendt, Alexander. *Quantum Mind and Social Science*. Cambridge: Cambridge University Press, 2015.

Wenger, Etienne. *Communities of Practice. Learning, Meaning, and Identity*. Cambridge: Cambridge University Press, 1998.

Wenger-Trayner, Etienne, Mark Fenton-O'Creevy, Steven Hutchison, and Beverly Wenger-Trayner, eds. *Learning in Landscapes of Practice: Boundaries, Identity, and Knowledgeability in Practice-Based Learning*. London and New York: Routledge, 2015.

White, Hayden. "The Value of Narrativity in the Representation of Reality." *Critical Inquiry* 7, no. 1 (1980): 5–27.

Whitehead, Alfred North. *Process and Reality: An Essay in Cosmology Gifford Lectures Delivered in the University of Edinburgh during the Session 1927–28*. Corr. ed. New York and London: The Free Press, 1978.

Wilcox, Lauren. "Practising Gender, Queering Theory." *Review of International Studies* 43, no. 5 (December 2017): 789–808.

Zarakol, Ayşe, ed. *Hierarchies in World Politics. Cambridge Studies in International Relations*. New York: Cambridge University Press, 2017.

Zhao, T. "Rethinking Empire from a Chinese Concept 'All-Under-Heaven' (Tianxia)." *Social Identities* 12, no. 1 (2006): 29–41.

3 Collective learning at the boundaries of communities of practice

This book looks at world ordering through the locus of communities of practice (CoPs) and collective learning. Collective learning involves a redefinition or reinterpretation of consensual knowledge about reality, that is, what people consider real, possible, and desirable at a given point in time. It is practical: it is a hermeneutic process of determining how to modify our actions in our day-to-day life, how we attribute meaning to these actions, and how those actions make sense in our broader environment. Collective learning thus implies a change in beliefs or a change in one's confidence in existing beliefs, which can result from exposure to new evidence, theories, or behavioral repertoires.[1]

While many factors have affected how Bank CoPs changed (and stayed stable) since the 1980s, focusing on how interactions in practice led to learning enables an understanding of the intricacies of *how* they evolved. Implicitly or explicitly building on Western social theories, non-Western philosophies, feminist approaches, management theories, and organizational sociology, a collective learning theory seeks to bolster the CoP literature by offering an empirically useful processual conceptual apparatus of a relational/processual ontology. This chapter argues that learning happens not only in actors' minds but also in and through their collective action, that IOs are, in fact, bundles of CoPs, and that learning happens primarily at the boundaries between those communities. Three processes of collective learning will be developed in this chapter: encounters between communities, boundary brokering, and the use of epistemic boundary objects.

Social practices

As introduced in the previous chapter, social practices are meaningful patterns of action recognized as competent actions by members of a given CoP. A broad range of social actions have been studied in practice-oriented IR, from private-security practices,[2] deterrence,[3] Iroquois diplomacy,[4] piracy,[5] sovereignty,[6] regionalism,[7] diplomacy,[8] European Union practices,[9] peacebuilding,[10] NATO practices,[11] international negotiations[12] to academic practices.[13] The so-called practice turn should not hide the fact that many IR scholars had pointed to practices as the basis of social life decades earlier: structural realists have analyzed states' balancing practices,

DOI: 10.4324/9781003529279-3

constructivists have analyzed practices of sovereignty, and feminists have studied gendered practices, to name a few.

Practice-oriented scholars in IR rely on insights from Michel Foucault,[14] Aristotle,[15] American pragmatists,[16] Ludwig Wittgenstein,[17] and, most commonly, Pierre Bourdieu.[18] If Theodore Richard Schatzki and others qualify the practice turn as a "family of theories,"[19] it is not, as some have argued, an "intellectual potluck."[20] If there is legitimate skepticism about the possibility of a unified language around the concept of practices,[21] practice-oriented scholars all study sets of routinized deeds that are sustained by the collectively held background knowledge of a group of competent practitioners arranged in a domain of knowledge (CoP). Attempts to lay out the practice turn's core commitments might make it look like a would-be ism[22], especially under the label of constructivism.[23] However, studying practices means adopting an additional analytical heuristic lens bounded by one ontological inevitability: the primacy of practices as processes through which social orders unfold.

Looking at practices makes for more amenable concepts to study the empirical world than interests, norms, rationality, or discursive structures. Embodied practices are objects of analysis that are more easily identifiable than looking inside actors' heads. A CoP (a domain of knowledge bounded by shared practice) implies criteria of competence, tools, and defined membership criteria from which we can infer cognitive and normative knowledge. Knowledge is produced, used, and has effects in and through patterned activities, not only in the heads of individual people.

One important concept that underlies the empirical analysis in this book is "anchoring practices," which make other practices possible. Anchoring practices embody rules and principles for a broader set of practices, and they structure the tools and resources actors need to "go on" and engage in other practices.[24] At a deeper level, anchoring practices define constitutive rules. Ann Swidler cites, for example, Elizabeth Armstrong's research on the proliferation of identities in the lesbian/gay community in San Francisco between 1964 and 1994.[25] After failed attempts to create a single unified organization for the community, community leaders started encouraging the proliferation of a multiplicity of smaller organizations organized around diverse identities, such as racial identities or sexual preferences. This growing diversity was captured in the Lesbian/Gay Freedom Day Parade, inaugurated in 1971. As a result, the "constitutive rule" defining the community changed from one common characteristic to diverse identities. Swidler argues that the parade has become an anchoring practice for this constitutive rule. Practices, like public participation ones at the World Bank, can thus organize, anchor, or constrain others.

Communities of practice

While often associated in IR with the practice turn, the concept of CoP in social theory is much broader. First defined by Lave and Wenger[26] and brought into IR by Adler,[27] a CoP is a domain of knowledge shared by practitioners with a common enterprise and like-mindedness in at least one shared practice. Definitions that refer to CoP as a "group of people" are misleading.[28] A CoP is not only a collective of individual members arranged in a group, a network, or a field. A CoP is the "social fabric of relations in action."[29] It is a "social configuration in which our enterprises are defined as worth pursuing and our participation is recognizable as competence."[30] It implies interactions within an activity system or social pattern in which participants know each other and understand the meaningfulness of each other's actions *in situ*.[31]

In other words, a CoP is a *domain of knowledge* in which individuals recognize each other as competent in the enactment of at least one practice.[32] A CoP implies a repertoire of shared resources (language, routines, tools, artifacts, concepts, stories, and historical events), and its members engage in practices together. Since the late 2000s, CoP approaches in IR have fruitfully refined our understandings of, for example, diplomacy, military attachés, international security, academic, maritime, and European communities.[33] More recently, explorations of the concept look at the case of the Association of Southeast Asian Nations (ASEAN),[34] feminist academics,[35] Chinese cyber practices,[36] the African Union,[37] or lethal weapon systems.[38] This book pushes this literature further by focusing on the central feature of CoP, that is, collective learning in and between communities, including through contestation of meaning and epistemic power. If we take seriously the fact that CoPs are domains of knowledge, what happens in them must be linked to collective learning, and most importantly, to social ordering.

As detailed in the previous chapter, CoP and their associated practices, as the social fabric of the international realm, make the world "hang together."[39] Examining international CoPs helps explain social ordering processes by looking at social orders' origins and evolution.[40] The focus is on how and why specific configurations of meaningful performances organize world politics and change. This is why a CoP framework points at power as a field of forces that create decentralized, relational, distributed, and productive epistemic and material authoritative social competence, which in turn constitutes the conditions of possibility for social reality to exist. Focusing on social interactions in the spaces between CoPs reveals how fields of knowledge are the social fabric of relations in action.[41] In short, social ordering is made of nexuses of practices, whose meaning derives from the domains of knowledge (CoP) they are embedded in. The emergence and evolution of social orders represent arrangements of people and material entities rendered meaningful collectively by fields of knowledge. This is why CoP socially orders the social world.[42]

How does one recognize a CoP? Compared to network members, individuals in a CoP interact with each other often, even if these interactions are not confined within organizational units. They are not just people who share a title or know each other; members of a CoP engage with each other regularly or in a routinized manner and recognize each other as competent in their shared practice. This regularity can be as infrequent as once a year in conferences or meetings, or as often as multiple times a day, and members of the community only need to interact with some members to still be part of the community. They can also "talk" through intermediaries such as professional journals, shared outlets, or datasets. What makes them a community is that their criteria of competence are reinforced and reified in communication. Some communities inside an IO often interact with outside communities (e.g., a World Health Organization country team in Madagascar engaging with Malagasy firms) while others mainly engage with communities inside the organization (e.g., IMF macroeconomists based in Washington, D.C.). A CoP is bound together by sustained interaction, shared background knowledge, a common identity, and recognized criteria of competence. Members of a CoP recognize each other as being part of the in-group. Most importantly, CoPs are in constant flux: "a community's 'nature' is not predetermined or fixed, but the contingent result of processes by which its members negotiate the meaning of its constitutional properties and boundaries qua practice."[43] Boundaries between communities represent sites of social interaction where identities and behaviors evolve.[44]

Interviewees for this research, when speaking of their day-to-day work, did not associate themselves with others based on similar professional affiliation but with people they were working closely with at a certain point in time. While professional affiliation sometimes defines a CoP, tasks or function can also be a criterion (e.g., top managers at the Bank). CoPs can also be topic-oriented working groups, country teams, social groups with similar interests, or a subset of professionals (bank engineers working in Brazil). Many interviewees for this research tend to distinguish themselves from "others" when speaking of other communities. "Their group" would argue with "this other group," or with this other individual who is not part of "their group." Finally, CoPs can be spontaneous or cultivated. If the European Union only intentionally sets up CoPs since 2016, the World Bank has been cultivating CoPs for a long time.[45]

CoP scholars agree that IOs are hierarchical bureaucracies. However, they argue that learning processes are also made in and through a constellation of horizontally organized CoP, or a collective of communities *within* and *outside* organizations, or what I call constellations of communities. Communities are organized in layers of embedded subcommunities in a fractal structure;[46] each subcommunity represents something more than a "subculture."[47] They are bound by shared background knowledge, tools, concepts, and criteria of competence. CoPs within institutional boundaries interact with each other, as well as with others outside these boundaries. They can emerge or be created across institutional divides, as CoPs internal to an institution sometimes have more in common with actors in a neighboring institution than with others inside their own organization. A trend of CoP scholarship looks at trans-organizations and extra-organizations CoPs,[48] like cross-boundaries practitioners' relationships and practical meaning-sharing between the EU and NATO.[49] Sometimes, CoPs within organizations are formed in reaction to their institutional culture, as in the German Federal Armed Forces, whereas practitioners established relationships within and outside organizational boundaries.[50] These interactions between CoPs within and outside IO collectively participate in social ordering processes in the international realms, outside of, or transcending, institutional boundaries.

Unlike many social theorists or management scholars,[51] this book extends the scope of communities beyond the organization, the firm, and the workplace. International CoPs often transcend these formal walls; for example, a working group on social development with members of the United Nations Development Program (UNDP), Médecins Sans Frontières, and the Red Cross who meet regularly, or an *ad hoc* group of development workers collaborating on an education project in Bangladesh, can become CoPs if they meet regularly for an extended period of time, recognize each other as competent, and develop tools or language to use toward a common goal. Nina Græger,[52] for example, has studied cross-boundary practitioners' relationships and practical meaning sharing between the EU and NATO.[53]

CoPs differ from epistemic communities, which are much more purposefully oriented toward knowledge creation. CoPs, in comparison, are geared toward performing a practice well, which simultaneously enables meaning-making processes.[54] Introduced to the field of IR in 1972 by John Ruggie, and promoted by Peter Haas 20 years later, an epistemic community is "a network of professionals with recognised expertise and competence in a particular domain and an authoritative claim to policy-relevant knowledge within that domain or issue-area."[55] To differentiate epistemic communities from networks or think tanks, Haas argued that they exclusively work in areas where "science matters," like environmental politics, instead of any normative fields like human rights.[56] As a subset of CoP, epistemic communities share normative and principled beliefs, causal/cognitive beliefs, notions of validity, and a common policy enterprise.[57] As such, specific epistemic practices of policy innovation and diffusion unite them, as well as the goal of developing and sharing knowledge. Epistemic communities have the power to suggest concepts or worldviews to institutions and societies, and thus, they can control knowledge and information, which can then influence practices and social orders in scientific realms.[58] While looking at epistemic communities also brings the focus on knowledge creation, it underplays the social construction of meaning and the unintended consequences of performances on social ordering. If epistemic communities are all CoPs, not all CoPs are epistemic communities.

The CoP concept is also different from international networks. Members of CoP are not individual nodes in relations with each other in an *ad hoc* fashion; they are the social fabric of relations in action. In short, individuals are intrinsically linked to the communities they are a part of, not unlike newborns entering society. Also, in comparison to network theories, power also does not refer to the possession of many relations but *multi-membership* in many CoPs.[59] If networks are interpersonal, intergroup, and interorganizational relationships through which information flows, CoPs involve social communication of knowledge through which practitioners negotiate meaning and develop their own distinctive identity.[60]

Collective learning in and through CoPs

Because CoPs are bounded not only by what their members know but also by what they do, practical know-how is at the basis of collective learning. In contrast to an individualist cognitive theory of knowledge, where knowledge is transferred in formal settings from a knower to a learner, organization theorists have studied relationality and interactions in situated learning. Learning is about cognitive evolution, "an active process of redefinition or reinterpretation of reality – what people consider real, possible and desirable – on the basis of new causal and normative knowledge."[61] This reinterpretation of reality does not happen only "in the head," but is tied to "doing" with other people. Knowledge does not evolve with the acquisition of new data, so to speak, but in performing a practice competently and in a slightly different way through constant contact with other practitioners.

Collective learning requires that communities compose, decompose, or recompose together how they deal with problems, regarding their background, practical, and forefront knowledge. The case study developed in this book will demonstrate that the institutionalization of inclusive practices followed two realizations: the rightness of including-qua-consulting borrowing governments and populations in the decision process (normative knowledge) and the failures of top-down structural adjustment programs and the effectiveness of government ownership, public participation, and civil society consultation (cognitive knowledge). Bank employees learned both that inclusive practices were "the right thing to do" (normative) *and* that they were more effective in achieving their goals (cognitive). A collective learning framework, focusing on acting and meaning-making processes, thus has the potential to contribute to norm-contestation frameworks.[62]

Learning does not imply knowing versus ignorance; there is never a stage of knowing *nothing* and then of knowing *something*. It implies changing existing knowledge – or the "temporary consensus of a group of practitioners that a 'problem' should be defined in a certain manner, the causes and effects arranged in a certain pattern that ends and means of 'solving' the problem identified."[63] What is often considered a rational choice in world politics is nothing more than conforming to this temporary consensus, including being restrained by perceived structural constraints. Changing this consensus implies that someone or something influences what we believe in because their practices, choices, and background knowledge generate something new that inform how we think about and do things.

Collective learning in CoPs situates itself mainly against two theories of learning. First, socialization scholars analyze how newcomers progressively gain the competence to be an integral part of a community. When they enter a community, new members of a CoP learn a specific language. They become familiar with the tools, documents, symbols, and procedures they should draw upon, as well as the set of routines they should adopt to deal with certain problems. They learn about the "implicit relations, tacit conventions, subtle cues, untold rules of thumb, recognizable intuitions, specific perceptions, well-tuned sensitivities, embodied understandings, underlying assumptions, and shared worldviews."[64] Socialization is successful when intersubjective understandings become taken-for-granted "objective facticities" for new adherents.[65] This concept has been applied at various levels to how states are socialized to self-help balancing behavior under conditions of anarchy;[66] how diplomats try to socialize others to their own beliefs;[67] how institutions socialize states to new behaviors;[68] how European standards and rules are internalized by new members – or not;[69] and more generally, how norms diffuse and spread.[70] This learning process does not end there, as community members confront each other with new ways of doing and constantly change how they do things, even if marginally.

Second, another type of learning studied in IR happens when community members negotiate meaning through their engagement in a routinized practice. This refers to learning once a person is inside an organization, among people who are already full members of a social group. While considered and recognized as masters of their practice, they continue to learn in their interactions with other competent community members.[71] Therefore, CoPs evolve because of internal factors. Adler's cognitive evolution framework is the latest attempt to theorize collective learning as arising because of, rather than despite, membership in a community. However, newcomers in a CoP can be socialized in the ways of doing of their new community, but they can also influence members of their new community. They can introduce successful tools or mechanisms, and they can even be hired specifically for this reason. Like contestation campaigns, peaceful encounters between two communities can also serve as learning catalysts, whereby one or both communities pick up on ways of doing from their counterparts. A report by one community can also travel in this boundary space and influence another domain of knowledge. If social learning comes from a process of interaction through which individuals shape one another's identities, this process goes both ways, whereas learners and teachers are interchangeable.

It needs to be emphasized again that compared to norms research in IR, studying collective learning refers to both normative *and* cognitive knowledge. If normative ideas refer to the "appropriateness" of a given action regarding the values attached to it,[72] cognitive knowledge specifies the recipes, guidelines, and maps for political action, often in a causal fashion: idea A is what works to deal with problem A.[73] Cognitive knowledge has sometimes been defined as tacit knowledge, which makes certain "strategies seem natural, appropriate, and effective, while others appear inappropriate, illegitimate, or even unthinkable."[74] Both cognitive and normative social knowledge are kinds of information that command a sufficient consensus at a given time to serve as a template to achieve a goal. They both inform the background knowledge of CoP members, as normativity and practices are deeply interlinked.[75] Learning is therefore concerned with norms as well as how to complicate, simplify, or redefine our understanding of the world by either following new evidence in the face of new problems or modifying old causal connections.

Learning through action

This book moves away from an old but still common tendency to treat knowledge as something substantial that can be grasped toward a definition of cognitive learning as a process of meaning-making out of the experience we have of the world.[76] Thinking of knowledge as something that can be owned—a "spectator theory of knowledge"[77]—is a fallacy of improper reification. Learning is behaving differently, performing a practice in a new way. Action is critical for individual learning, but action needs to be coupled with reflection and an interpretation of those actions and previous experiences.[78] This also means that practices (especially procedural ones) do not necessarily follow rational policy change.[79]

Meaning is intrinsically linked to action because it is enacted, corporeal, and situated.[80] Collective learning and meaning-making processes concern individuals engaging in action regarding their beliefs, desires, episteme, and values. Similar to Aristotle's phronesis[81] or James Scott's practical knowledge,[82] learning is linked to acting because it represents the motivations, intentions, and justifications surrounding acting. Collective learning is therefore a negotiation of meaning with others in intersubjective relations. Furthermore, knowledge is not thought of before the fact but during the enactment of a practice; it is built, sustained, and modified during action. By doing so, practices and knowledge are not causally created; they dynamically enable reality to unfold as it does in rendering it meaningful. Like cognitive evolution theory,[83] a collective learning framework departs from studies about norms and classic constructivism by explaining changes of practice not only through concepts such as internalization or socialization but also by the very nature of enacting with others' meaningful patterns of actions.

Unlike Bourdieu's habitus, which tends to be stable over time through social capital, Anthony Giddens emphasizes the constant evolution of practical consciousness through reflexivity. Background knowledge for Giddens is not as static as the habitus can be for Bourdieusian scholars; it is constantly being reflected on, expanded, and modified. Giddens' structuration theory offers an "ontology of potentials," reflecting agents' ability to produce historical variations or to always "act otherwise."[84] Background knowledge is mostly not only taken for granted but also "constantly actualized, displayed, and modified by members of society in the course of their interaction."[85] Practical consciousness is continuously evolving because of what Giddens calls a constant monitoring of action: "individuals reflect upon, monitor and modify their actions on an ongoing basis" instead of prior to action.[86] This concept complements rational and normative logics of actions, which both suppose that intentionality precedes action. Both the rational pathway of thinking (rational intention-action-achievement of goal) and the normative one (normative influence-intention-action-achievement of purpose) are flawed because in reality action often precedes intention.[87] However, through practical consciousness, practitioners reflexively monitor their practice while acting, not before.

Morten Andersen and Iver B. Neumann's case of wampum diplomacy exemplifies how background knowledge is constantly monitored and re-enacted through practice. The wampum, a belt strung with various fibers, is a material artifact that the Iroquois believe gives life to the messengers' words: "Messages transmitted between tribes were literally read into the wampum before it was taken by a messenger to be presented to another tribal council where the messenger lent the message voice."[88] A messenger could not deliver a message without using the wampum; it was impossible not to use it in diplomatic relations. However, this type of practice evolved with the arrival of colonizers and became a shared practice as Europeans used the wampum as a mnemonic device. It evolved because of a logic of action that was reflexively monitored and not rationalized: "What we observe in the case of wampum is a practice creating and re-creating actors and a social environment by being practiced."[89]

Norm scholars in IR have recently made the same move about the close relationship between normativity and action: norms are increasingly seen less as discrete units to grasp but as normativity within action.[90] Norms are seen less as substantive items promoted, shared, and internalized but as "momentary snapshots" of the rules of the game.[91] This followed pragmatist ideas: consider mind and action as intertwined ongoing processes; reflection and creativity are ongoing in action, not reserved for definite, discursively enacted conscious moments.

Learning also often leads to cognitive changes linked to action instead of normative shifts. When a Bank hydroelectricity-project relocation team must deal with pressure from vulnerable populations who prefer to stay close to their ancestral territory instead of being moved to urban centers, they can learn to modify their relocation plan accordingly, not because it is the "right thing to do" (normatively) but because it is a more effective way to gain social legitimacy or time-efficient results (cognitively).

Learning by translating at the boundaries

Learning does not happen on a tabula rasa, which means negotiation happens *through* existing background knowledge, not apart from it. In Bruno Latour's sense, translation (or chains of translation) refers to how actors translate contradictory interests.[92] Translation is the mediation of knowledge between actors, which is done not only through background knowledge but also through cognitive schemes and political values. Zeynep Gulsah Capan, Filipe dos Reis, and Maj Grasten (2021) have developed a model of translation as transformation, highlighting the productive power of translation. In short, translation creates something new, and the politics happen in the encounters between multiple worlds. Indeed, the process of translation itself is always political, not only where it originates or where it ends. In a collective learning framework, because of constant practical contestation, translation can serve not only transformation but also resistance to transformation. The translation of new knowledge, or interpretation through translation, mobilizes one's repertoire of resources (language, routines, and tools) and background knowledge to understand (and eventually use) a new concept or tool.[93] This means that new information, even if radically different from existing knowledge, often reinforces existing preferences or predispositions of CoPs instead of challenging them.[94]

If domains of knowledge bind practitioners together, the liminal space between CoPs is where they translate knowledge from other communities. Learning does not happen only through socialization or from negotiation between members of one CoP. It also, or perhaps mainly, happens when CoPs interact with members of other communities. Practitioners constantly negotiate meaning with community members, but they negotiate meaning at least as frequently with practitioners in other communities. Boundaries are not *lines* that outsiders can cross and that lock insiders in – they are conceptual *spaces* where members of at least two communities negotiate knowledge. Sometimes called liminal spaces in feminist studies[95] or *seuil* ("threshold") in translation studies,[96] boundaries are markers for social, cultural, or political differences or "sites of differences."[97] They delimit identities-in-difference.[98] What provokes learning is not differences between communities per se, but the smooth or confrontational interaction of differences. Boundaries, of which state borders are only one example, are not only fixed lines in space or time; they are spaces of differentiation.[99] Following interactionists like Andrew Abbott, many scholars drawing on the CoP concept define boundaries between (or through) relationally enmeshed "things," in this case, domains of knowledge and action, which are constantly in flux. These spaces between CoPs are thus conceptual sites where differences interact, learning happens and identifies are transformed.[100]

By giving even greater ontological primacy to social relations than other practice-oriented scholars, a CoP framework to study social orders focuses on the interactions between multiple communities within organizations, but does not limit itself to communities within formal boundaries. International organizations are *constellations of communities of practice* interacting with each other as well as with CoPs outside of the organization. This book analyzes both formal and informal communities nested inside an organization and communities that are external to or transcend strict organizational structures. Organizations are made of sub-cultures not only based on employees' disciplinary backgrounds and regional units[101] but also based on different background knowledge, shared tools, and concepts (as in working groups or informal networks).

An external CoP could be an international or national social group surrounding an international or intergovernmental organization. For example, external communities to the United Nations could be members of a think tank on human development, an advocacy network on children's rights, a community of herders in Mongolia, or economists at the IMF. An internal CoP is defined as one that exists formally inside the organization. IOs are home to multiple communities that perform highly different practices, such as an operations evaluation team, a professional unit, a working group, a board of directors, a group of senior managers, a learning group, or a country team. CoPs at the World Bank, for example, include project managers, a participatory development learning group, a working group on trade policies, the board of directors, or the Bolivia country team. These external and internal communities interconnect through their practices, and they learn to act differently through repeated contact.

Because members in a CoP share background knowledge, culture, tools, and understandings, communities might appear stable. However, change frequently occurs since members need to negotiate or "translate" meaning with other domains of knowledge. This is why boundaries are where exciting stuff happens: they are the spaces where members of at least two communities negotiate meaning. Collective learning thus does not happen only internally through socialization or from negotiation between community members, but also when CoPs interact with members of other communities, as boundaries are where the "unexpected can be expected, where innovative or unorthodox solutions are found, where serendipity is likely, and where old ideas find new life and new ideas propagate."[102] Calling interactions at the boundaries "hallways" for collective learning, organizational sociologist Nancy Dixon studies these discrepancies between old and new thinking: "To the extent that we all agree, or that we detect no difference, we will not learn."[103]

In those liminal spaces between international CoPs, differences are confirmed but challenged "through the clash of practices," but it is also where "commonly shared understandings can be generated through encounters."[104] Learning at the boundaries, either through shared epistemic objects, boundary encounters, or boundary brokers, is maximized for communities that are more familiar with each other because they have more constant interaction and a greater acknowledgment of the validity of the other community's competence. While American diplomats and Indian workers might be dissimilar on too many levels to accept some of their counterparts' practices or knowledge as useful, the United Nations High Commissioner for Refugees and the International Organization for Migration will cross-fertilize each other's practices regularly, and more consciously. Even at the boundaries of two very similar communities, like the World Bank and IMF macroeconomists, there is a space in which differences interact, even very slight ones. This promotes small fluctuations that can (sometimes) add up to bigger changes. However, encounters can be more transformational between highly dissimilar CoPs, when the very existence of practices, knowledge, or tools is contested.

Interestingly, CoPs within the Bank often interact with each other, and they sometimes have more in common with an external community than with a community inside their organization; for example, Bank macroeconomists have more in common with IMF economists than with the Bank's NGO Unit. Therefore, this book does not focus on one community (or one organization), but on a *constellation* of communities inside and outside the World Bank. The multiple domains of knowledge analyzed in this book are the ones that my empirical research identified as having impacted the emergence and institutionalization of inclusive practices. These groups include the community of managers in Washington, D.C., country teams, learning groups, advocacy coalitions, UNDP or IMF teams, national governments, and others.

There can be a total absence of commonality between very different communities: no common knowledge, no recognized criteria of competence, and no communal resources. An example of such an encounter could be between European police officers and Syrian refugees, IMF economists and Burkinabè midwives, or American diplomats and a union of Indian workers. Boundaries define where/when the different competences and experiences are translated. Change happens in this space because individuals are confronted with new/different knowledge that they can import if they include it in their practice before "going back" to their community. This knowledge can be mimicked intentionally or unintentionally.

A collective learning framework aims to contribute to the organizational sociology literature, which looks at both levels (internal and external), but generally attribute different logics to each level. For example, Antje Vetterlein suggests that the first step is for state donors of IOs to enable the conditions of possibilities for change externally, and the second, primarily internal step is where change happens.[105] While explaining the two worlds of the World Bank, Catherine Weaver similarly divides them according to a different logic: the Bank's world (pressure from the external political and ideational environment) and the World Bank (internal culture and bureaucratic politics).[106] Similarly, Barnett and Finnemore bracket the external influence of states, which they explain according to a principal-agent logic that focuses on IOs' internal pathologies and bureaucratic culture.[107] This book aims to contribute to this literature by looking at a meso-level between the internal and the external.

This book analyzes how the two levels of analysis interact through transcending CoPs. It blurs not only the boundaries between inside and outside the walls of an organization but also the boundaries between communities within an organization. Collective learning is related to *interactions* between internal, external and in-between communities. When a CoP evolves, it impacts other communities; practitioners can consciously (e.g., through advocacy or shaming) or unconsciously (e.g., through example-setting or joint practices) influence the temporary consensus of knowledge of members of another CoP. Reifying institutions and analytically reconstructing their bureaucratic cultures, like some organizational sociologists do, may be analytically helpful, but it simplifies the diversity existing within these organizations.

Learning through practice contestation

While the process of learning at the boundaries could point to how collective learning happens smoothly when CoPs interact, conflict is also part of the story. Contestation can make individuals realize how wrong they were about how they were doing things or discover better ways to solve a problem. Practice contestation does not *necessarily* happen purposively, consciously, or discursively when policymakers decide at a specific point in time to discard parts of what they know to be true or to select new knowledge that "fits" reality better. Integrating criticisms can be made to increase legitimacy or social acceptability. For example, if humanitarian workers suffer many criticisms during a specific participatory survey technique on the ground, they can decide not to reuse it in the future. This is not a judgment on the inherent ineffectiveness of their previous practice, but a redefinition of what they believed was effective, following contestation by external actors.

To counteract Bourdieusian practice scholarship, CoP scholars often focus on commonalities and like-mindedness instead of conflict and hierarchy. On the one hand, Vincent Pouliot, Rebecca Adler-Nissen, Jérémie Cornut, and others developed a Bourdieusian praxeology to focus primarily on conflict and power and to theorize hierarchies based on social positions. This suggests a very high level of stability, as hierarchies are hard to challenge and power dynamics based on habitus are often very stable. On the other hand, Emanuel Adler, Niklas Bremberg, Federica Bicchi, myself, and others focus on the shared and communal aspect of practices. However, this does not mean (in theory) that we strip away power dynamics and contestation.

Most CoP scholars will admit that participation in a community involves conflictual and competitive dynamics as well as harmonious ones. While CoP approaches can sometimes mistakenly be seen as overly "quiescent and consensual," like-mindedness does not mean an absence of power dynamics and contestation.[108] As the philosopher Davide Nicolini mentions, social scientists have tended to overromanticize communities as an "idealized form of sociality," which wrongly strips away the conflictual character of practices.[109] Sustained mutual relationships can be harmonious, conflictual, or both, and these conflicts over meaning are inherently linked to epistemic power.

However, CoP scholars are often criticized for not taking questions of conflict and hierarchy seriously enough.[110] Even when a shift in practice seems gradual and inevitable, it is improbable that this change occurred without disagreements and contestation about previous background knowledge or accepted tools.[111] If conflict can arise through negotiation when new members integrate a CoP,[112] interactions at the boundaries between communities are where most contestation happens. These more constant interactions between members of two or more communities gave Bank employees examples of how to implement inclusive practices and made them realize the importance of inclusiveness to improve the effectiveness of their projects and policies. Similar processes happened when communities within the Bank contested each other's interpretation of their human rights framework.[113]

Without these interactions with CoPs of activists or NGOs, Bank employees might have realized the failure of structural adjustment but not adopted inclusive practices; they could have been criticized but responded differently, or a new president could have tried but failed to change the narrative. Learning happens through negotiation of meaning in action but also through practice contestation. More recently, a few IR scholars have started delving into contestation as a main feature of CoPs[114] even from an intersectional perspective.[115]

Contestation in practice does not mean that CoP members discard old background knowledge, tools, or practices altogether in the face of confrontation. Practices in organizations are periodically contested, which often leads to their reinterpretation instead of them being fully deleted. Furthermore, contestation is not always a power struggle; it often refers to day-to-day reformulation of knowledge through social interactions. Practice contestation can often lead community members to reformulate what they know or reorganize tools and concepts. No matter how radical they appear, shifts in practices are often combinations and permutations of what was there before.[116] Through this process of contestation, parts of existing knowledge are validated, some are erased, and others are reconstructed.

Scholars have often formulated the reactions to contestation in a rationalistic way, as if the Bank wanted to "secure its legitimacy" by adopting inclusive practices.[117] However, practice contestation does not necessarily happen purposefully – policymakers do not decide at a specific moment to discard parts of what they know to be true or to adhere to new ideas that fit their reality at a specific moment. Instead, in the constant flux of unfolding of practices, practitioners make day-to-day practical choices that observers can reconstruct only to determine later what has been contested, selected, and discarded. For example, when nuclear deterrence practices were contested globally, they were not discarded altogether but permeated into other less aggressive deterrence practices.[118] It would be a reconstruction *post hoc* to say that "the Bank responded to criticisms" in a certain way.

In a groundbreaking move from the early norm literature, Antje Wiener described the principle of norm "contestedness" as a meta-organizing principle of global governance.[119] She defines norm contestation as one type of social practice.[120] For Wiener, critically engaging with norms means contesting "global normative structures of meaning-in-use," what actors ought to do (appropriate standards of behavior): "These interventions occur at the site of norm 'cracks'; that is, when stakeholders' interpretations of norms differ and distinct meanings come to the fore through utterances on the site of the engagement".[121] Such discrepancies between the interpretation and contestation of existing norms were studied in such cases as whaling,[122] slavery,[123] responsibility to protect,[124] anti-corruption,[125] global governance,[126] and financial policies.[127] Importantly, norm contestation is mostly "constituted by discursive interventions."[128]

By contrast, practice contestation is not one specific social practice but is enacted in the course of all practices. It is not only a discursive intervention directed at norms, values, and rules but comprises actions that challenge tools, concepts, guidelines, and causal understanding. Collective learning adds to the norm-contestation literature the concept of cognitive knowledge or the consensus among actors about causes and effects and how to deal effectively with given problems. If early constructivists in IR focused on normativity and norms,[129] more recent constructivist leaning scholars have looked at meaningful actions that are infused with cognitive (and normative) knowledge. In short, like norm contestation, practice contestation is a meta-organizing principle of world orders, but it differs from it by focusing on contestation *in action* instead of through discursive interventions and on cognitive as well as normative knowledge.

Practice contestation, and collective learning in CoPs in general, can thus refer to actions directed at normative knowledge (what is good or bad) as well as cognitive knowledge (what causes what and how to deal with problems).[130] Both types of knowledge have instantiations *in practice*, which is where learning can be initiated. Additionally, while certain moments can be considered instances of contestation, practice contestation in a CoP is an ongoing and productive process. A practice is never universally accepted or internalized once and for all; meaning is always contested, discursively, or in action. "Contestation is necessary for learning to take place in communities of practice. It is a process by which practitioners dynamically define their practice, adapt to environmental challenges, and adopt a common identity."[131]

How can CoPs be sites of commonality *and* conflict? Focusing on norm contestation, Wiener, expressly distances herself from communitarian ontologies and what she believes are "fixed and stable communities" (2014, viii) to build an individualist understanding of contestation, where individuals contest structures of meaning-in-use. However, sustained mutual relationships always involve conflictual interactions that do not negate the communal character of a CoP. In other words, what binds a community together is not their constant agreement and harmony but rather like-mindedness. The fact that CoPs are driven by mutual engagement in a joint enterprise does not mean that they always agree on every aspect of this enterprise.[132] Some things can be shared but contested simultaneously, such as the background knowledge, tools, and concepts used to deal with a problem.

Constant practice contestation can still fit within a relational and processual ontology. Through contestation, practitioners *collectively* adapt to changes in their environment and forge new tools to deal with problems. Without constant practice contestation, practices might simply be discarded when they reach a high level of mismatches with their environment. Disagreement is thus a productive part of the joint enterprise of CoPs, and mutual engagement does not require homogeneity to count as a joint enterprise. The enterprise is joint not because everybody "believes the same thing or agrees with everything, but in that it is communally negotiated."[133]

There are different types of practice contestation in CoPs; for and against change as well as inside or outside formal boundaries. First, internal disruption for change happens when community members contest an existing practice on normative or cognitive grounds. These disruptions do not always provoke change but always open possibilities for learning. The more disruption there is, the more probable a tipping point for change. Newly formed units managing the Bank's engagement with NGOs or individuals less socialized in the Bank's internal CoPs, such as previous chief economist Joseph Stiglitz, became internal disrupters at the World Bank. Second, external pressure for change happens when external practitioners contest existing practices and push a CoP to change how it does things. It comes from the contestation by external communities against a CoP within an international organization or specific CoPs' practices. Third, internal resistance to change happens when community members contest an attempted change in practice or resist this change. It refers to contestation of new practices by community members who do not want to see them spread or institutionalized. Those practitioners within a CoP with the most internalized or fixed background knowledge are the most likely to engage in internal contestation. In my research, senior economists who have worked for many decades within the Bank tended to be internal resisters to new practices of inclusion. Fourth, external resistance to change happens when an external community or actor resists attempted changes in practices and pressures a community into stability. The IMF, for example, was highly resistant to the Bank becoming more inclusive and open to civil society actors, and member states were very resistant to adopting structural adjustment programs, which they considered a waste of money. This division of types of practice contestation serves an analytical purpose and is not representative of an ontological division. This double process of contestation (for and against change) at both levels (inside or transcending formal boundaries) highlights that contestation does not always lead to change, as in most cases of normative contestation studied in IR. This *post hoc* typology pictures practice contestation as multidirectional.

Learning through epistemic power

Contestation, especially success in contestation claims, is inherently linked to epistemic power. Practice contestation is enacted through the ability to yield epistemic power. Research on power as the capacity to achieve something by influence, force, or control has been done by scholars on the World Bank, to emphasize either the power of the United States to sway the Bank's orientations[134] or the power of corporations or global capitalism to reinforce its neoliberal ideology.[135] Instead, power in this book is linked to the authority to validate, confirm, or formulate new knowledge, ergo to construct subjectivity and social facts.[136] Not everyone in every social situation has the same ability to negotiate meaning effectively or in a desired direction. Power in that sense mediates the acquisition, maintenance, and transformation of meaning, to the extent that it influences what is deemed legitimate and valid by a group.

Epistemic power thus refers to the ability to be recognized as competent in meaning negotiation. Qin situates this type of relational power between agential power or resource endowments (military capabilities, economic power, etc.) and structural power (the systemic distribution of capabilities or ideas). He suggests the example of complex interdependence, for example, as an intersubjective relationship supported by power, which "is not possessed by any actor."[137] In an alliance arrangement where one state has access to the resources possessed by an ally, this access to power resources is relational because it is usable by said ally. It is relational because it is usable through "relationships" instead of "ownership."[138] For example, in an organization, the president is not the only powerful actor. Being close to the president may give one manager significant epistemic power through relations. Having more trustful working relationships with employees may also give a manager lower in the hierarchy greater relational power than the president. In the case of the imposition of a radically new practice that requires employees to work longer hours, if the president is the source and messenger of the new practice, it might create uneasiness among the employees and an impression that the president does not understand their work. However, if the manager is on board and builds on existing trusting relationships with employees to implement the new practice, it might be accepted more readily. Epistemic power also refers to the capacity to create constituencies to support a contestation claim.

The power of relations implies that it is sharable and dynamic. Not everyone holds the same power in every situation; it all depends on the configuration of relationships and the environment. Building on Chinese dialectics, relational power can be empowering for many actors simultaneously: "A power relationship can be unilaterally commanding and domineering as mainstream IR theories tend to believe, but it can also be mutually empowering, making both actors engaged in a power relationship more powerful."[139] Looking at relational power not only contributes to a more fine-grained picture of world politics and social ordering but also contributes to the CoPs literature in focusing on non-hierarchical, non-coercive power.

Epistemic power, as a relational form of power, can trigger or impede learning processes in IOs in five ways. First, following Lave and Wenger's concept of peripherality, some individuals closer to the center of a community have more capacity to influence their colleagues.[140] Suppose a member has been part of a CoP for longer, for example. In that case, they will have more capacity to influence their CoP through practice contestation because their contestation claim will have more political weight. The most powerful individuals are, therefore, those who are already full CoP members and who have mastered its tools and practices. Newcomers or novices have less influence to contest existing practices because they cannot set the agenda and their input can be more easily dismissed. Finally, if a member is far from the center, s/he has less power and status, and others will grant less legitimacy to her/his contestation claims.[141]

Second, hierarchy inside the international organization or institution the CoP is nested in can impede or orient learning processes. Pressures from senior managers and Bank leadership have a greater capacity to direct the negotiation of meaning for lower-level employees.[142] Materially, senior managers can fire or hire people who will support their contestation claims and/or resist others' claims that are incongruent with those of the manager; finance new initiatives; impose time constraints; or create *ad hoc* CoPs. A development community that is funded by the United States' aid program will be more likely to follow contestation claims by a US representative than a Canadian one. This power may follow a top-down imposition of material capabilities and increases the epistemic claim's perceived value. In cases like these, more powerful individuals can constrain the potential for learning to originate and the ways it takes place. However, while leading individuals can inform informal practices, collective learning only happens partially or primarily through top-down imposition. Indeed, horizontal learning is enhanced when "hierarchies are broken down and power relations are (temporarily) set aside."[143]

Third, proximity to global capitalist centers of power, or access to financial or material capabilities, gives individuals more capacity to influence the adoption of new tools or concepts. Indeed, meaning often continues to reflect the dominant sources of power.[144] Material power does not only refer to coercive power or the ability to set the agenda vertically but also shapes predispositions and what is even available to put on the agenda. In the field of development, capitalist elites frame the problem of development in certain terms and determine how project success should be conceived of and measured. This framing limits radical rethinking of cognitive and normative knowledge. Then again, even less economically powerful countries like Norway can also greatly influence new initiatives at the Bank by creating new financial instruments to support them.

Fourth, proximity to centers of knowledge production influences learning processes. Even as an outsider to a community, being an expert can give significantly more influence when contesting a community's cognitive knowledge.

> While workers may be full participants in their own community of practice, their knowledge, despite its relevance for the formulation of strategy, is not necessarily recognized within the formal organizational hierarchy where, so called, expert knowledge, acquired from external consultants, is preferred.[145]

For example, Stephen Fox observed a community of fishermen in Saint-Brieuc Bay where marine researchers successfully framed a new problem relating to declining stocks of scallops.[146] The "experts" then succeeded in framing the solution as a technological device for domesticating the scallops' breeding patterns, rendering themselves an "obligatory point of passage" in the practice of the fishermen. Experts also have the power to regulate access to certain discourse or evidence, in that they are listened to, but more importantly, their knowledge claims are respected.

Fifth, meaning negotiation is necessarily linked to an intersectional understanding of power. The positionality of individuals in a community in their day-to-day interaction, based on gender, ethnicity, geographical provenance, education levels, social class, sexual orientation, and other identity markers, influences learning processes.[147] At the Bank, wealthy white males who studied in Ivy League universities in the United States have historically had more status than poorer women from African NGOs or Indigenous activists from South America. While intersectionality is not an addition of variables to calculate the amount of power someone can yield, some configurations of identities will give individuals more privilege and capacity to influence knowledge production. It is not insignificant that all presidents of the Bank have been males with US citizenship, named by the US government. Considering these identity markers does not (only) mean that the United States has a firm grip on the Bank actions,[148] but that a male was systematically chosen. In the end, social positionality influence your capacity to influence practices, narratives, and knowledge. For example, despite a greater inclusion of NGOs in Bank practices, American economists still have greater leverage over Bank practices than civil society workers. This is not only due to their institutional power (based on their position in the institution), but also due to their positionality (based on identity and systems of oppression). These power differentials should be considered in analyzing who confronts Bank projects, who has access to the organization's hallways, and who successfully triggers learning through contestation. Oppressive social structures make up a world where white privilege and patriarchy dictate who will be listened to and invited to the table.[149] Not everyone has equal access to certain meetings or higher management cars.

Learning through coloniality of epistemic power

Collective learning in world politics should also be understood through the concept of *coloniality* of epistemic power.[150] If social interactions in domains of knowledge are mediated by various structures of differentiation, colonial devaluation of epistemic value is arguably the most important one. Practices of inclusion of civil society actors by multilateral organizations in a North/South context have especially meant a renewal of coloniality of power in novel forms. The question is: *how* was coloniality of power reproduced, despite Bank practitioners' best intentions to challenge existing policymaking procedures? The answer is not only that Bank CoPs did not fully democratize their procedures (which is only part of the answer), but also that when they do include NGOs and civil society actors, the coloniality of power mediates the ability to influence meaning-making, as does class and gender.[151] As will be detailed in Chapter 8, coloniality of epistemic power is visible in the selection of NGOs, the definition of what is the "right" data, and the control of participation processes.

In short, inclusive practices have not fully challenged the asymmetry of recognized competence to influence meaning-making, not only because the Bank still has financial leverage but also because they perpetuated Western epistemes and ways to do things. If scholars have successfully argued that the Bank's overall political rationality remained technocratic and neoliberal,[152] interactions between CoPs are also still mediated by colonial/racial stratification. Inclusive practices slightly changed the attitudes of Bank employees toward aid-targeted communities, but inclusion did not suppress the international power inequalities between the Global North and South, especially regarding how members of different domains of knowledge are listened to. These inequalities were perpetuated at least partly through informal rules and interactions.

Even if she does not use that terminology, the colonial/racial hierarchies described by Sévérine Autesserre in humanitarian aid are similar in the development field. Despite being "well meaning individuals who have devoted their lives to combating injustice, violence, and poverty,"[153] humanitarian and development workers tend to reproduce old ways of doing in daily interactions, which end up reproducing hierarchies with the populations they aim to "help." These divisions created in practice between so-called "expatriates" and so-called "local" populations endure. This book aims to add a layer of complexity about how the coloniality of epistemic power penetrates these interactions, even if many observers keep seeing these power relationships as "race-neutral" or "colorblind."[154]

For the evolution of international social orders, this means new practices participate in the constant fluctuation of the architecture of the international realm. New practices reconfigure how people do things and how CoPs interact with each other, even if it does not equate to a paradigm change. This specification is significant for scholars on social ordering and international practices, as well as for IR scholarship in general. When studying CoPs in international settings where actors from the Global North and the Global South are involved, one must look at colonial remnants of dehumanization, especially through epistemic devaluation. Studies on international hierarchies, diplomacy, IOs, or INGOs would gain from adding the layer of understanding that Global South scholars have developed for years now about racial and colonial inequalities.

Closeness to the center of a community, expertise, and the delegation of authority to define competence are also mediated by the coloniality of epistemic power, defined as racial stratifications in meaning-making processes.[155] Colonial relationships in meaning-negotiation have tainted the relationships between Bank practitioners and Global South NGOs in policymaking or project elaboration. However, most practice-oriented and CoP researchers ignore the colonial undertone of whose knowledge is accepted as valid and whose competence is recognized.[156] Epistemic power is about epistemic violence: the processes of "appropriating, assimilating, ignoring, undermining and degrading [indigenous] knowledge."[157] The destruction of Indigenous knowledge has been qualified as "epistemicides,"[158] with its gendered undertones frequently underlined.[159] On top of the destruction of modes of thought through colonial education systems in the Global South,[160] colonization has also "demonized" Indigenous and non-Western epistemes, worldviews, and knowledge systems, rendering them incompetent.[161] This is still visible in North/South interactions in meaning negotiation today, especially in international "development," arguably the field most influenced by a white or Western gaze.[162]

Epistemic violence in and between CoPs is not only the project of the constitution of colonized subjects as "Other," as analyzed in postcolonial and subaltern studies literature.[163] It also consists in "asymmetric occultation of the trace of this Other in its precarious subjectivity."[164] Gayatri Spivak, in her book *Can the Subaltern Speak,* argues that the subaltern (the non-specialists, non-academic from the Global South) "can talk and know their condition" but are not listened to.[165] Their knowledge is subjugated, disqualified, and deemed inadequate, beneath not only the level of valid cognition but also the level of humanity. This "intellectual imperialism"[166] or "imperial reason" of colonizers reduced human beings to the category of sub-humans devoid of thinking capacities.[167] This process kept influencing relationships between Global North agents and Global South ones long after formal colonization ended, including in how international CoPs interact with each other.[168]

Because the euro-descendant thinking became the episteme *par excellence,*[169] Western modes of knowledge became the only way of producing universal and objective knowledge: "this concerns ideas about organizing, classifying and storing knowledge, yet it is specifically by hiding its locus of enunciation that its claims toward universality are facilitated."[170] Western epistemic subjects then came to understand themselves as unique, objective, and void of "socio-political and spatio-temporal determination."[171] This influenced how Bank CoPs believed the knowledge developed by Western NGOs was more universal than Global South ones and thus more valid. After centuries of associating Western knowledge with science and Global South knowledge with superstition, it is now difficult for western agents to engage in fair meaning negotiation in the 21st century. The difficulty in being heard or influencing policymaking does not come from a "deficiency" of the discourse itself but from a deficiency in hermeneutic resources.[172]

Furthermore, the "colonial library"[173] influenced how Global South communities perceived themselves. As a result, many NGO's CoPs interacting with the Bank started to auto-regulate their own discourse simultaneously to write what Bank teams wanted to hear but also because many started to believe the Bank's prescriptions. Mechanisms like self-censorship and mirroring reinforced the adherence to technocratic principles by Global South NGOS,[174] proving that NGOs are not only exogenous forces to global institutions but are also shaped by them.[175] Coloniality of epistemic power is thus linked to epistemic violence and epistemic racism, which go beyond stating that knowledge is partial or biased. It is about the "geopolitical" location of epistemic subjects and goes against the assumption that we can interact with different knowledge systems and knowledge producers independently from their "[e]thnic/racial/gender/sexual epistemic location."[176] This geopolitical location is crucial in how Bank employees interact with Global South communities, even if they invite them to the table. Relationships are not created in a void. Because practice-oriented scholars are interested in local contexts of interactions, they should also consider how broader systemic systems of oppression are enacted locally in day-to-day interactions.[177]

Collective learning processes

The relational processual ontology detailed in the previous chapter presented processes as the source of variation in how reality unfolds. Processes are more or less general sequences or sets of social events by which social reality unfolds. They are not mechanisms; they are not mechanical causes producing some effect on the world. Instead, processes are analytical constructs rendered logical by social scientists to understand the reality we want to depict, which can be observed, unobserved, or is in principle unobservable.[178] Three processes illustrate how collective learning happens at the boundaries between CoPs: encounters between communities, boundary brokering, and the use of epistemic boundary objects.

These processes are "responsible" for collective learning because they detail the nuts and bolts that concatenate an explanans (collective learning) and an explanandum (practice change). They do not presuppose an individual agent, as in mechanism-based approaches, but presuppose an act and a set of connections in time and space. The preference is thus given to action (intended or unintended) over purposeful actors. For example, when Victor Hugo wrote the beginning of the play *Hernani*, he knew he was going against the established rules of writing plays in Alexandrine. However, he ignored that he was going to open a new era in the history of drama through public unrest over his decision. We can thus say that *Hernani* "caused" the end of a cultural practice, but it was not Hugo who purposefully triggered this change. It was an intricate process already ongoing in other theaters, albeit less important ones.

These processes of collective learning can unfold independently; for example, a boundary encounter with no boundary object can lead to one specific instance of learning. Parts of a broader social change can happen when only one mechanism is present, but the propensity of it happening will be greater, or more visible, when there is a multiplication of processes. Furthermore, one instance of boundary encounter can lead to adopting a new tool rather than to an overall change in practice. The accumulation of instances of learning thus leads to a threshold, that is, when a practice is institutionalized broadly in a community or an organization.

Learning can happen quickly or slowly, depending on the type of organization and its surrounding environment. The frequency of sustained interaction and the number of points of contact at the boundaries will render an organization more prone to learn and, therefore, to change. In that sense, the World Bank is more flexible than the IMF because the former interacts more often with NGOs, Global South populations, other IOs, and bilateral agencies. However, even the IMF has become increasingly heterogeneous in recent decades.[179]

There will also be more instances of learning in an organization where employees and managers develop a conscious desire to learn. An organization can promote "learning initiatives" to encourage its employees to adopt new mechanisms and tools; they can even cultivate formal CoPs.[180] The Bank-wide Learning Group on Participatory Development, founded in the 1990s, is one such example. There were also many similar initiatives in regional or country offices in the 1990s and 2000s. For example, the Central and Indian Ocean Division of the Africa Department dealing with agriculture and the environment hired participation specialists at the beginning of the 1990s to review existing projects and select which participatory practices could be applied. They then promoted those practices to various CoPs inside the Bank.[181] In the South Asia Region in the same period, two departments created *ad hoc*, informal learning groups on participatory mechanisms for interested employees.[182] Learning new practices may then reduce the cost of practice change in other settings. Adopting practices by some actors can provide relevant information about the benefits of adopting the practice for others.[183] So, if change is attempted successfully in one unit, it is more likely to spread to other units, thus increasing the chance for an exponential acceleration of practice change.

Despite unfolding over time, it is essential to mention that the processes defined in this book happened in a non-linear and non-sequential fashion, that is, without chronological or hierarchical order. This is so because the processual ontology at the basis of a collective learning framework focuses on how processes unfold in a continuous motion and not at discrete moments in time. The processes conceptualized, therefore, do not act in a predetermined sequence, where the first mechanism happens, then the second mechanism, then the third, like the norm life cycle;[184] the spiral normative model;[185] or in intergovernmental-organizations theories, where the principals give autonomy to IOs (first step), which then change according to their bureaucratic culture (second step).[186] Therefore, these co-constitutive processes promote a type of change that is dynamic and fluid rather than discrete; analytically reconstructing these processes in a chronology or a sequence would not aptly represent the complexity of reality.

Finally, collective learning processes must happen between at least two internal or external CoPs to be considered as taking place at the boundaries between CoPs. The processes must also be at the heart of a situated activity, involve negotiation of meaning, and not be routinized as part of a regular practice. Novelty and change mostly happen in an unusual setting where/when differences between two communities interact, when there is a mismatch between two communities' tools, understandings, competences, or resources. The processes of learning developed in this book are useful analytical tools to understand better how this specific change in practices unfolded through time. They can be helpful as mid-level generalizations and could apply to other IOs encompassing multiple interacting CoPs. The analytical decision to point at a multiplicity of those processes in multiple CoPs over time instead of focusing on only one was made to emphasize that collective learning is a constant feature of social ordering.

Process 1: Boundary encounters

A boundary encounter occurs when more than one community member meet in time and space. Encounters can be diachronic events such as a dinner, end-of-the-day drink, informal lunch, conference, or visit to another community's practice site. In those informal encounters where a practice, tool, or concept is discussed, members of another community draw on their background, experience, and competence to give meaning to the practices of other communities. For example, Thomas

Kwasi Tieku and Afua Boatemaa Yakohene studied how CoPs work together through informality despite the rigid bureaucratic and institutional boundaries they inhabit.[187] They argue that informal encounters often helped resolve political crises at the African Union, the Economic Community of West African States (ECOWAS), and the UN. Boundary encounters can also be synchronic, such as a joint practice, policy, or project where differences interact over a more extended period.

Boundary encounters like a joint project promote learning on both sides because practitioners need to negotiate meaning. They confront each other with other ways of doing and understanding, which can subsequently influence their understanding of their tools, routines, or concepts. It is a two-way interaction where both CoPs negotiate meaning with each other—if both are ready to challenge their way of thinking.[188] The World Social Forum is an example of a boundary encounter between various international CoPs (Indigenous, feminist, labor unions, and religious groups) that influence each other through setting examples, discussing informally, and sharing experience. In an IO, encounters can happen at both levels of communities: at the boundaries of communities within the organization or with external communities. For example, a project can be developed and implemented between the United Nations Children's Fund and the UNDP, between the World Bank's Civil Society Unit and its Ghana country team (boundary between internal communities), or between the UNDP and the Bank's Civil Society Unit (boundary between internal and external communities). An encounter is not a *boundary* encounter if it is routinized over time, involves people from only one subcommunity, or if nothing concerning a given practice is discussed, acted on, or exemplified. An end-of-the-day drink between World Bank economists and IMF employees in which they only discuss family issues is not a boundary encounter. A boundary encounter must involve negotiation of meaning, not be routinized, and not be a defining feature of any community.

Process 2: Boundary brokering

Boundary brokering is a social process where new practices or tools from one CoP appear in a boundary space or are included in the practice of another community (e.g., through consultants or new employees). While someone can be part of more than one community, brokering means an actor has yet to regularly interact with another community or acquire the formal status of a community member. Unlike the type of interaction enacted by newcomers who bring new knowledge within a community,[189] boundary brokering happens when actors are part of two communities simultaneously and translate knowledge from one to the other.[190]

Most scholars looking at CoPs analyze how new community members are socialized into the new group or learn its activities. However, these new employees can also broker new ideas by bringing their resource and background knowledge to the Bank. Going back to Eric Wolf's classic definition of brokers between communities and states, brokering means "facing in two directions at once."[191] This multiple membership gives brokering a unique role in collective learning because it brings one CoP's background knowledge, communal resources, and routines into another one. In comparison, scholars who have studied change agents[192] often see multi-membership as an impediment: if social movements become too close to mainstream agents, for example, they risk losing their comparative advantage and authority.[193]

Brokering can happen between CoPs inside an international organization or between internal and external communities. Inside an organization, a manager moving from one subcommunity to another, or individuals working in multiple communities simultaneously, can participate in brokering. Hiring external consultants, appointing external advisory boards, or integrating new permanent employees involves brokering between internal and external communities. Brokers promote learning by importing or translating another community's knowledge, tools, routines, understandings, skills, or know-how.[194] Brokering can influence learning processes, depending on epistemic positionality. For example, *ceteris paribus*, a female intern will be less influential when contesting a practice than a male Nobel Prize winner in economics.

Practitioners involved in boundary brokering are different from brokers in networks, norm entrepreneurs, and change agents, even we can reconstruct *post hoc* their individual influence in learning processes. The power of boundary brokering does not come from individual positions as nodes with the most connections, which gives individuals the ability to control the flow of information within a network of actors.[195] Their epistemic power rather comes from their closeness to the center of the community, their recognized expertise, their positionality or their multiple memberships. Participation in a network speaks to actors' ability to "increase their power by enhancing and exploiting their network positions."[196] In CoP analysis, even "boundary brokers" do not rely on "positional power," but influence practices by setting a creative example of how to perform a practice, thus bringing something different to a community.[197] Relational power in CoPs, as it relates to expertise, intersectionality, and the capacity to set new practices, is more fluid and less measurable than in networks, where one of the goals of research is to measure networks' shapes and members' endowments.[198] Indeed, the degree of centrality of a node depends on its position in a network, or "the sum of the value of the ties between that node and every other node in the network."[199] Many networks' theorists, with the intent of calculating power and centrality in a defined set of relationships, tend to look at nodes, actors, and relationships as apparently static things instead of "fundamentally dynamic, transactions, and doings."[200] In short, the main difference between brokering at the boundary and acting as a powerful actor in a network is that in the latter, meaning negotiation loses its importance, and threads (fixed ties) become more important than the social fabric (fluid set of relations in motion).

This definition of brokers also differs from the socialization scholarship, which focuses on how newcomers are socialized into the norms and habits of a community, like in Lave and Wenger's[201] concept of "legitimate peripheral participation." Newcomers or outsiders can participate in brokering change because their actions follow their previous community's knowledge and communal resources. Brokering can be done through setting an example, active lobbying, forging coalitions of like-minded advocates inside or outside the organization, using external critiques to support their claims, or providing NGOs with information.[202]

The social ontology required to look at boundary brokering also differs from norm entrepreneurs[203] or change agents,[204] who prioritized individual agency and discursive consciousness. Often, agents of change are pictured individually, as in the case of organizations' top managers.[205] However, if changing presidents can trigger important changes through norm entrepreneurship and imposition of views, it cannot explain all changes in bureaucracies. Scholars who have defined "development brokers" (*courtier locaux du développement*)[206] go even further in the rationality of actors: brokers intentionally seek to bring resources from funders to communities. Like community chefs in some African societies, they mediate resources between institutional actors and their populations.[207] Even if such scholars say they focus on bundles of social practices, their definitions of brokerage emphasize individual or reified agents. Boundary brokering rather emphasizes process and practices rather than actors (individual or collective). Even if sometimes reconstructed as such *post hoc*, brokering is not about the agency of individual brokers who seek their own interests, but about a set of social practices of mediation happening in between communities.

Process 3: Use of epistemic boundary objects

The use of epistemic boundary objects points at objects used in at least two CoPs; for example, reports produced in one community and used in another. Susan Leigh Star and James R. Griesemer called boundary objects "intersecting social worlds."[208] Boundary objects in social theory are objects inhabiting several intersecting communities and interpreted flexibly by each. Boundary objects are something that people act toward and with. They appear like objects with a clear meaning, but they are subject to a constant process of interpretation, that is, translating the object's content into something that fits a particular understanding of the world. A forest, for example, can be a boundary object interpreted and used differently by various communities of hikers, conservationists, and biologists. More specifically, *epistemic* boundary objects are documents with encoded information, such as reports, memos, or research notes, that are produced and understood by members of one community and used and understood by members of another. Even a report intended for use within an organization will be interpreted and used in ways concordant with the distinct practices, knowledge, and routines of each community within the organization.

Boundary objects always require translation and interpretation. Information contained in an epistemic boundary object is not transferred but transformed; thus a report, for example, is a boundary object, not a mere container of data.[209] Discussing ambiguity, Jacqueline Best[210] argues that while organizations' manuals are less ambiguous than poems, they are still open to interpretation because each epistemic object pertains to a network of other texts and is interpreted in the context of the other texts the reader has read. When a practitioner reads a memo, the relation goes beyond the person and the piece of paper – it happens at the boundary between two communities' background knowledge, language, and concepts. Translation mobilizes one's repertoire of resources (language, routines, and tools). However, an unread or unused report or memo, produced by only one CoP, or which the recipients reject, does not become a boundary object. For example, a country assessment made by a World Bank country team is not an epistemic object if it is not shared with other communities inside the Bank, that is, if it only informs their practice. Similarly, most NGO reports about the Bank's work in the 1980s were dismissed for not having sound methodologies and therefore lost their potential as epistemic boundary objects. Like many organizational-learning theorists, this framework rejects transfer models of knowledge that dissociate knowledge from its meaning.[211]

Conclusion

A theoretical framework based on CoP and collective learning has a lot of moving parts. There are many other less complicated ways to tell the story of the institutionalization of inclusive practices at the World Bank. Historically, most IR scholars (including constructivists and organizational sociologists) have preferred analytical elegance to theoretical intricacies – the most obvious examples being the unproblematic enactment of rational action or reified norms. While analytical simplicity might be a helpful way to explain the world, IR now needs multifaceted frameworks (including relational/processual ones) to make sense of the messiness of the social world. An applicable processual/relational approach can be useful to give us a better understanding of how the world is in a constant state of becoming, even if it's not meant as a recipe where all parts need to always be present. In the following pages, some processes and concepts will be more readily visible in some instances than others.

This lack of simplicity also means that a collective learning framework is not a predictive tool. The presence of contestation and interaction at the boundaries will not *necessarily* or *always* lead to a change in practice. There can be events preventing change or intervening processes, such as the election of a new government or the appointment of a Bank president who disagrees with the overall direction an organization is taking. There can be sharper breaks or turns in collective learning. James Wolfensohn's election as the World Bank president in 1995 may represent a more significant break with previous practices, but his participation in brokering processes was still part of an ongoing social process. Together, the concepts devised in this book may shed new light on social ordering and could be used to understand other cases; for example, how contestation contributed to the adoption of gender norms at the IMF or how epistemic boundary objects played a role in changing peacekeeping practices at the United Nations.

Notes

1 Levy, "Learning and Foreign Policy."
2 Abrahamsen and Williams, "Privatization in Practice."

3 Morgan, "The Practice of Deterrence."
4 Andersen and Neumann, "Practices as Models."
5 Bueger, "Practice, Pirates and Coast Guards."
6 Schmidt, "Foreign Military Presence and the Changing Practice of Sovereignty"; Loh and Heiskanen, "Liminal Sovereignty Practices."
7 Glas, "Habits of Peace."
8 Neumann, "Returning Practice to the Linguistic Turn"; Cornut, "To Be a Diplomat Abroad"; Pouliot, *International Pecking Orders*; Glas, *Practicing Peace*; Martel, "The Polysemy of Security Community-Building."
9 Bremberg, "The European Union as Security Community-Building Institution"; Adler-Nissen, "Towards a Practice Turn in EU Studies"; Hofius, "Community at the Border or the Boundaries of Community?"
10 Pingeot, "International Peacebuilding as a Case of Structural Injustice"; Bian, "The Racialization of Expertise and Professional Non-Equivalence in the Humanitarian Workplace."
11 Græger, "European Security as Practice?"
12 Adler-Nissen and Drieschova, "Track-Change Diplomacy."
13 Sondarjee, "We Are a Community of Practice, Not a Paradigm!"
14 Hansen, *Security as Practice*.
15 Brown, "The 'Practice Turn', Phronesis and Classical Realism."
16 Adler, "The Spread of Security Communities"; Schmidt.
17 Frost and Lechner, "Two Conceptions of International Practice."
18 Pouliot; Cornut; Chudzikowski and Mayrhofer, "In Search of the Blue Flower?"; Adler-Nissen, "Symbolic Power in European Diplomacy."
19 Schatzki, Knorr Cetina, and Von Savigny, *The Practice Turn in Contemporary Theory*.
20 Erik Ringmar, "The Search for Dialogue as a Hindrance to Understanding," 3.
21 Kratochwil, "Making Sense of 'international Practices."
22 Bueger and Gadinger, "The Play of International Practice"; Pouliot and Cornut, "Practice Theory and the Study of Diplomacy."
23 McCourt, *The New Constructivism in International Relations Theory*.
24 Sending and Neumann, "Banking on Power," 237.
25 Swidler, "What Anchors Cultural Practices," 90.
26 Lave and Wenger, *Situated Learning*.
27 Adler, *Communitarian International Relations*; Adler, "Europe as a Civilizational Community of Practice."
28 For example, Bicchi, "Communities of Practice and What They Can Do for International Relations," 3.
29 Adler, Bremberg, and Sondarjee, "Communities of Practice in World Politics," 2.
30 Wenger, *Communities of Practice*, 3; Adler, *World Ordering*.
31 Nicolini, *Practice Theory, Work, and Organization An Introduction*, 87.
32 For a review of the concept, see Adler, Bremberg, and Sondarjee; Bueger, Hofius, and Edwards, "Global Ordering and the Interaction of Communities of Practice"; Bicchi.
33 Adler; Bicchi, "The EU as a Community of Practice"; Bueger; Kornprobst, "From Political Judgements to Public Justifications (and Vice Versa)"; Bremberg; Græger; Hofius; Vitelli, "The South American Defense Council"; Banerjee and MacKay, "Communities of Practice, Impression Management, and Great Power Status."
34 Glas and Martel, "Boundary Work, Overlapping Identities, and Liminality in Communities of Practice"; Martel, *Enacting the Security Community*; Nair, "Sociability in International Politics."
35 Sondarjee.
36 Qiao-Franco, "An Emergent Community of Cyber Sovereignty."
37 Tieku and Yakohene, "Exploring Communities of Practice from an Informality Perspective."
38 Bode, "Emergent Normativity."
39 Ruggie, "What Makes the World Hang Together?" 2–3.
40 Adler; Adler, Bremberg, and Sondarjee.

41 Bueger, Hofius, and Edwards.
42 Adler, Bremberg, and Sondarjee; Bueger, Hofius, and Edwards.
43 Hofius, *European Union Communities of Practice*, 46.
44 Glas and Martel; Qiao-Franco.
45 Bicchi, Federica, *Global Studies Quarterly*.
46 Wenger, "Communities of Practice and Social Learning Systems," 243.
47 Sarfaty, "Doing Good Business or Just Doing Good," 93.
48 Adler; Bueger; Banerjee and MacKay.
49 Græger, "European Security as Practice"; Græger, " 'High Politics' and Everyday Practices at the Border."
50 Schulte, Andresen, and Koller, "Exploring the Embeddedness of an Informal Community of Practice within a Formal Organizational Context."
51 Wenger, McDermott, and Snyder, *Cultivating Communities of Practice*; Bechky, "Sharing Meaning across Occupational Communities"; Daft and Weick, "Toward a Model of Organizations as Interpretation Systems."
52 Græger.
53 See also Banerjee and MacKay; Vitelli.
54 5/11/22 9:52:00 AM.
55 John G. Ruggie, "Collective Goods and Future International Collaboration"; Haas, "Introduction," 3; Adler and Haas, "Epistemic Communities, World Order, and the Creation of a Reflective Research Program," 371.
56 Haas, *Science and Progress in International Relations*.
57 Haas, "Introduction," 3.
58 Antoniades, "Epistemic Communities, Epistemes and the Construction of (World) Politics."
59 Hafner-Burton, Kahler, and Montgomery, "Network Analysis for International Relations"; Mérand, Hofmann, and Irondelle, "Governance and State Power."
60 Adler, Bremberg, and Sondarjee, 4; Glas and Martel.
61 Adler and Barnett, *Security Communities*, 43.
62 Welsh, "Norm Contestation and the Responsibility to Protect"; Hofmann, *Ten Years R2P—What Doesn't Kill a Norm Only Makes It Stronger?*; Bural, "Parody as Norm Contestation"; Wiener, *Contestation and Constitution of Norms in Global International Relations*; Gutterman and Lohaus, "What is the 'Anti-Corruption' Norm in Global Politics?"; Deitelhoff and Zimmermann, "Things We Lost in the Fire."
63 Haas, *When Knowledge is Power*, 219.
64 Wenger, 47.
65 Berger and Luckmann, *The Social Construction of Reality*, 44.
66 Waltz, *Theory of International Politics*, 127.
67 (Johnson 2008).
68 Checkel, "International Institutions and Socialization in Europe."
69 Mérand, *European Defence Policy*.
70 Klotz, "Norms Reconstituting Interests"; Finnemore and Sikkink, "International Norm Dynamics and Political Change"; Wong, "Is Trafficking Slavery?"
71 Yanow, "Translating Local Knowledge at Organizational Peripheries."
72 Finnemore and Sikkink; Risse, Ropp, and Sikkink, *The Power of Human Rights International Norms and Domestic Change*; Hoffmann, "Norms and Social Constructivism in International Relations."
73 Schmidt, "Discursive Institutionalism," 306–307.
74 Autesserre, *Peaceland*, 38.
75 Gadinger, "The Normativity of International Practices."
76 Dixon, *The Organizational Learning Cycle*; Revans, *ABC of Action Learning*.
77 Rescher, *Process Metaphysics*, 125.
78 Dixon, 59.
79 Mosse, "Is Good Policy Unimplementable?"
80 Suchman, *Plans and Situated Action*; Brown and Duguid; Law, *Organizing Modernity*; Weick.

81 Brown.
82 Scott, *Seeing like a State*.
83 Adler.
84 Cohen, *Structuration Theory*.
85 Giddens, "Functionalism," 107.
86 Loyal, *The Sociology of Anthony Giddens*, 53.
87 Giddens, *The Constitution of Society*, 3.
88 Andersen and Neumann, 477.
89 Andersen and Neumann, 478.
90 Wiener.
91 (Pratt 2020, 8).
92 Latour, *Reassembling the Social*.
93 Daft and Weick, 286.
94 Roberts, "Limits to Communities of Practice," 630.
95 Anzaldúa, Borderlands.
96 Sofo, "Du Pont Au Seuil."
97 Abbott, "Things of Boundaries."
98 Spivak, "Can the Subaltern Speak?" 72.
99 Van Houtum and Van Naerssen, "Bordering, Ordering and Othering," 126.
100 Hofius, "Community at the Border or the Boundaries of Community?"; Hofius, *European Union Communities of Practice*; Græger; Sondarjee, "Collective Learning at the Boundaries of Communities of Practice"; Qiao-Franco; Glas and Martel.
101 Sarfaty, "Why Culture Matters in International Institutions," 667.
102 Wenger, 254.
103 Dixon, 53.
104 Hofius, 947.
105 Vetterlein, "Change in International Organizations," 133; see also Stone and Wright, *The World Bank and Governance*.
106 Weaver, "The World's Bank and the Bank's World."
107 Barnett and Finnemore.
108 Marshall and Rollinson, "Maybe Bacon Had a Point," 74.
109 Nicolini, 89.
110 Fox; Contu and Willmott, "Re-Embedding Situatedness," 200; Marshall and Rollinson.
111 Græger, "European Security as Practice: EU-NATO Communities of Practice-in-the-Making?"; Græger, "Grasping the Everyday and Extraordinary in EU-NATO Relations."
112 Fox.
113 Sarfaty.
114 Sondarjee, "Coloniality of Epistemic Power in International Practices"; Glas and Martel; Qiao-Franco.
115 Chessé and Sondarjee, "A Feminist Critique of International Practices."
116 Padgett and Powell, *The Emergence of Organizations and Markets*.
117 Clegg, *Controlling the World Bank and IMF Shareholders, Stakeholders, and the Politics of Concessional Lending*, 20.
118 Morgan.
119 Wiener, "Contested Compliance"; Wiener, *A Theory of Contestation*; Wiener, *Contestation and Constitution of Norms in Global International Relations*.
120 Wiener, *Contestation and Constitution of Norms in Global International Relations*, 2.
121 Wiener, 11.
122 Bailey, "Arrested Development."
123 Wong.
124 Welsh.
125 Gutterman and Lohaus.
126 Ba and Hoffmann, *Contending Perspectives on Global Governance*.
127 Chwieroth, "Normative Change from Within."

128 Wiener, 189.
129 Finnemore and Sikkink; Risse, Ropp, and Sikkink; Park and Vetterlein, *Owning Development.*
130 Schmidt.
131 Adler, 114.
132 Collins, Patricia Hill. "The New Politics of Community." *American Sociological Review* 75(1) 7–30 (2009).
133 Wenger, 78.
134 Wade; Peet, *Unholy Trinity*; Andersen, Hansen, and Markussen, "US Politics and World Bank IDA-Lending"; Babb and Buira, "Mission Creep, Mission Push and Discretion."
135 Haslam, "The Firm Rules"; Ruckert, "Producing Neoliberal Hegemony?"; McGoey, Darren, and West, "Le Philanthrocapitalisme et Les 'crimes Des Dominants'."
136 Adler and Bernstein, "Knowledge in Power."
137 Qin, *A Relational Theory of World Politics*, 241.
138 Qin, 261.
139 Qin, 242.
140 Lave and Wenger.
141 Yanow.
142 Contu and Willmott.
143 Huzzard, "Communities of Domination?" 358.
144 Roberts, 627.
145 Yanow.
146 Fox.
147 Collins and Bilge, *Intersectionality*; Collins, *Intersectionality as Critical Social Theory*; Crenshaw, *On Intersectionality*; Chessé and Sondarjee.
148 Peet; Wade; Andersen, Hansen, and Markussen; Stones, *Controlling Institutions.*
149 hooks, *Feminist Theory*; Niemann, Gutiérrez y Muhs, and Gonzáles, *Presumed Incompetent.*
150 Sondarjee.
151 Chessé and Sondarjee; Nair; Neumann, "The Body of the Diplomat"; Bian.
152 Sondarjee, "Change and Stability at the World Bank."
153 Autesserre, 5.
154 Bian, 1; Pampinella, "'The Way of Progress and Civilization'."
155 Quijano, "Colonialidad y Modernidad/Racionalidad"; Maldonado-Torres, "On the Coloniality of Being: Contributions to the Development of a Concept"; Lugones, "Toward a Decolonial Feminism."
156 Sondarjee; Pingeot; Pampinella.
157 Simpson, "Aboriginal Peoples and Knowledge," 138.
158 Boaventura de Sousa Santos, *Epistemologies of the South*; Dladla, "Towards an African Critical Philosophy of Race."
159 Lugones; Tamale, *Decolonization and Afro-Feminism.*
160 Thiong'O, *Decolonising the Mind.*
161 Tamale, 28; Simpson; Mohanty, *Feminism without Borders*; Spivak, *Les subalternes peuvent-elles parler ?*; Grosfoguel, "The Epistemic Decolonial Turn."
162 Pailey, "De-centring the 'White Gaze' of Development"; Sondarjee, "Decentring the Western Gaze in International Relations."
163 Grosfoguel.
164 Spivak, 45.
165 Spivak, 52.
166 Ake, *Social Science as Imperialism*, xiv.
167 De Sousa Santos, *Crítica de la razón indolente.*
168 This does not mean that formal colonization ended everywhere (Palestine being a prominent example), but that where it ended, colonial thinking has endured.
169 Amin, *Eurocentrism.*

170 Van Milders and Toros, "Violent International Relations," 122.
171 Mbonda, *Une décolonisation de la pensée*, 16.
172 Mbonda, 25.
173 Mudimbe, *The Invention of Africa*.
174 Sondarjee, 358.
175 Hopewell, "Multilateral Trade Governance as Social Field," 1128.
176 Grosfoguel, 213.
177 Chessé and Sondarjee.
178 Hedström and Swedberg, *Social Mechanisms*.
179 Momani, "Recruiting and Diversifying IMF Technocrats."
180 Bicchi.
181 Operations Policy Department, *The World Bank and Participation*, 9.
182 Operations Policy Department, 9.
183 Elkins, "Embedding the Vulnerable into the Millennium Development Goals."
184 Finnemore and Sikkink.
185 Risse, Ropp, and Sikkink.
186 Hawkins et al., *Delegation and Agency in International Organizations*; Weaver.
187 Tieku and Yakohene.
188 Wenger, 113.
189 Fox.
190 Sarfaty, 105.
191 Wolf, "Aspects of Group Relations in a Complex Society," 66.
192 Mitlin, Hickey, and Bebbington, "Reclaiming Development?"
193 Anderl, *Broken Solidarities*.
194 Græger.
195 Goddard, "Brokering Change," 250; Mérand, Hofmann, and Irondelle, 128.
196 Hafner-Burton, Kahler, and Montgomery, 573.
197 Sondarjee; Qiao-Franco; Glas and Martel.
198 Glas et al., "Understanding Multilateral Treaty-Making as Constitutive Practice."
199 Hafner-Burton, Kahler, and Montgomery, 563.
200 Nexon and Pouliot, " 'Things of Networks'," 342.
201 Lave and Wenger.
202 Vetterlein, "Seeing Like the World Bank on Poverty."
203 Finnemore and Sikkink.
204 Mitlin, Hickey, and Bebbington.
205 Finnemore, "Redefining Development at the World Bank."
206 Olivier De Sardan and Bierschenk, "Les Courtiers Locaux Du Développement"; Bierschenk, Chauveau, and Olivier de Sardan, *Courtiers En Développement*; Lewis and Mosse, "Theoretical Approaches to Brokerage and Translation in Development."
207 Bierschenk, "Afterword."
208 Leigh Star and Griesemer, "Institutional Ecology, 'Translations' and Boundary Objects," 388.
209 Bechky.
210 Best, "Bureaucratic Ambiguity," 90.
211 Lave and Wenger; Brown and Duguid.

References

Abbott, Andrew. "Things of Boundaries." *Social Research* 62, no. 4 (1995): 857–82.

Abrahamsen, Rita, and Michael C. Williams. "Privatization in Practice: Power and Capital in the Field of Global Security." In *International Practices*, 310–32. New York: Cambridge University Press, Emanuel Adler and Vincent Pouliot, 2011.

Acharya, Amitav. "How Ideas Spread: Whose Norms Matter? Norm Localization and Institutional Change in Asian Regionalism." *International Organization* 58, no. 2 (2004): 239–75.

Adler, Emanuel. *Communitarian International Relations. The Epistemic Foundations of International Relations*. London and New York: Routledge, 2005.
Adler, Emanuel. "The Spread of Security Communities: Communities of Practice, Self-Restraint, and NATO's Post–Cold War Transformation." *European Journal of International Relations* 14, no. 2 (2008): 195–230.
Adler, Emanuel. "Europe as a Civilizational Community of Practice." In *Civilizations in World Politics*, edited by Peter Katzenstein, 24. New York: Routledge, 2009.
Adler, Emanuel. *World Ordering. A Social Theory of Cognitive Evolution*. Cambridge: Cambridge University Press, 2019.
Adler, Emanuel, and Michael Barnett. *Security Communities*. Cambridge: Cambridge University Press, 1998.
Adler, Emanuel, and Steven Bernstein. "Knowledge in Power: The Epistemic Construction of Global Governance." In *Power in Global Governance*, 294–318. Cambridge: Cambridge University Press, 2005.
Adler, Emanuel, Niklas Bremberg, and Maïka Sondarjee. "Communities of Practice in World Politics: Advancing a Research Agenda." *Global Studies Quarterly* 4, no. 1 (2024): ksad070.
Adler, Emanuel, and Patricia Greve. "When Security Community Meets Balance of Power: Overlapping Regional Mechanisms of Security Governance." *Review of International Studies* 35 (2009): 59–84.
Adler, Emanuel, and Peter M. Haas. "Epistemic Communities, World Order, and the Creation of a Reflective Research Program." *International Organization* 46, no. 1 (1992): 367–90.
Adler-Nissen, Rebecca. "Symbolic Power in European Diplomacy: The Struggle Between National Foreign Services and the EU's External Action Service." *Review of International Studies* 40, no. 4 (2014): 657–81.
Adler-Nissen, Rebecca. "Towards a Practice Turn in EU Studies: The Everyday of European Integration." *Journal of Common Market Studies* 54, no. 1 (2016): 87–103.
Adler-Nissen, Rebecca, and Alena Drieschova. "Track-Change Diplomacy: Technology, Affordances and the Practice of International Negotiations." *International Studies Quarterly* 63, no. 3 (2019): 531–45.
Ake, Claude. *Social Science as Imperialism: The Theory of Political Development*. Lagos: Ibadan University Press, 1979.
Amin, Samir. *Eurocentrism: Modernity, Religion, and Democracy: A Critique of Eurocentrism and Culturalism*. 2nd ed. New York, NY: Monthly Review Press, 2009.
Anderl, Felix. *Broken Solidarities: How Open Global Governance Divides and Rules*. Bristol: Bristol University Press, 2022.
Andersen, Morten Skumsrud, and Iver B. Neumann. "Practices as Models: A Methodology with an Illustration Concerning Wampum Diplomacy." *Millennium – Journal of International Studies* 40, no. 3 (2012): 457–81.
Andersen, Thomas Barnebeck, Henrik Hansen, and Thomas Markussen. "US Politics and World Bank IDA-Lending." *The Journal of Development Studies* 42, no. 5 (July 2006): 772–94.
Antoniades, Andreas. "Epistemic Communities, Epistemes and the Construction of (World) Politics." *Global Society* 17, no. 1 (January 2003): 21–38. https://doi.org/10.1080/0953732032000053980.
Anzaldúa, Gloria. *Borderlands: The New Mestiza = La Frontera*. 3rd ed. San Francisco: Aunt Lute Books, 2007.
Autesserre, Séverine. *Peaceland: Conflict Resolution and the Everyday Politics of International Intervention*. Cambridge: Cambridge University Press, 2014.
Ba, Alice D., and Matthew J. Hoffmann. *Contending Perspectives on Global Governance. Coherence, Contestation and World Order*. London and New York: Routledge, 2005.
Babb, Sarah, and Ariel Buira. "Mission Creep, Mission Push and Discretion: The Case of IMF Conditionality." In *The IMF and the World Bank at Sixty*. London: Anthem, 2005.

Bailey, Jennifer L. "Arrested Development: The Fight to End Commercial Whaling as a Case of Failed Norm Change." *European Journal of International Relations* 14, no. 2 (2008): 289–318.
Banerjee, Kiran, and Joseph MacKay. "Communities of Practice, Impression Management, and Great Power Status: Military Observers in the Russo-Japanese War." *European Journal of International Security* 5, no. 3 (October 2020): 274–93.
Barnett, Michael, and Liv Coleman. "Designing Police: Interpol and the Study of Change in International Organizations." *International Studies Quarterly* 49 (2005): 593–619.
Barnett, Michael, and Martha Finnemore. *Rules for the World: International Organizations in Global Politics*. Ithaca and London: Cornell University Press, 2004.
Bebbington, Anthony, David Lewis, Simon Batterbury, Elizabeth Olson, and M. Shameem Siddiqi. "Of Texts and Practices: Empowerment and Organisational Cultures in World Bank-Funded Rural Development Programmes." *The Journal of Development Studies* 43, no. 4 (May 2007): 597–621.
Bechky, Beth A. "Sharing Meaning across Occupational Communities: The Transformation of Understanding on a Production Floor." *Organization Science* 14, no. 3 (2003): 312–30.
Berger, Peter L., and Thomas Luckmann. *The Social Construction of Reality. A Treatise in the Sociology of Knowledge*. New York: Anchor Books, 1966.
Best, Jacqueline. "Bureaucratic Ambiguity." *Economy and Society* 41, no. 1 (February 2012): 84–106.
Bian, Junru. "The Racialization of Expertise and Professional Non-Equivalence in the Humanitarian Workplace." *Journal of International Humanitarian Action* 7, no. 3 (December 2022): 1–14.
Bicchi, Federica. "The EU as a Community of Practice: Foreign Policy Communications in the COREU Network." *Journal of European Public Policy* 18, no. 8 (2011): 1115–32.
Bicchi, Federica. "Communities of Practice and What They Can Do for International Relations." *Review of International Studies* 48, no. 1 (2021): 24–43.
Bicchi, Federica. "Cultivating Communities of Practice: From Institutions to Practices." *Global Studies Quarterly* 4, no. 1 (2024): 1–10.
Bierschenk, Thomas. "Afterword: Brokerage as Social Practice." *Cultural Dynamics* 33, no. 4 (November 2021): 418–25.
Bierschenk, Thomas, Jean-Pierre Chauveau, and Jean-Pierre Olivier de Sardan, eds. *Courtiers En Développement: Les Villages Africains En Quête de Projets. Collection "Hommes et Sociétés"*. Paris : Mainz: Karthala ; Association euro-africaine pour l'anthropologie du changement social et du développement, 2000.
Bode, Ingvild. "Emergent Normativity: Communities of Practice, Technology, and Lethal Autonomous Weapon Systems." *Global Studies Quarterly* 4, no. 1 (2024): 1–11. https://doi.org/10.1093/isagsq/ksad073.
Bremberg, Niklas. "The European Union as Security Community-Building Institution: Venues, Networks and Co-Operative Security Practices." *JCMS: Journal of Common Market Studies* 53, no. 3 (May 2015): 674–92.
Brown, Chris. "The 'Practice Turn', Phronesis and Classical Realism: Towards a Phronetic International Political Theory?" *Millennium – Journal of International Studies* 40, no. 3 (2012): 439–56.
Brown, John Seely, and Paul Duguid. "Organizational Learning and Communities of Practice." *Organization Science* 2 (1991): 40–57.
Brunsson, Nils. *The Organization of Hypocrisy: Talk, Decisions, and Actions in Organizations*. Chichester and New York: Wiley, 1989.
Brunsson, Nils. "Organized Hypocrisy." In *The Northern Lights: Organizational Theory in Scandinavia*, edited by Barbara Czarniawska and Guje Sevon, 201–22. Oslo: Liber/Abstrakt/Copenhagen Business School Press, 2003.
Bueger, Christian. "Practice, Pirates and Coast Guards: The Grand Narrative of Somali Piracy." *Third World Quarterly* 34, no. 10 (2013): 1811–27.

Bueger, Christian, and Frank Gadinger. "The Play of International Practice." *International Studies Quarterly*, no. 59 (2015): 449–60.
Bueger, Christian, Maren Hofius, and Scott Edwards. "Global Ordering and the Interaction of Communities of Practice: A Framework for Analysis." *Global Studies Quarterly* 4, no. 1 (January 27, 2024): ksad079. https://doi.org/10.1093/isagsq/ksad079.
Bural, Erna. "Parody as Norm Contestation. Russian Normative Justifications in Georgia and Ukraine and Their Implications for Global Norms." *Global Society* 30, no. 1 (2016): 67–77.
Burke, W. Warner. *Organization Change: Theory and Practice. Foundations for Organizational Science*. Thousand Oaks, CA: Sage Publications, 2002.
Capan, Zeynep Gulsah, Filipe dos Reis and Maj Grasten. 2021. The Politics of Translation in International Relations. New York: Springer International Publishing.
Checkel, Jeffrey. "International Institutions and Socialization in Europe: Introduction and Framework." *International Organization* 59 (2005): 801–26.
Chessé, Alice, and Maïka Sondarjee. "A Feminist Critique of International Practices." *International Studies Quarterly* 68, no. 2 (2024): 1–10.
Chudzikowski, Katharina, and Wolfgang Mayrhofer. "In Search of the Blue Flower? Grand Social Theories and Career Research: The Case of Bourdieu's Theory of Practice." *Human Relations* 64, no. 1 (2011): 19–36.
Chwieroth, J. M. "Normative Change from Within: The International Monetary Fund's Approach to Capital Account Liberalization." *International Studies Quarterly* 14, no. 2 (2008): 289–318.
Clegg, Liam. *Controlling the World Bank and IMF Shareholders*, Stakeholders, and the Politics of Concessional Lending. London, UK: Palgrave MacMillan, 2013.
Cohen, Ira J. *Structuration Theory: Anthony Giddens and the Constitution of Social Life. Contemporary Social Theory*. Houndmills, Basingstoke and Hampshire: Macmillan, 1989.
Collins, Patricia Hill. "The New Politics of Community." *American Sociological Review* 75 no. 1 (2009): 7–30.
Collins, Patricia Hill. "Social Inequality, Power, and Politics: Intersectionality and American Pragmatism in Dialogue." *Journal of Speculative Philosophy* 26, no. 2 (2012): 442–57.
Collins, Patricia Hill. *Intersectionality as Critical Social Theory*. Durham: Duke University Press, 2019.
Collins, Patricia Hill, and Sirma Bilge. *Intersectionality. Key Concepts Series*. Cambridge, UK and Malden, MA: Polity Press, 2016.
Contu, Alessia, and Hugh Willmott. "Re-Embedding Situatedness: The Importance of Power Relations in Learning Theory." *Organization Science* 14, no. 3 (June 2003): 283–96.
Cook, S., and Dvora Yanow. "Culture and Organizational Learning." *Journal of Management Inquiry* 2, no. 3 (1993): 373–90.
Cornut, Jérémie. "To Be a Diplomat Abroad: Diplomatic Practice at Embassies." *Cooperation and Conflict* 50, no. 3 (2015): 385–401.
Cornwall, Andrea, and Karen Brock. "What Do Buzzwords Do for Development Policy? A Critical Look at 'Participation', 'Empowerment' and 'Poverty Reduction.'" *Third World Quarterly* 26, no. 7 (October 2005): 1043–60.
Crenshaw, Kimberlé. *On Intersectionality: Essential Writings*. New York: New Press, 2019.
Daft, Richard L., and Karl E. Weick. "Toward a Model of Organizations as Interpretation Systems." *The Academy of Management Review* 9, no. 2 (April 1984): 284.
Danaher, Kevin, ed. *50 Years Is Enough: The Case against the World Bank and the International Monetary Fund*. Boston, MA: South End Press, 1994.
Dardot, Pierre, and Christian Laval. *La nouvelle raison du monde: essai sur la société néolibérale. La decouverte poche 325*. Paris: Éd. La Découverte, 2009.
De Sousa Santos, Boaventura. *Crítica de la razón indolente: contra el desperdicio de la experiencia : para un nuevo sentido común: la ciencia, el derecho y la política en la transición paradigmática*. Bilbao: Desclée de Brouwer, 2003.

Deitelhoff, Nicole, and Lisbeth Zimmermann. "Things We Lost in the Fire: How Different Types of Contestation Affect the Robustness of International Norms." *International Studies Review* 22 (2020): 51–76.

Dixon, Nancy M. *The Organizational Learning Cycle: How We Can Learn Collectively*. 2nd ed. Brookfield, VT: Gower, 1999.

Dladla, Ndumiso. "Towards an African Critical Philosophy of Race: Ubuntu as a Philo-Praxis of Liberation." *Filosofia Theoretica: Journal of African Philosophy, Culture and Religions* 6, no. 1 (2017): 39–68.

Downs, Anthony. *Inside Bureaucracy*. Glenview: Scott Foresman, 1967.

Easterby-Smith, Mark, Mary Crossan, and Davide Nicolini. "Organizational Learning: Debates Past, Present And Future." *Journal of Management Studies* 37, no. 6 (September 2000): 783–96.

Elkins, Meg. "Embedding the Vulnerable into the Millennium Development Goals: Social Protection in Poverty Reduction Strategy Papers." *Journal of International Development* 26 (2014): 853–74.

Erik Ringmar. "The Search for Dialogue as a Hindrance to Understanding: Practices as Inter-Paradigmatic Research Program." *International Theory* 6, no. 1 (2014): 1–27.

Finnemore, Martha. "Redefining Development at the World Bank." In *International Development and the Social Sciences: Essays on the History and Politics of Knowledge*, edited by Frederick Cooper and Randall M. Packard. Berkeley: University of California Press, 1997.

Finnemore, Martha, and Kathryn Sikkink. "International Norm Dynamics and Political Change." *International Organization* 52, no. 4 (1998): 887–917.

Fiol, C. M., and M. A. Lyles. "Organizational Learning." *Academy of Management Review* 10 (1985): 803–13.

Fox, Stephen. "Communities of Practice, Foucault and Actor-Network Theory." *Journal of Management Studies* 37, no. 6 (September 2000): 853–68.

Frost, Mervyn, and Silviya Lechner. "Two Conceptions of International Practice: Aristotelian Praxis or Wittgensteinian Language-Games?" *Review of International Studies* (2015): 1–17.

Gadinger, Frank. "The Normativity of International Practices." In *Conceptualizing International Practices: Directions for the Practice Turn in International Relations*, edited by Alena Drieschova, Christian Bueger, and Ted Hopf, 100–21. Cambridge, United Kingdom and New York, NY: Cambridge University Press, 2022.

Gherardi, Silvia. "Practice-Based Theorizing on Learning and Knowing in Organizations." *Organization* 7, no. 2 (2000): 211–23.

Gherardi, Silvia, and Davide Nicolini. "Learning in A Constellation of Interconnected Practices: Canon or Dissonance?" *Journal of Management Studies* 39, no. 4 (June 2002): 419–36.

Giddens, Anthony. "Functionalism: Après La Lutte." *Social Research* 43, no. 2 (1976): 325–66.

Giddens, Anthony. *The Constitution of Society*. Cambridge, USA: Polity Press with Blackwell Publishing, 1984.

Glas, Aarie. "Habits of Peace: Long-Term Regional Cooperation in Southeast Asia." *European Journal of International Relations* 23, no. 4 (2017): 833–56.

Glas, Aarie. *Practicing Peace: Conflict Management in Southeast Asia and South America*. New York, NY: Oxford University Press, 2022.

Glas, Aarie, and Stéphanie Martel. "Boundary Work, Overlapping Identities, and Liminality in Communities of Practice: Diplomacy within and beyond ASEAN." *Global Studies Quarterly* 4, no. 1 (January 27, 2024): ksad072. https://doi.org/10.1093/isagsq/ksad072.

Glas, Aarie, Clifton van der Linden, Matthew J. Hoffmann, and Robert Allen Denemark. "Understanding Multilateral Treaty-Making as Constitutive Practice." *Journal of Global Security Studies* 3, no. 3 (2018): 339–57.

Goddard, Stacie E. "Brokering Change: Networks and Entrepreneurs in International Politics." *International Theory* 1, no. 2 (2009): 249–81.
Græger, Nina. "European Security as Practice: EU-NATO Communities of Practice-in-the-Making?" *European Security* 25, no. 4 (2016): 478–501.
Græger, Nina. "Grasping the Everyday and Extraordinary in EU-NATO Relations: The Added Value of Practice Approaches." *European Security* 26, no. 3 (2017): 340–58.
Græger, Nina. " 'High Politics' and Everyday Practices at the Border: Emerging Communities of Practice in the High North." *Global Studies Quarterly* 4, no. 1 (January 27, 2024): ksad075. https://doi.org/10.1093/isagsq/ksad075.
Grosfoguel, Ramón. "The Epistemic Decolonial Turn: Beyond Political-Economy Paradigms." *Cultural Studies* 21, no. 2–3 (March 2007): 211–23.
Gutterman, Ellen, and Mathis Lohaus. "What is the 'Anti-Corruption' Norm in Global Politics? Norm Robustness and Contestation in the Transnational Governance of Corruption." In *Corruption and Norms. Why Informal Rules Matter*, edited by Ina Kubbe and Annika Engelbert. London: Palgrave MacMillan, 2018.
Haas, Ernst. *When Knowledge is Power. Three Models of Change in International Organizations.* Berkeley, Los Angeles and Oxford: University of California Press, 1990.
Haas, Ernst B. *Science and Progress in International Relations: Conversation with Ernst B. Haas. Interview by Institute of International Studies*, October 6, 2001. http://globetrotter.berkeley.edu/people/Haas/haas-con3.html.
Haas, Peter M. "Introduction: Epistemic Communities and International Policy Coordination." *International Organization* 46, no. 1 (1992): 1–35.
Hafner-Burton, Emilie M., Miles Kahler, and Alexander H. Montgomery. "Network Analysis for International Relations." *International Organization* 63 (2009): 559–92.
Hansen, Lene. *Security as Practice. Discourse Analysis and the Bosnian War.* New York: Routledge, 2006.
Haslam, Paul Alexander. "The Firm Rules: Multinational Corporations, Policy Space and Neoliberalism." *Third World Quarterly* 28, no. 6 (September 2007): 1167–83.
Hatch, Mary Jo, and Ann L. Cunliffe. *Organization Theory: Modern, Symbolic, and Postmodern Perspectives.* 3rd ed. Oxford, United Kingdom: Oxford University Press, 2013.
Hawkins, Darren G., David Lake, Daniel L. Nielson, and Michael J. Tierney, eds. *Delegation and Agency in International Organizations.* Cambridge: Cambridge University Press, 2006.
Hedberg, B. "How Organizations Learn and Unlearn." In *Handbook of Organizational Design*, edited by Paul Nystrom and William Starbuck. New York: Oxford University Press, 1981.
Hedström, Peter, and Richard Swedberg, eds. *Social Mechanisms: An Analytical Approach to Social Theory. Studies in Rationality and Social Change.* Cambridge and New York: Cambridge University Press, 1998.
Hoffmann, Matthew J. "Norms and Social Constructivism in International Relations." In *The International Studies Encyclopedia*, edited by Robert Allen Denemark. Malden, MA: Wiley-Blackwell, 2010.
Hofius, Maren. "Community at the Border or the Boundaries of Community? The Case of EU Field Diplomats." *Review of International Studies* 42, no. 5 (2016): 939–67.
Hofius, Maren. *European Union Communities of Practice: Diplomacy and Boundary Work in Ukraine. Routledge Global Cooperation Series.* London and New York: Routledge, 2023.
Hofmann, Gregor. *Ten Years R2P—What Doesn't Kill a Norm Only Makes It Stronger? Contestation, Application and Institutionalization of International Atrocity Prevention and Response. PRIF Report.* Frankfurt: Peace Research Institute, 2015.
hooks, bell. *Feminist Theory: From Margin to Center. South End Press Classics.* Vol. 5, 2nd ed. Cambridge, MA: South End Press, 2000.
Hopewell, Kristen. "Multilateral Trade Governance as Social Field: Global Civil Society and the WTO." *Review of International Political Economy* 22, no. 6 (November 2, 2015): 1128–58.

Huzzard, Tony. "Communities of Domination? Reconceptualising Organisational Learning and Power." *The Journal of Workplace Learning* 16, no. 6 (2004): 350–61.
Johnson, Alastair Iain. "Socialization in International Relations Theory." In *Social States China in International Institutions, 1980–2000*, 280. Princeton, NJ: Princeton University Press, 2008.
Klotz, Audie. "Norms Reconstituting Interests: Global Racial Equality and U.S. Sanctions Against South Africa." *International Organization* 49 (1995): 451–79.
Kornprobst, Markus. "From Political Judgements to Public Justifications (and Vice Versa): How Communities Generate Reasons upon Which to Act." *European Journal of International Relations* 20, no. 1 (March 2014): 192–216.
Kranke, Matthias. "Exclusive Expertise: The Boundary Work of International Organizations." *Review of International Political Economy* 29, no. 2 (March 4, 2022): 453–76. https://doi.org/10.1080/09692290.2020.1784774.
Kratochwil, Friedrich. "Making Sense of 'international Practices." In *International Practices, Emanuel Adler and Vincent Pouliot*, 36–60. New York: Cambridge University Press, 2011.
Latour, Bruno. *Reassembling the Social: An Introduction to Actor-Network Theory*. Oxford and New York: Oxford University Press, 2005.
Lave, Jean, and Etienne Wenger. *Situated Learning. Legitimate Peripheral Participation*. Cambridge: Cambridge University Press, 1991.
Law, J. *Organizing Modernity*. Oxford: Blackwell Publishers, 1994.
Leigh Star, Susan, and James R. Griesemer. "Institutional Ecology, 'Translations' and Boundary Objects: Amateurs and Professionals in Berkeley's Museum of Vertebrate Zoology." *Social Studies of Science* 19 (1989): 387–420.
Levy, Jack S. "Learning and Foreign Policy: Sweeping a Conceptual Minefield." *International Organization*, no. 48 (1994): 279–312.
Lewis, David, and David Mosse, eds. "Theoretical Approaches to Brokerage and Translation in Development." In *Development Brokers and Translators: The Ethnography of Aid and Agencies*, 1–26. Bloomfield, CT: Kumarian Press, 2006.
Loh, Dylan M. H., and Jaakko Heiskanen. "Liminal Sovereignty Practices: Rethinking the Inside/Outside Dichotomy." *Cooperation and Conflict* 55, no. 3 (2020): 284–304.
Loyal, Stephen. *The Sociology of Anthony Giddens*. London: Pluto Press, 2003.
Lugones, Marìa. "Toward a Decolonial Feminism." *Hypatia* 25, no. 4 (2010): 742–59.
Maldonado-Torres, Nelson. "On the Coloniality of Being: Contributions to the Development of a Concept." *Cultural Studies* 21, no. 2–3 (2007): 240–70.
March, James G., and Johan P. Olsen. *Ambiguity and Choice in Organizations*. Bergen: Universitetsforlaget, 1976.
March, James G., Martin Schulz, and Xueguang Zhou. *The Dynamics of Rules: Change in Written Organizational Codes*. Stanford, CA: Stanford University Press, 2000.
Marshall, Nick, and Jeanette Rollinson. "Maybe Bacon Had a Point: The Politics of Interpretation in Collective Sensemaking." *British Journal of Management* 15, no. 51 (2004).
Martel, Stéphanie. "The Polysemy of Security Community-Building: Toward a 'People-Centered' Association of Southeast Asian Nations (ASEAN)?" *International Studies Quarterly* 64, no. 3 (September 1, 2020): 588–99. https://doi.org/10.1093/isq/sqaa040.
Martel, Stéphanie. *Enacting the Security Community: ASEAN's Never-Ending Story. Studies in Asian Security*. Stanford, CA: Stanford University Press, 2022.
Mbonda, Ernest-Marie. *Une décolonisation de la pensée: études de philosophie afrocentrique*. Paris: Sorbonne Université Presses, 2021.
McCourt, David M. *The New Constructivism in International Relations Theory*. 1st ed. Bristol University Press, 2022. https://doi.org/10.2307/j.ctv293p48m.
McGoey, Linsey, Thiel Darren, and Robin West. "Le Philanthrocapitalisme et Les 'crimes Des Dominants'." *Politix* 121 (2018): 29–54.

Mérand, Frédéric. *European Defence Policy: Beyond the Nation State*. New York: Oxford University Press, 2008.

Mérand, Frédéric, Stéphanie C. Hofmann, and Bastien Irondelle. "Governance and State Power: A Network Analysis of European Security." *Journal of Common Market Studies* 49, no. 1 (2011): 121–47.

Meyer, John W., and Brian Rowan. "Institutionalized Organizations: Formal Structure as Myth and Ceremony." *American Journal of Sociology* 83, no. 2 (1977): 340–63.

Mitlin, Diana, Sam Hickey, and Anthony Bebbington. "Reclaiming Development? NGOs and the Challenge of Alternatives." *World Development* 35, no. 10 (October 2007): 1699–720.

Mohanty, Chandra Talpade. *Feminism without Borders: Decolonizing Theory, Practicing Solidarity*. Durham: Duke University Press, 2003.

Momani, Bessma. "Recruiting and Diversifying IMF Technocrats." *Global Society* 19, no. 2 (April 2005): 167–87. https://doi.org/10.1080/13600820500044878.

Morgan, Patrick M. "The Practice of Deterrence." In *International Practices*, edited by Emanuel Adler and Vincent Pouliot, 139–73. New York: Cambridge University Press, 2011.

Mosse, David. "Is Good Policy Unimplementable? Reflections on the Ethnography of Aid Policy and Practice." *Development and Change* 35, no. 4 (2004): 639–71.

Mudimbe, V. Y. *The Invention of Africa: Gnosis, Philosophy, and the Order of Knowledge. African Systems of Thought*. Bloomington: Indiana University Press, 1988.

Nair, Deepak. "Sociability in International Politics: Golf and ASEAN's Cold War Diplomacy." *International Political Sociology* 14, no. 2 (June 1, 2020): 196–214. https://doi.org/10.1093/ips/olz024.

Neumann, Iver B. "Returning Practice to the Linguistic Turn: The Case of Diplomacy." *Millennium – Journal of International Studies* 31, no. 3 (2002): 627–51.

Neumann, Iver B. "The Body of the Diplomat." *European Journal of International Relations* 14, no. 4 (December 2008): 671–95.

Nexon, Daniel H., and Vincent Pouliot. " 'Things of Networks': Situating ANT in International Relations." *International Political Sociology* 7, no. 3 (2013): 342–45.

Nicolini, Davide. *Practice Theory, Work, and Organization an Introduction*. Oxford: Oxford University Press, 2012.

Nicolini, Davide, and M. B. Meznar. "The Social Construction of Organizational Learning: Conceptual and Practical Issues in the Field'." *Human Relations* 48, no. 7 (1995): 727–46.

Niemann, Yolanda Flores, Gabriella Gutiérrez y Muhs, and Carmen G. Gonzáles, eds. *Presumed Incompetent: The Intersections of Race and Class for Women in Academia*. Boulder, CO: University Press of Colorado, 2012.

Oliver, Christine. "Strategic Responses to Institutional Pressures." *Academy of Management Review* 16, no. 1 (1999): 145–79.

Olivier De Sardan, Jean-Pierre, and Thomas Bierschenk. "Les Courtiers Locaux Du Développement." *Bulletin de l'APAD*, no. 5 (June 1, 1993). https://doi.org/10.4000/apad.3233.

Operations Policy Department. *The World Bank and Participation*. Washington, DC: The World Bank, 1994.

Padgett, John Frederick, and Walter W. Powell, eds. *The Emergence of Organizations and Markets*. Princeton: Princeton University Press, 2012.

Pailey, Robtel Neajai. "De-centring the 'White Gaze' of Development." *Development and Change* 51, no. 3 (May 2020): 729–45.

Pampinella, Stephen. " 'The Way of Progress and Civilization': Racial Hierarchy and US State Building in Haiti and the Dominican Republic (1915–1922)." *Journal of Global Security Studies* 6, no. 3 (March 1, 2021): 1–17.

Park, Susan, and Antje Vetterlein. *Owning Development. Creating Policy Norms in the IMF and the World Bank*. Edited by Susan Park and Antje Vetterlein. Cambridge: Cambridge University Press, 2010.

Peet, Richard. *Unholy Trinity. The IMF, World Bank and WTO*. New York: Zed Books, 2003.

Pingeot, Lou. "International Peacebuilding as a Case of Structural Injustice." *International Peacekeeping* 27, no. 2 (March 14, 2020): 263–88.

Pouliot, Vincent. *International Pecking Orders: The Politics and Practice of Multilateral Diplomacy*. New York: Cambridge University Press, 2016.

Pouliot, Vincent, and Jérémie Cornut. "Practice Theory and the Study of Diplomacy: A Research Agenda." *Cooperation and Conflict* (2015): 1–19.

Pratt, Simon Frankel. "From Norms to Normative Configurations: A Pragmatist and Relational Approach to Theorizing Normativity in IR." *International Theory* 12, no. 1 (March 2020): 59–82.

Qiao-Franco, Guangyu. "An Emergent Community of Cyber Sovereignty: The Reproduction of Boundaries?" *Global Studies Quarterly* 4, no. 1 (January 27, 2024): ksad077.

Qin, Yaqing. *A Relational Theory of World Politics*. Cambridge: Cambridge University Press, 2018.

Quijano, Aníbal. "Colonialidad y Modernidad/Racionalidad." *Peru Indigena* 13, no. 29 (1991): 11–29.

Rescher, Nicholas. *Process Metaphysics: An Introduction to Process Philosophy*. Albany: State University of New York Press, 1996.

Revans, Reg. *ABC of Action Learning*. Milton: Taylor & Francis, 2017.

Risse, Thomas, Stephen C. Ropp, and Kathryn Sikkink. *The Power of Human Rights International Norms and Domestic Change*. Cambridge: Cambridge University Press, 1999.

Roberts, Joanne. "Limits to Communities of Practice." *Journal of Management Studies* 43, no. 3 (2006): 623–39.

Ruckert, Arne. "Producing Neoliberal Hegemony? A Neo-Gramscian Analysis of the PRSP in Nicaragua." *Studies in Political Economy* 79 (2007): 91–118.

Ruggie, John G. "Collective Goods and Future International Collaboration." *American Political Science Review* 66 (1972): 874–93.

Ruggie, John G. "What Makes the World Hang Together? Neo-Utilitarianism and the Social Constructivist Challenge." *International Organization* 52 (1998): 855–85.

Sarfaty, Galit A. "Why Culture Matters in International Institutions: The Marginality of Human Rights at the World Bank." *The American Journal of International Law* 103, no. 4 (2009): 647–83.

Sarfaty, Galit A. "Doing Good Business or Just Doing Good: Competing Human Rights Frameworks at the World Bank." In *The Intersection of Rights and Regulation: New Directions in Sociolegal Scholarship*. 1st ed., edited by Bronwen Morgan, 93–106. London and New York: Routledge, 2017.

Schatzki, Theodore Richard, Karin Knorr Cetina, and Eike Von Savigny. *The Practice Turn in Contemporary Theory*. Edited by Theodore R. Schatzki, Karin Knorr Cetina, and Eike Von Savigny. London and New York: Routledge, 2001.

Schimmelfennig, Frank. "Introduction: The Impact of International Organizations on the Central and Eastern European States: Conceptual and Theoretical Issues." In *Norms and Nannies: The Impact of International Organizations on the Central and East European States*, edited by Ronald Linden, 1–32. Lanham, MD: Rowman & Littlefield, 2002.

Schmidt, Sebastian. "Foreign Military Presence and the Changing Practice of Sovereignty: A Pragmatist Explanation of Norm Change." *American Political Science Review* 108, no. 4 (2014): 817–29.

Schmidt, Vivien. "Discursive Institutionalism: The Explanatory Power of Ideas and Discourse." *Annual Review of Political Science* 11 (2008): 303–26.

Schulte, Benjamin, Florian Andresen, and Hans Koller. "Exploring the Embeddedness of an Informal Community of Practice Within a Formal Organizational Context: A Case Study in the German Military." *Journal of Leadership & Organizational Studies* 27, no. 2 (May 2020): 153–79.

Scott, James C. *Seeing Like a State: How Certain Schemes to Improve the Human Condition Have Failed. Yale Agrarian Studies*. New Haven: Yale University Press, 1998.

Sending, Ole Jacob, and Iver B. Neumann. "Banking on Power: How Some Practices in an International Organization Anchor Others." In *International Practices*, edited by Emanuel Adler and Vincent Pouliot, 231–54. New York: Cambridge University Press, 2011.
Shrivastava, P. "A Typology of Organizational Learning." *Journal of Management Studies* 20 (1983): 7–28.
Simpson, Leanne. "Aboriginal Peoples and Knowledge: Decolonizing Our Processes." *The Canadian Journal of Native Studies* 21, no. 1 (2001): 137–48.
Sofo, Giuseppe. "Du Pont Au Seuil : Un Autre Espace de La Traduction." *TRANS*, no. 24 (April 1, 2019). https://doi.org/10.4000/trans.2335.
Sondarjee, Maïka. "Change and Stability at the World Bank: Inclusive Practices and Neoliberal Technocratic Rationality." *Third World Quarterly* 42, no. 2 (2021a): 348–65.
Sondarjee, Maïka. "Collective Learning at the Boundaries of Communities of Practice: Inclusive Policymaking at the World Bank." *Global Society* 35, no. 3 (2021b): 307–26.
Sondarjee, Maïka. "We are a Community of Practice, Not a Paradigm! How to Meaningfully Integrate Gender and Feminist Approaches in IR Syllabi." *International Studies Perspectives* 23, no. 3 (2022): 229–48.
Sondarjee, Maïka. "Decentring the Western Gaze in International Relations: Addressing Epistemic Exclusions in Syllabi in the United States and Canada." *Millennium – Journal of International Studies* 51 (2023).
Sondarjee, Maïka. "Coloniality of Epistemic Power in International Practices: NGO Inclusion in World Bank Policymaking." *Global Society* 38, no. 3 (2024): 328–50.
Sousa Santos, Boaventura de. *Epistemologies of the South: Justice Against Epistemicide*. London and New York: Routledge, 2014.
Spivak, Gayatri Chakravorty. "Can the Subaltern Speak?" In *Marxism and the Interpretation of Culture*, edited by C. Nelson and L. Grossberg, 271–313. Basingstoke: Macmillan, 1988.
Spivak, Gayatri Chakravorty. *Les subalternes peuvent-elles parler ?* Paris: Éditions Amsterdam, 2006.
Steinberg, Richard H. "In the Shadow of Law or Power? Consensus-Based Bargaining and Outcomes in the GATT/WTO." *International Organization* 56, no. 2 (2002): 339–74.
Stone, Diane, and Christopher Wright, eds. *The World Bank and Governance: A Decade of Reform and Reaction. Routledge/Warwick Studies in Globalisation 14*. London and New York: Routledge, 2007.
Stones, Rob. *Controlling Institutions: International Organizations and the Global Economy*. Cambridge: Cambridge University Press, 2011.
Suchman, L. *Plans and Situated Action*. Cambridge: Cambridge University Press, 1987.
Swidler, Ann. "What Anchors Cultural Practices." In *The Practice Turn in Contemporary Theory*, edited by Karin Knorr Cetina, Theodore Richard Schatzki, and Eike Von Savigny. New York: Routledge, 2000.
Tamale, Sylvia. *Decolonization and Afro-Feminism*. Ottawa: Daraja Press, 2020.
Thiong'O, Ngugiwa. *Decolonising the Mind: The Politics of Language in African Literature. Reprint. Studies in African Literature*. Oxford: Currey [u.a.], 2005.
Tieku, Thomas Kwasi, and Afua Boatemaa Yakohene. "Exploring Communities of Practice from an Informality Perspective: Insights from the AU, ECOWAS, and UN in West African Mediation Theaters." *Global Studies Quarterly* 4, no. 1 (January 27, 2024): ksad074. https://doi.org/10.1093/isagsq/ksad074.
Van Houtum, Henk, and Ton Van Naerssen. "Bordering, Ordering and Othering." *Tijdschrift Voor Economische En Sociale Geografie* 93, no. 2 (May 2002): 125–36.
Van Milders, Lucas, and Harmonie Toros. "Violent International Relations." *European Journal of International Relations* 26, no. 1_suppl (September 2020): 116–39.
Vetterlein, Antje. "Change in International Organizations: Innovation or Adaptation? A Comparison of the World Bank and the International Monetary Fund." In *The World Bank and Governance: A Decade of Reform and Reaction. Routledge/Warwick Studies in*

Globalisation 14, edited by Diane Stone and Christopher Wright. London and New York: Routledge, 2007.

Vetterlein, Antje. "Seeing Like the World Bank on Poverty." *New Political Economy* 17, no. 1 (2012): 35–58.

Vitelli, Marina Gisela. "The South American Defense Council: The Building of a Community of Practice for Regional Defense." *Revista Brasileira de Política Internacional* 60, no. 2 (November 9, 2017).

Wade, Robert. "US Hegemony and the World Bank: The Fight Over People and Ideas." *Review of International Political Economy* 9, no. 2 (2002): 215–43.

Waltz, Kenneth. *Theory of International Politics*. Long Grove, IL: Waveland Press, 1979.

Weaver, Catherine. "The World's Bank and the Bank's World." *Global Governance, Poverty Alleviation and Human Development in the Twenty-First Century: The Role of the World Bank* 13, no. 4 (2007): 493–512.

Weaver, Catherine. *Hypocrisy Trap: The World Bank and the Poverty of Reform*. Princeton: Princeton University Press, 2008.

Weick, Karl E. *Sensemaking in Organizations. Foundations for Organizational Science*. Thousand Oaks: Sage Publications, 1995.

Welsh, Jennifer. "Norm Contestation and the Responsibility to Protect." *Global Responsibility to Protect* 5, no. 4 (2013): 217–38.

Wendt, Alexander. *Quantum Mind and Social Science*. Cambridge: Cambridge University Press, 2015.

Wenger, Etienne. *Communities of Practice. Learning, Meaning, and Identity*. Cambridge: Cambridge University Press, 1998.

Wenger, Etienne. "Communities of Practice and Social Learning Systems." *Organization* 7, no. 2 (2000): 225–46.

Wenger, Etienne, Richard A. McDermott, and William Snyder. *Cultivating Communities of Practice: A Guide to Managing Knowledge*. Boston, MA: Harvard Business School Press, 2002.

Wiener, Antje. "Contested Compliance: Interventions on the Normative Structure of World Politics." *European Journal of International Relations* 10, no. 2 (2004): 189–234.

Wiener, Antje. *A Theory of Contestation*. Heidelberg, New York, Dordrecht and London: Springer, 2014.

Wiener, Antje. *Contestation and Constitution of Norms in Global International Relations*. Cambridge: Cambridge University Press, 2018.

Wolf, E. "Aspects of Group Relations in a Complex Society: Mexico." In *Peasants and Peasant Societies: Selected Readings*, edited by Teodor Shanin, 50–68. Harmondsworth: Penguin Books, 1984. Reprint. Penguin Modern Sociology Readings.

Wong, Wendy. "Is Trafficking Slavery? Anti-Slavery International in the Twenty-First Century." *Human Rights Review* 12 (2011).

Yanow, Dvora. "Translating Local Knowledge at Organizational Peripheries." *British Journal of Management* 15 (2004): 9–25.

Zimmermann, Lisbeth. *Global Norms with a Local Face: Rule-of-Law Promotion and Norm Translation*. 1st ed. Cambridge: Cambridge University Press, 2017.

4 Inclusive procedural practices at the Bank

The structural adjustment period of the 1980s and 1990s became associated with an expert-led culture in which Bank experts were considered better able to prescribe policies that would lead to development and growth than borrowing governments or their populations. The Bank's authority in policymaking did not come (only) from its attributes (i.e., financial assets or expertise) but also the Bank's *relations* with borrowing countries; that is, the latter conceded authority to the former. Of course, these relations were influenced by colonial relations of power, spanning from formal colonization onwards. With independence movements in the 1960s, colonial offices became development offices, often with colonial officers re-branding themselves. Formal decolonization processes did not necessarily hinder the superiority attributed to whiteness in North/South relations or the "white gaze of expertise."[1] While this hierarchy has not fully vanished, the Bank attempted to decentralize its policymaking practices.

The historically top-down approach of the World Bank had created resentment among borrowing governments' officials and a tense rapport with aid-targeted populations. To answer criticisms and improve their projects' success rates, the Bank enacted major decentralizations of its activities in 1987 and 1997 and became more open to the inputs of the Global South populations it aimed to serve. Although observers and employees repeatedly criticized the Bank's new narrative to put borrowing governments "in the driving seat,"[2] most people interviewed for this research agree that the relationship between Bank country teams and government officials improved in the 1990s and 2000s. Many broad-based inclusive practices vanished but became anchoring practices for others to emerge. Bank teams also became more inclined to hire employees for country teams directly from the countries they were working in, working groups increasingly studied how to mainstream participatory development, and consultative mechanisms multiplied. One major innovation was, of course, the adoption by the board of directors of the participatory poverty reduction strategy papers (PRSPs) in 1999.

Are NGOs and civil society organizations now "in the driver's seat" of multilateral development policies? No. Has there been a transfer of power between the Bank and borrowing governments? Sometimes yes, sometimes no. Are more stakeholders more often recognized as legitimate interlocutors? Definitely. As a set of new policymaking mechanisms, more inclusive *procedural* practices changed

DOI: 10.4324/9781003529279-4

Bank teams' perceptions of borrowing governments and civil societies in Global South countries. While global asymmetries of power endure (colonial and others), mainly because the World Bank remains a lending institution and borrowing countries remain borrowers, a change in procedural practices modified the relationships between them, especially since the 1990s and the 2000s.

While this book focuses on procedural changes, more inclusion also led to substantive changes in projects and policies, especially regarding development's social aspects, if not macroeconomic policies. For example, participatory rural approaches such as the rural poverty assessments started to integrate social aspects of poverty, which were overlooked by traditional measures like the gross domestic product, income, or consumption-based measurements.[3] Participatory poverty assessments also triggered a reflection on what poverty means, and, as a result, many projects and policies became more focused on the actual needs of the people they targeted.

After years in the field organizing broad consultations with Global South populations around the world (close to 60,000 people), Deepa Narayan and her team published a three-part report titled *Voices of the Poor*.[4] This research also informed the 2000–2001 *World Development Report* (WDR) on *Attacking Poverty*. Interpretative information about poverty was included to go away from material and "objective" measures. Redefining poverty as a process, many interviewees for *Voices of the Poor* talked about issues such as a lack of access to affordable health care, not just as the cause of their inability to get treatment for illness but instead as a source of vulnerability and social destitution.[5]

Before delving into collective learning mechanisms in the following chapters, this one describes the evolution of the Bank's structure and policymaking practices regarding loan elaboration and disbursement. It provides the backdrop to the book's overall argument that Bank practitioners slowly modified what they believed were the means to efficient development policies. The following pages detail how they learned that these practices were more effective (i.e., how they changed the consensus of shared cognitive and normative knowledge). It must be noted that with an organization with so many communities in constant and simultaneous interaction, however, it is impossible to connect all the dots in an intelligible story that does not strip away the complexity. This chapter thus presents a story made of analytical choices rather than depictions of an untamed ontological reality. To represent the complexity of the fluctuation of practices, it does not focus on one community but explores the variety of simultaneous changes of practices and background knowledge. You might skip ahead to the following chapters if you are more interested in digging deeper as to how interactions at the boundaries between CoPs, the use of boundary objects, and boundary brokering sustained these changes or how coloniality of power mediates those new practices.

Learning to be more effective

Bank employees learned that inclusive practice were more effective. Increased effectiveness means that inclusive practices improved the expected results of programs, as determined by Bank employees' evaluation standards. In short, greater inclusion increased the commitment of borrowing governments to macroeconomic reforms, improved the social acceptability of projects, allowed Bank employees to gain more accurate and comprehensive data on poverty, eventually decreased the need for supervision, led to better measurable outcomes, and decreased operational costs – even if they increased elaboration costs. As a general indicator, the level of satisfaction with project outcomes according to Bank standards from 1980 to 1988 was in steep decline. At that point, only 56 percent of projects were considered satisfactory by Bank employees' own evaluation. By contrast, by 2006, the approval rate had risen to 83 percent, matching levels seen immediately following the very popular presidency of Robert McNamara in the 1970s.[6] The overall argument is not only a functional one about more effective practices but is also about how individuals in communities redefined a "successful" practice and how inclusive practices reformulated the relationship between Bank employees and borrowing governments.

Five factors contributed to the growing perception by many Bank communities that inclusive practices were effective (such as ownership of policies by borrowing governments, participation of the Global South population, and consultation with NGOs) as compared to top-down practices. First, inclusive practices came to be seen as increasing the commitment of governments and populations to development policies and projects. Setting conditionalities in the structural adjustment programs proved to be highly ineffective in getting governments to commit to a set of reforms. Governments will only follow policy prescriptions that fit their existing policy options, which are themselves influenced by national politics (Dollar and Svensson 1998; Killick, Gunatilaka, and Marr 1998). According to the Bank itself, "[e]xperience indicates that where more meaningful participation of borrowing governments has been achieved, it often enhances government commitment and ownership for the Bank-financed activity."[7] Getting more commitment increases governments' willingness to share costs and improves the sustainability of projects and policies. An annual review of the Operations Evaluation Department in 1992 indicated "borrower ownership" and "beneficiary participation" as two crucial factors for the success of 24 lending operations described as "outstanding."[8] In a report on public participation in 121 rural water supply projects, Deepa Narayan also identifies the participation of aid-targeted populations as the most critical determinant for the success of the implementation of projects.[9] Their participation influenced, among other things, the proportion of water systems in good condition and the extent of the population that had access to and control over water resources. Narayan defines participation as the process by which citizens from borrowing countries influenced or partly controlled the project that affected them.

Second, inclusive practices also made projects and policies more acceptable to the public and thus prevented criticisms down the road. The growing inclusion of a more significant number of stakeholders was partly due to the Bank's need to address contestation by external actors. Including NGOs and Global South populations was a way to render Bank projects more effective regarding social acceptability and maybe even palliate the decrease in Bank funding from external sources. Even if many criticisms are still directed at Bank practices, their intensity has decreased, and the readiness of NGOs and civil society actors to work with the Bank on development projects has increased. In May 2003, of 2,600 opinion leaders surveyed in 35 countries of the Global South, the majority responded that the Bank had become more responsive to the demands of borrower governments, if not necessarily to civil society groups. Close to 59 percent believed that the Bank had become more responsive over the past few years, while only 18 percent said it had become less responsive, 16 percent said there had been no change, and 9 percent did not answer.[10] A 2016 survey by Latino Barometer mentioned by one senior Bank official also noted that the World Bank had become the second most popular development organization in Latin America, right after the United Nations.[11] By comparison, Bank projects in the 1980s were very unpopular, perceived as "overdesigned," "too complex," and a poor reflection of the needs of poor people, which significantly contributed to their unpopularity.[12]

Third, Bank employees started to view discussions with borrowing governments to decrease tight supervision later on and to avoid the imposition of a complex system of conditionalities. This is one of the main reasons why more and more World Bank country teams included government officials in determining the pace and content of the conditionalities associated with macroeconomic policies. Bank teams eventually switched from hard-core conditionalities, which demanded the adoption of specific policies before adopting a new loan, to pro forma conditions attached to each new tranche of money. Despite the cost and additional time needed in the preparation phase,[13] "a number of task managers believe this extra effort spent in the early years of the projects will be offset by lower intensity supervision in later years."[14] In specific projects, the delegation of planning and organization could prevent the need for tight daily supervision once the project was up and running.

Fourth, consultation with civil society organizations and NGOs has supplemented the Bank's data collection. Global South organizations could supply "local knowledge" in the policy process and "give voice to the opinions and experiences of the poor."[15] More knowledge attuned to each context of work led to better results, and using existing context-specific knowledge sometimes decreased the need for independent and costly research. Consultations also led to hiring service providers that were more familiar with aid-targeted communities and could reach goals more effectively and in a more timely fashion. Hiring local providers was often more cost-effective than organizing *ad hoc* mechanisms.

Fifth, inclusive practices were also a way for the Bank to seek more legitimacy in its work with borrowing governments and communities. While legitimacy is very contested, an organization is seen as legitimate when its authority is accepted and perceived as justified. Positive perceptions of Bank teams in borrowing countries were thus crucial in increasing the Bank's effectiveness. Moreover, despite ongoing discontent about the Bank's activities, many stakeholders consider the Bank to be more legitimate to work with now than in the 1980s. Best explains, "although simply believing that something is legitimate does not necessarily make it so, if enough people believe that a particular institution or practice is legitimate and then act on that belief, they contribute to its legitimacy."[16] While this book does not examine this issue in depth, many officials interviewed for this research confirmed that contestation by civil societies in borrowing countries is much less virulent today than it was 30 years ago.[17] In that sense, the adoption of inclusive practices increased the Bank's legitimacy following the infamously top-down policies of the Washington Consensus, thus facilitating its day-to-day work in borrowing countries.

Overall, environmental pressures that affected the legitimacy of the Bank as the world's principal development institution (like contestation by civil society and Indigenous populations) reinforced this move toward more inclusion. Without environmental factors, the change might not have happened as quickly or have been institutionalized in this specific period. Already in 1987, *World Development* was publishing an issue entitled "Development Alternatives: the Challenge of NGOs."[18] Environmental factors put additional pressure on Bank employees to learn new ways of improving effectiveness. One of the main factors was the impasse reached by international development institutions at the end of the 1980s, with a fall in GDP per capita in most countries in the Global South and the subsequent increase in global and national inequalities. At this point, mainstream approaches to development were determined to have failed, even according to World Bank measurements.

Researchers and activists alike also increasingly challenged the dominant paradigm promoted by the Bank and the other Bretton Woods institutions (World Trade Organization and International Monetary Fund (IMF)); moreover, strong proponents of strict top-down structural adjustments were growing ever scarcer. The 1994 *Fifty Years is Enough* campaign, led by international NGOs and activists, was a very public demonstration of the growing disapproval of the Bank as an organization. Non-governmental actors and researchers criticized the Bank for forcing the governments of weaker states to integrate into a global system in which they were structurally economically unequal. These activists accused the Bank of not listening to the populations the organization wanted to help and of having caused a debt and social crisis in many of the countries the Bank was meant to be assisting. Leonor Briones of the Freedom from Debt Coalition in the Philippines argues that the logic of structural adjustment required "the repression of democratic rights."[19]

Activists eventually organized around "anti-globalization" or "global justice" agendas that contested the legitimacy of the existence of the World Bank and the IMF. During that period, Bank employees felt unwelcome in many communities or government ministries; this isolation decreased the potential success of their projects and policies. This diminution in social acceptability and the failures of the Bank prescriptions in the 1980s and 1990s also led many governments in sub-Saharan Africa and South Asia to turn their back on Bank loans in favor of loans from China or other new lenders from the Global South. Bank employees could not do business as usual if they wanted to avoid criticism.[20] The professionalization of international and national NGOs and civil society organizations in the 1990s enabled these groups to collect better data and use the Bank's own language to criticize its projects. They standardized participatory techniques and mechanisms in a manner that is understandable and applicable to Bank teams. Their criticisms finally reached receptive ears by the American government in Washington, D.C.

The capacities of borrowing governments were also more significant in the 1980s, which encouraged Bank economists to include them in the policymaking process. Many finance ministers in borrowing governments were then trained at Ivy League universities teaching neoclassical economics precepts. This rendered tight conditionalities less necessary because these governmental officials more readily adopted the macroeconomic policies emanating from the mainstream paradigm. The changing relationship between Bank officials and borrowing governments would have been impossible if governments with left-wing tendencies continued to disagree on basic neoliberal economic principles, such as the fight against inflation or the privatization of state-owned enterprises. These factors created a favorable environment for Bank employees to be open about changing their practices. They did not cause the change toward inclusion practices, but they facilitated the learning process, thus increasing the probability that inclusive practices would be institutionalized.

How is the Bank different from the 1980s?

Observers have differing views on the extent or the meaningfulness of these new practices of inclusive policymaking in an institution that has historically upheld very top-down and expert-based practices. On the one side, some Bank managers and observers claim that a new paradigm has emerged in Bank practices and behavior,[21] suggesting that the Bank has "engaged civil society" on an unprecedented scale[22] and celebrate the new participatory PRSPs for having been successful in improving well-being.[23] Xu Yi-Chong and Patrick Weller (2009) show how the day-to-day actions of staff have changed the Bank as a whole, moving it toward the greater inclusion of other stakeholders. Joel Lazarus shows the potential of the participation mechanisms under the PRSP adopted in 1999.[24] Dani Rodrik celebrates this new emphasis on humility, policy diversity, and selective and modest reforms.[25] For him, the Bank's 2005 report, *World Bank Economic Growth in the 1990s: Learning from a Decade of Reform,* proves that the Bank is undergoing a shift in thinking. In the foreword of this report, Gobind Nankani, former vice president for Africa at the World Bank, calls this period the end of a conviction.[26] This enthusiasm was echoed at a conference in Barcelona in 2004 entitled "From the Washington Consensus towards a new Global Governance," which reunited renowned economists such as Olivier Blanchard, Paul Krugman, José Ocampo, and Jeffrey Sachs.

On the other side, because of the peculiar character of the change toward more inclusive procedures and the fact that it went against usual Bank practices, other scholars have qualified this change as rhetorical, dishonest, or manipulated or to hide neoliberal policies. Some observers dismiss the broad-based participation of populations, the inclusion of NGOs, or country ownership as being only rhetorical,[27] inefficient,[28] recycling of prior policies with only a marginal change to include poverty,[29] a neoliberal strategic response,[30] or neoliberal colonization.[31] Bonnie

Campbell and Bruno Losch argue that the Bank's ideological commitments endure (e.g., the underestimation of inequalities, disqualification of policies of redistribution, omission of conflicts of interests of key actors, such as labor unions),[32] and Angela Wood calls these inclusive practices "one step forward, two steps back."[33] Many observers have pointed to the similarity in the content of the structural adjustment programs of the 1980s and the more participatory poverty reduction strategy of the 1990s, suggesting that this proves the lack of substantive input from central governments.[34] Arguably, the macroeconomic framework and the end goal of economic development remain largely the same over time, even according to the senior Bank officials interviewed for this research. On the effects of inclusive practices on the livelihoods of aid-targeted populations, scholars have pointed to the failing results of the PRSP.[35] Critical development scholars conclude that if there has been a procedural change but no positive impacts, then the change must be rhetorical, or this procedural change was intentionally to co-opt populations.

A disagreement is thus rampant concerning the extent of the change toward inclusive practices and the effectiveness of the results. Nonetheless, even if they can debate the meaningfulness, the significance, or the impact of this change on policies, most observers would agree that there has been a *procedural change* in policymaking practices at the Bank in how projects are elaborated. Even if this change was defined as only minimal or hypocritical, this would still be an ideal case for studying how practice change happens and why it happened at this specific time. While macroeconomic practices might be very similar to the 1980s, policies and projects are no longer written *only* by Bank employees in Washington, D.C., Bank country teams and employees in various departments consult aid-targeted populations and integrate government officials and stakeholders into the policymaking process in a more concrete way. With an interpretative methodology giving weight to what practitioners say about what they do, it is impossible to avoid noticing how differently Bank employees explain their day-to-day practices from the 1980s to the 2010s.

To further a conversation between optimists and pessimists, change and stability are hereby both defined as integral parts of social ordering. Of course, despite many changes in policymaking practices, there are great similarities in policy content and the political rationality of the Bank.[36] For example, despite important differences in the policy elaboration process between the policy framework paper (PFP) of the 1980s and the PRSPs of the 2000s, there remained a high level of similarity in policy content and priorities. Both targeted poverty and social concerns and relied on macroeconomic precepts and suggestions. "While targets are more refined in the PRSP, focus is still on policies where outcomes can actually be measured and quantified."[37] However, the procedures to develop such policies were more inclusive in the case of the PRSP. In other words, goals were similar, but the procedures to reach these goals differed. This stems from the fact that learning happens either at a tactical level – how to achieve better a particular goal (to increase the efficiency of development projects and policies) – or at a deeper level – which goals should be pursued (in this case, a neoliberal and technocratic type of development).[38] The conclusion of this book addresses the question of how there can be meaningful change in the process of policymaking and project elaboration but stability in the content of policies and the overall neoliberal technocratic ethos of the Bank. In the end, this book examines the emergence of international practices of inclusion of new stakeholders to devise development policies and programs as a *procedural change* at the Bank, not a substantive or philosophical change.

Environmental changes

The 1973 international oil shock jolted many economies of the Global South, whose current balance of payment deteriorated quickly, especially in East Africa. Between 1973 and 1975, Zambia, Kenya, and Tanzania took additional loans from the World Bank with policy conditions attached. Making matters worse, a second oil crisis occurred in 1979 due to an oil shortage and the fall of the Shah of Iran during the Iranian Revolution. As a result, the price of oil rose to provoke an economic emergency in most oil-importing countries. Coupled with the sharp increase in the interest rates of international loans at the end of the 1970s, a financial crisis pushed countries of the Global South, which were unable to balance their budget into a vicious circle of debt. Amid this debt crisis, international financial institutions more easily persuaded governments to enact policy reforms as preconditions for bailout funds. Privatization became attractive both for multilateral lenders and for governments in dire need of revenues: "Governments also came to rely on the advice of US-trained economists in high government posts, whose presence helped foster investor confidence."[39]

The election of Margaret Thatcher as Prime Minister of the United Kingdom in 1979 and Ronald Reagan as her counterpart in the United States in 1980 kicked off the next decade of financial austerity. Promoting policies of laissez-faire, free markets, and the strict control of labor movements to deal with the financial crisis, these governments became associated with the conservative trend of neoliberalism, whose intellectual roots lay in monetarist theories associated with Friedrich von Hayek. These shifts in economic thinking in the Western world shaped the structural adjustment policies of the Bank, along with the weakening of socialist governments in the Global South. In an op-ed in the journal *issue*, Edward Jaycox, then the World Bank's vice president for Africa (1987–1996), used Thatcher's most famous quote to describe the structural adjustment period: "Adjustment is a fact of life – for everyone, for every country. It is a continual process, not a one-time correction. *There is no alternative.*"[40] While initially, not all Bank macroeconomists were on board with micromanaging national debts, practices of conditionalities were slowly adopted as the way to deal with the debt crisis.

On March 15, 1980, the Bank's first structural adjustment loan was approved to Turkey for US$200 million in three tranches to support the structural adjustment program presented by the Turkish government. In the two decades following the adoption of the concept of structural adjustment by its board of directors, the Bank made 537 very similarly drafted adjustment loans to 109 countries, totaling nearly $100 billion.[41] However, the debt crisis accelerated on August 13, 1982, when Mexico's finance minister, Jesus Silva Herzog, publicly announced that they could not repay their debts to the IMF that were due two days later. This marked the beginning of the 1980s debt crisis, which forced governments of the Global South in the International Development Association to seek quick fund disbursements to stabilize their balance of payments. Starting in mid-1986, the structural adjustment loans were linked to the policies and data presented in each country's Policy Framework Paper (PFP). A PFP was a document written by Bank employees that describes a country's major problems, its short-term objectives and priorities, its suggested macroeconomic and structural policies, and its need for and sources of external financing. Washington-based economists mainly wrote these documents on behalf of borrowing countries.

The formulation of the so-called Washington Consensus in 1989 by the American economist John Williamson further articulated an already creditable neoliberal economic turn in the policy advice of multilateral institutions. The formalization of this consensus was epitomized by a list of ten policy prescriptions designed by the Bank, the IMF, and the American Treasury and destined for Latin American countries.[42] According to Williamson, the list was the lowest common denominator of policy advice that Washington economists agreed to. In this period, the neoliberal guideline focused on market orientation, fiscal discipline, liberalization, outward-oriented economic policies, foreign direct investment, privatization, and deregulation. In most cases elaborated by Bank economists based in Washington, D.C., these guidelines became the basis for the conditionalities associated with the World Bank and the IMF's structural adjustment programs. However, the Washington Consensus' strongest detractors criticized it for being a neoliberal manifesto imposed on countries of the Global South.[43]

Becoming the sixth president of the World Bank in 1981, Alden W. Clausen stated that the most outstanding achievement of his presidency was the acceleration of disbursements and the quality of the lending associated with the structural adjustment loans.[44] Moving the Bank away from the focus on poverty of the previous president, Robert McNamara, Clausen was much more concerned with correcting economic policies to promote macroeconomic stability. Journalists and the public now remember the 1980s as a dark period for the Bank: "[T]his shift in the public message of the Bank made it all too easy to paint it as heartless."[45]

Top-down policymaking practices in the 1980s

The Bank's practices and narrative in the 1980s were based on prioritizing external expertise to deal with national development problems. This external expert stance, or expert-led, was deeply embedded in Bank officials' understanding of producing results. This stance was reiterated in many reports and memos: "[T]he project sponsors and designers place themselves outside the local system they are investigating and about which they are making decisions – even if they happen to come from or live within the local system."[46]

To gain access to new capital, the Bank offered countries a set of conditions designed by Bank economists based in Washington, D.C. This predefined set of conditions accompanied each tranche of money, and borrowing governments risked losing their loans at every stage if they did not implement them. Additionally, the pace and the sequence to complete the conditionalities associated with each tranche were as short as a few months to a year or two.[47] The power of the Bank to implement top-down policies with strict conditionalities came from a long process in which borrowing governments came to accept the Bank's conditions not only because of material incentives but also because of the Bank's perceived expert authority. Moreover, most Bank employees ignored the input of borrowing governments and non-governmental actors, creating a lot of resentment.

One senior Bank economist recalled that the private sector and other international organizations often hired highly educated people in countries of the Global South, which created an imbalance between them and those who decided to keep working for the public service. Therefore, he said, borrowing governments "needed Bank staff to do the footwork."[48] He added that even finding research assistants or consultants in borrowing countries to do simple tasks like using Microsoft Excel or finding documents was difficult. In a speech in 1988, while the seventh Bank President Barber Conable admitted that structural adjustment could sometimes hurt aid-targeted populations and poor people "often lack[ed] voice and influence," he concluded that the Bank has "a special duty to encourage and finance measures that protect them."[49] The Bank believed they had a duty to externally protect "poor" populations instead of allowing them to develop means to empower themselves.

I would argue that Bank economists, trained in the United States, were prompting structural adjustment programs in Washington, D.C., not because they *consciously* wanted to advance a neoliberal ideology or impose their hegemony but because they *believed* they were helping governments that did not have the required expertise to build effective development programs. They believed the theories and principles they were espousing, having been influenced by Chicago school economists and the general intellectual and political environment at the time. Most Bank economists believed that the best way to trigger development was to help countries with deeply needed external expertise on balance of payments, and inflation control. Staff members recalled that the hegemonic discourse at the Bank in the 1980s was, "we tell them what to do."[50] The question of intentionality will be further explored in the conclusion of this book.

In this period, Bank teams would include borrowing governments in framing national policies if they gave consent to neoliberal conditionalities. However, many governments in borrowing countries had other ideas about how to deal with the debt crisis. In Latin America, many governments had just implemented an import-substitution industrialization strategy, and in Africa, many countries had elected socialist or pan-Africanist governments, like that of Thomas Sankara in Burkina Faso, and the Congolese Labor Party in the People's Republic of the Congo. Most of these governments agreed on conditionalities devised by Bank macroeconomists in order to access funds quickly; they were in dire need of new funds to reimburse piling up debts. A "subordinate actor may very well reflect on and assess the contents of a superordinate actor's prescriptions and disagree with it yet defer to that actor."[51] Borrowing governments developed a pattern in Bank dealings in this period in which they would agree to very restrictive sets of conditionalities but have no intentions to fulfill them. According to many Bank macroeconomists interviewed for this research, many structural adjustment programs were agreed upon by countries, but the prescribed conditionalities were never implemented.[52]

A lack of borrowing governments' ownership of economic programs especially created a lack of coordination in implementing the policies. Bank economists designed structural adjustment conditions and got them approved by finance ministers or Central Bank representatives without ensuring that they corresponded to other government ministries' vision of their long-term development plan (e.g., agriculture, education). One senior Bank economist said that this lack of coordination delayed the fulfillment of many conditionalities associated with each tranche: "There were far too many conditions, far too many. Sometimes, the minister of finance would say 'yes, we'll agree to reduce tariffs on this or that,' without telling the minister of commerce, who was actually in charge of that."[53] In the end, people inside and outside the Bank now qualify the structural adjustment period as a development failure. In a column in the *New York Times*, American economist Paul Krugman described in the early 2000s those countries that followed structural adjustment prescriptions as economic failures ranging from disappointing to catastrophic.[54] According to a regional chief economist at the Bank, the 1980s were a complete failure *even according to Bank standards*; this conclusion led to the realization in the mid-1990s that "you could not do business as usual."[55]

Furthermore, during the 1980s and 1990s, civil society CoPs organized about 150 social protests against the institutions of Bretton Woods. Bank management and employees were confronted with failure and contestation both inside the organization, by civil society organizations and activists, as well as by well-respected external experts. The "Fifty Years Is Enough" 1994 campaign, organized by various civil society organizations and activists, was especially successful in publicizing dissatisfaction with Bank policies. This discontent had its paroxysm in 1999 with major anti- or alter-globalization protests organized against the World Trade Organization and the institutions of Bretton Woods. As a result, the social acceptability of the Bank and other international financial institutions, especially given their decisions for and relationships with borrowing populations and national governments, was crumbling.

All of the senior officials and economists interviewed for this research recognize, at least partly, the failure of the policies of the structural adjustment period. A senior manager for the african region admitted that the 1980s were a "completely lost" decade: "This is a decade during which fiscal adjustment policy brought investment down to one percent of GDP across the board. No matter how you look at it, from a development perspective, it was a failure."[56] Governments that had no other choice than to sign onto a structural adjustment program had a strong feeling that international financial institutions "ganged up" against them.[57] In some countries, the implementation of the programs even became a verb: "[W]e have been 'SAP-ed.'"[58] The social acceptability of these programs kept decreasing as the 1980s went on, and Bank economists were increasingly faced with failure regarding economic outcomes, macroeconomic stability, and social acceptability. The main reason cited by senior officials at the Bank for the failure of structural adjustment was not the inappropriateness of the policies but their imposition as a universal template. As a Bank economist explained, "the real problem was not that it was the wrong policies but it was the wrong people designing them."[59] Another Bank economist recalled that it was easy to make a government sign a document, but it was more difficult to make it commit to a set of policy recommendations: "You can take the horse to the water but you will not make it drink."[60]

The relationship between Bank employees and civil society actors was even more distant than with governmental agencies. A senior Bank economist recalled that in the 1980s, Bank representatives were simply "not allowed" to talk to civil society actors or private stakeholders.[61] For example, he recalled that for the first structural adjustment loan in Morocco, the main condition was lowering trade tariffs. However, the Bank team was prevented from meeting with any actors from the private sector, NGOs, or union representatives.[62] Bank agencies were very secretive and kept their distance from civil society organizations, and their relationship ranged from distrust to outright hatred. Bank employees in the 1980s, a majority of whom were economists trained in Western countries, did not trust the reliability of NGO inputs, and some didn't believe in the principle of consulting with them. As a result, many Bank employees saw civil society more as a nuisance than as potential allies.

In an interview, the NGO leader Warren Nyamugasira asserted that in the early 1990s, NGO workers "could not speak unless spoken to," and that the "whole structure was designed to underline the dependence of the Africans upon the donors."[63] Similarly, a Bank official recalled that even when she was supposed to write the section of a report on women's issues in Romania in the 1980s, she "just could not consult women's organizations."[64] She did not have the resources or the mandate to do so. The Bank especially did not want civil society organizations to have access to documents that could be used to criticize the organization. During the structural adjustment period, the Bank was very opaque regarding the elaboration of its projects and internal communication: "Every single policy on every page had at the bottom: 'this is strictly for internal use.'"[65] This secrecy created frustration in civil society actors, who had to develop their analysis of Bank projects using their own data and measurements. The relationship between them and Bank teams was tense and oppositional.

Many senior Bank officials noted that there were also "growing political capacities" in borrowing governments, which was having an impact on their willingness to include government officials in policy discussions. This apparently contributed to changing the relationship between Bank teams and borrowing governments. "The changed attitude of mind of our clients, that's very important. It dramatically changed the context of work."[66] According to a former United Nations official, the leverage of the Bank has changed since the 1980s:

> Bank officials just can't act like this anymore. It is no longer politically, socially, or culturally acceptable. The days when Bank delegations would descend with incredible arrogance are over. Maybe they can in really poor or fragile states, but in general, they can't do that anymore.[67]

Intense on-the-ground contestation was organized against specific projects and structural adjustment plans, especially by activists in countries impacted by the policies. Facing growing contestation from all over the world, Bank economists had to streamline conditionalities. The top-down conditionality system between 1980 and 2014 has evolved from "hard core" to "pro forma." The former version recommended strict prerequisites to enforce involuntary actions by borrowing governments, which were required to obtain loans or debt relief. The latter, while still a requirement to obtain money, had to be discussed and agreed upon by both parties. This shift came from the difficulty the Bank had enforcing and implementing strict conditionalities and dealing with domestic constituencies in day-to-day practices. The need for new loans often led countries to sign off on conditionalities on which they did not fully agree, so Bank teams realized that including governments in drafting conditionalities reduced the risk of non-compliance. Indeed, in general, there has been much more commitment to loan conditionalities from borrowing governments in the 2010s than in the 1980s, even though the economic policies were not incredibly different.

Openness to other stakeholders

Until the 1990s, Bank economists told me that they often dismissed NGOs' criticisms, and comforted themselves in the idea that NGOs did not understand their expertise. They would rarely engage with NGOs' data or reports, especially what they considered NGOs' "caricatural" criticisms of the Bank's projects.[68] However, two factors encouraged Bank employees to consider NGO research anew in the 1990s and 2000s. On the one hand, although many NGOs produced similar kinds of reports in the 1990s as in the 1980s, their research became epistemic boundary objects when the Bank started to hire sociology and anthropology experts who recognized the value of, for example, qualitative and ethnographic methodologies. On the other hand, NGOs started to adopt a language and methodology that was more congruent with the Bank's teams. For those reasons, NGO reports started to be read and considered more seriously in the 1990s. Oxfam, which was "the biggest critic of the Bank ever," started to be "listened to" by Bank employees at the end of the 1990s.[69] NGOs and civil society organizations have always written reports and articles to criticize the Bank's actions, but eventually, civil society leaders were also able to convince internal brokers in a variety of Bank CoPs to support their contestation claims.

The first Bank-NGOs Committee, chaired by the Policy Adviser for External Relations Javed Burki, was established in 1981 to organize annual meetings between Bank officials and international NGO leaders. In the following years, after sustained discussions within the Bank-NGOs Committee, employees started to receive requests from Bank managers to identify projects in which NGOs could be more deeply involved.[70] A few years later, the first regional Bank-NGOs committees were formed. In the 1980s, interviewees for this research told me that annual meetings with NGOs were less a genuine dialogue than a way for the Bank to orient the debate. A formal NGO Unit was then established in 1986 (which later became the NGO and Civil Society Unit). At first, the NGO Unit was more of a resource for NGOs to monitor the activities of the Bank than a mechanism to include NGOs in the practices of the Bank. As Michelle Miller-Adams explains, the unit's status as a peripheral concern was evident in the organizational chart.[71] Until 1993, the unit was much more part of the Bank's external relations than in the central operational departments.

The NGO and Civil Society Unit eventually promoted a "disclosure policy,"[72] which led to the establishment of the World Bank's official policy on disclosure of information.[73] Thus, NGOs gained more direct access to information previously kept secret at the Bank. For years, the NGO Unit functioned as an intermediary between what Bank CoPs tried to tell the NGOs' CoPs and what the NGOs tried to respond. In January 1994, the board of executive directors adopted an expanded Information Disclosure Policy, making access to information easier for civil society organizations. With this policy, it was easier for NGOs to access information regarding specific project proposals, staff appraisal reports, Operations Evaluation Department documents, environmental assessments, analysis and action plans, final results of economic and sector work, sectoral policy papers, and legal opinions of the General Counsel.[74] This policy also led to the establishment of the Public Information Center at the Bank's headquarters and information centers in many borrowing countries, in addition to London, Paris, and Tokyo. These centers were used by civil society organizations to monitor Bank activities as they became more fluent in the Bank's language.

A Strategic Framework for Mainstreaming Citizen Engagement was launched in 2013 to strengthen the Bank's relationship with civil society, and to provide the latter with "opportunities to find synergies and collaborate on public campaigns and education efforts."[75] The inclusion of these stakeholders was increasingly viewed as essential to increasing social acceptability and the success of social projects. According to a senior Bank health specialist, starting to work with NGOs in the 1990s changed how he perceived the usefulness of NGOs in the Bank's work:

> It was actually very helpful. In the many things you wanted to do, you now had support from local NGOs. For very little money you could pull them in, they would start to do the things that you knew were important to support the project. That was . . . one of the biggest things we did. When we broke this barrier and started working with NGOs. There were a lot of opportunities for task managers to experiment, listen to the local people, recognize local initiatives.[76]

Alexander Shakow explained that shifts toward more communication and partnership with NGOs happened partly because senior managers were giving the "signal" that "working with NGOs is okay" and partly because country-level employees recognized that "success depends on being able to reach out at the local level and that NGOs have a way of doing that." The shift in the narrative was not a direct order to start consulting but enabled new possibilities of practices. Wolfensohn's new calls for openness also positively affected NGO readiness to work with the

Bank. According to his unofficial biographer, the shift in Wolfensohn's discourse opened a new era in the relationship between civil society actors and World Bank officials:

> For Africa, it signaled that the World Bank's new leader would go out of his way to visit a promising new democracy, and that he would listen to its people; the years of harsh structural-adjustment conditionality were over. For [NGOs], including the many that had assailed the Bank in Madrid the previous year, it signaled that the Bank's new president had instincts much like theirs: that he wanted to sit under baobab trees, eating nuts with village leaders.[77]

In the early 1990s, the Bank slowly became (at least discursively) open to external voices from NGOs, but also borrowing governments, their citizens, and other stakeholders. In the last year of his tenure, in 1994, then President Lewis Preston acknowledged in a letter to employees the need for the Bank to become "even more effective than it is today" and "more client-centered."[78] The Bank's official publications in the 1990s started to change regarding the emphasis on the need for ownership of policies:

> Although the government may receive help in designing the program, the authorities must understand it fully and be satisfied that it is the appropriate course of action for the country. It is desirable that, in whatever way is appropriate, the government publicly proposes and justify the overall strategy of the adjustment program and take a sequence of highly visible actions to implement the program.[79]

The Bank kept on promoting structural adjustments but emphasized the need for other stakeholders to be "satisfied that [a certain course of action] is the appropriate course of action."[80] Official publications reinforced this change in the Bank's narrative: "Admittedly, in the past, sponsors and designers may not have always listened to all the people or consulted poor and disadvantaged members of society, but this is changing."[81] The change was underway.

In 2000, after consulting with more inclusive organizations, the NGO and Civil Society Unit – which contained many boundary brokers who had just been hired in the Strategic Compact turnover – published general guidelines to support Bank employees in processes of consultation with civil society organizations. This practical guide, an epistemic boundary object, states five key aspects to effective consultation:

> giving civil society organizations ownership by involving representatives in the design of the consultation process; being clear from the outset about what is and is not under consideration, to avoid unrealistic expectations; demonstrating respect for those consulted through careful follow-up and feedback; using appropriate selection procedures to ensure that all the relevant interests

are represented; tailoring types of interactions to the knowledge and capability of different groups.[82]

In 2001, an informal Joint Facilitation Committee phased out the Bank-NGOs Committee to establish a second-generation mechanism for the Bank's engagement with civil society. The committee was initially composed of Bank employees and 15 representatives of civil society networks of trade unions, Indigenous groups, faith-based organizations, NGOs, and private foundations. This inclusion enabled more inclusion, as those organizations promoted new mechanisms and contested the Bank's practices even more directly. In particular, the committee contested the tendency of the Bank to involve civil society in the initial stages of Bank projects (i.e., information sharing and consultation) but not in later stages (i.e., collaboration and empowerment).[83]

In July 2010, the Bank launched an Access to Information policy based on the US' and India's Freedom of Information Acts to democratize access to Bank resources and to establish a "practitioner exchange," a program of relationship building between practitioners worldwide in which participants shared best practices in a range of different fields. After that, the Bank launched new technological instruments to share data with civil society groups, each with various degrees of success. The online platform *PovcalNet* allowed users to access and replicate the Bank's poverty assessments under different assumptions, and *Isimulate* enabled users to access Bank forecasting models as well as to design and share their own.[84] In the 2010s, there was also a multiplication of online consultations in the form of open forums with government officials and civil society leaders. The Bank was seeking the knowledge of NGOs and civil society actors to better understand sector-specific conditions and data, but some topics were still not covered in these consultations, such as trade and fiscal policies. While the inclusion of stakeholders such as NGOs, village associations, municipal governments, private-sector businesses, and unions in policymaking processes was prohibited in the 1980s, it became gradually accepted and even promoted by boundary brokers in the following decades. Other stakeholders started to be included in various aspects of Bank employees' day-to-day practices. In the 2000s, "it was a lot easier to engage with critics of the Bank" than ever before.[85]

According to the World Bank's website, the "involvement" of NGOs in Bank policymaking, in general, went from 21 percent of all projects in 1990 to 82 percent in 2012.[86] Consultations with NGOs in Bank projects and policymaking were recognized at the Bank to have "improved the quality of policymaking, positively influenced the direction of country programs, strengthened national ownership of key reforms, and promoted public sector transparency and accountability."[87] In total, from 1973 to 1988, only six percent of projects financially supported by the Bank involved NGOs, and the role of NGOs in these projects was mostly confined to service delivery.[88] By contrast, an internal review of project loans states that in 2004, 74 percent (194 of 262) of projects approved by the executive board had some form of civil society participation.[89] In addition, new tools to consult NGOs were developed, and guidelines and sourcebooks were published by the NGO and Civil Society Unit.[90]

Many financial instruments were put in place to encourage participatory development. Field-based learning opportunities and training programs for employees and managers were also set up.[91] In 1993, new financial instruments were established to promote innovation in development strategies. The Participation Fund and its successor, the Fund for Innovative Approaches in Human and Social Development, were set up to finance NGOs to find new ways to promote participation and human and social development. Social funds also became a symbol of the Bank trying to reach out to the poor through community development projects. Each mechanism set an example of a potentially reproducible tool, and reports shared those experiences with communities inside the Bank. At the end of the 1996 fiscal year, the Bank approved 51 social funds in 32 countries, totaling approximately US$1 billion.[92] In the mid-1990s, managers implemented other small lending instruments that encouraged participatory development, such as learning and innovation loans, flexible program lending, and loans for less than US$5 million for innovative projects.

From the policy framework to the poverty reduction strategy

At the beginning of the 1990s, the Bank started to produce country assistance/partnership strategies (replaced in 2014 by the country partnership framework), which were usually a four-year overall Bank strategy for each country. These papers were generally prepared by the International Bank for Reconstruction and Development and the International Development Association and intended to summarize the Bank assistance program to a given country regarding poverty reduction and development goals.[93] In short, it was a "Bank-owned" document.[94] Compared to previous documents, these strategies encouraged the participation of various levels of government, civil society organizations, the private sector, and other stakeholders. According to the Bank's information disclosure policy, all country offices had to issue a "public information notice" to NGOs, civil society organizations, and all interested citizens concerning drafting a country assistance strategy. As a result, the involvement of civil society in the writing of country-assistance strategies became increasingly important throughout the years. From 20 percent of strategies involving other stakeholders in the fiscal year 1998, the participation rate increased to over 80 percent in the fiscal years 2000 and 2001.[95] These strategies eventually led to the PRSPs.

A significant evolution in the 2000s concerning the ownership of multilateral development programs was the replacement of the PFP (associated with structural adjustment programs) with the PRSPs (associated with development policy loans). A PFP had to support each structural adjustment loan. These documents, which were written by Bank employees, described a country's political economy, suggested short- and medium-term priorities, and established aid-financing needs. Adopting a PFP led to the disbursement of funds under the IMF Structural Adjustment Facility and various funds from the Bank. In principle, they were made in "close collaboration of the applicant country and the employees of the Fund and the Bank."[96] Borrowing governments were supposed to participate in joint Bank-IMF meetings and the drafting of the papers. However, many Bank officials confirmed in interviews that Bank and IMF employees wrote them in Washington before taking them to the various boards within the institution for approval.[97]

As a former Bank regional chief economist said, the general attitude at the Bank during that period was "we are right and they are wrong" and "they don't know anything."[98] The PFPs, which supported structural adjustment loans in the 1980s and 1990s, were indicative of this attitude. Many Bank officials confirmed in interviews for this research that Bank and IMF employees mainly wrote the PFP and the associated structural adjustment programs in Washington, D.C., before seeking approval by the board of governors.[99] As many Bank economists recalled, PFP had very little input from borrowing governments.[100]

As a senior Bank economist recalled, PFP "were looked at and commented upon by donors. It wasn't really the borrowing governments' documents. They didn't contribute to their finding."[101] Then again, the frameworks, which were a prerequisite for a structural adjustment program leading to debt relief, were often agreed upon but never implemented because of a lack of ownership. Malawi, for example, committed to the same reforms in seven successive PFPs without achieving them.[102] Another Bank economist said: "we were not supposed to write these letters but, hey, the government is giving us their stationery, we've been to meetings and the minister said: 'you have power at night, we don't.'"[103] The Bank was then rightly accused of deploying a "'cookbook' approach" because of the very similar content between each country's PFP and lacking sensitivity to variations in social, economic, and political conditions of borrowing countries.[104] Moreover, the top-down approach of the PFP created resentment in some borrowing governments' offices, those that had, at the time, very different ideas about how to achieve development.

In an interview with Bank archivists, Paul Cadario remembered the process of developing the structural adjustment program in Senegal in the 1980s when he was a junior loan officer: "We cooked it up with the Ministry of Finance, and then they'd sign because they wanted the money, but there was neither the willingness nor the capacity to implement the undertakings that were there."[105] Failures of the structural adjustment programs came not only from an overly strict adherence to certain economic principles that hurt the poor in the name of economic development but also from this lack of commitment by borrowing governments.

The main reason cited by Bank employees for the failure of structural adjustment is not the inappropriateness of the policies but instead their *coercive imposition* as a universal template. As one Bank economist explained, "the real problem was not that it was the wrong policies but it was the wrong people designing them."[106] Another Bank economist recalled that it was easy to make a government sign a document but difficult to make it commit to a set of policy recommendations: "You can take the horse to the water but you will not make it drink."[107] In their recollection, the problem was not the policies themselves, but that the borrowing government did not adhere to them. Since the 1980s, there has been a social diffusion of neoliberal technocratic standards of action, rendering the direct imposition of such programs unnecessary. A Bank economist explained that this change in attitude by borrowing governments and their agreement to basic economic principles rendered the relationship between the two more productive, as their "clients" changed their attitude from the previous period."[108] This "virtuous" circle was the spread of a certain way of thinking about development.

In December 1999, a team led by people from Poverty Reduction and Economic Management, under the leadership of Jeni Klugman, presented a paper to the board of governors about the PRSPs, which were to be associated with debt reliefs under the Highly Indebted Poor Countries initiative.[109] The minutes of the December 20 meeting reveal general agreement about the principles underlying the PRSPs, namely

> that they should be country-driven with broad participation of elected bodies, civil society and development partners; they should reflect the country-specific nature and determinants of poverty; and that they should be results-oriented and link public actions to poverty outcomes, especially through faster and broad-based growth.[110]

The PRSP, therefore, replaced the PFP in laying out a country's poverty data and development plan. Produced in parallel with the Bank-owned country assistance strategy, the PRSPs were supposed to be managed and owned by the country. As a result, the country assistance strategy writers often used the PRSP or similar country-owned documents to define the Bank strategy.

The poverty reduction initiative was designed to give debt relief or restructuring to low- and medium-income countries. PRSPs were to be presented and accepted by the executive board in 1999 as a new requirement for funds and debt relief.[111] Made to be a collaboration between the World Bank, the IMF, and borrowing governments, PRSPs were macroeconomic, social, and structural programs based on growth and poverty reduction. In other words, PRSPs were supposedly country-led development programs based on economic growth at the macro level (liberalization, taxation, balance of payment, and budget management) and on poverty reduction in each context. Because they were written with governments and were meant to represent country-specific determinants of poverty, PRSPs became the main condition for obtaining debt relief under the Highly Indebted Poor Countries initiative.[112]

One of the main substantive differences between the PFP and the PRSP is that the latter was much more comprehensive. The PFP, on the one hand, was between 20 and 30 pages and addressed issues relating mainly to economic efficiency, as it was necessary for the adoption of structural adjustment programs. The PRSPs, on the other hand, were much longer documents, up to 200 pages, and included social aspects and government priorities that were not considered in the PFP. In short, PRSPs encompassed six main features:[113] be locally appropriated (i.e., involve broad participation of civil societies and private sectors in all operational steps); be focused on results on the poor; present a holistic and global understanding of poverty; formulate the implementation process of institutional as well as fiscal policies; be oriented toward the establishment of partnerships and coordination with a variety of aid actors (bilateral, multilateral, and NGO); and be based on a long-term perspective of poverty reduction.

Most importantly, while PFP was primarily written in Washington, D.C., the PRSP had a public participation component and theoretically had to be written by borrowing governments, with the help of Bank experts if needed. The PRSPs were established to build inclusive policies within a neoliberal framework while preserving the interests of civil society.[114] The macroeconomic policies and the focus on growth were very similar in the PFP and the PRSP. However, the outcomes were very different regarding growth, macroeconomic stability, and social acceptability. This means that there was no sharp break or paradigm shift between the two eras but that something significant changed to improve results, which has to do with changes in the procedures of writing those documents. As a former World Bank chief economist for Africa stated:

> You had the same policies in both cases, roughly, and you had a dramatic difference in the growth rates. So it could not be the policies themselves. It was who was designing them. They undertook policies and implemented them. And then there was a virtuous circle going on in Africa.[115]

Some senior officials at the Bank pointed out that the distinctive feature of the PRSP was not so much the focus on poverty ("it was a continuing trend" since the presidency of Robert McNamara),[116] but the idea of country ownership. A board discussion paper from December 10, 1999, presented many ways in which NGOs could be involved in the development of the PRSP, including verifying the reliability of information collected and undertaking independent research.[117] NGOs and civil society organizations were supposed to participate in the writing of PRSPs to ensure that they were on board with what the Bank was expecting, to avoid future criticisms of Bank policies, and to gain social acceptability. These consultations were supposed to be organized by the primary client, that is, borrowing governments. The paper underlined the importance of participation and empowerment in the PRSP:

> Empowerment is a key outcome, as well as an instrument for improving poverty outcomes more generally, through better diagnosis of priorities and causes, as well as monitoring. Levers for public action to improve governance include strengthened governmental processes, like budgetary management backed by audits, as well as broader-based accountability.[118]

As pointed out by various observers, the first PRSPs, even if they were supposed to be written by borrowing governments, only represented a partial transfer of ownership to borrowing countries. A senior official recalled a "bumpy" process of getting from a situation where borrowing-government officials were told to "sit and shut up and listen to experts" to one where you are told, "you are the boss, tell us what to do."[119] Bank teams were still the only ones in the driving seat of the first generation of PRSPs in the early 2000s:

> Basically it was done by our team working with governments. . . . Even if there was capacity, we did not want governments to do it. The governments were not organized in any fashion to do it. Then, progressively, countries started to organize themselves to do it.[120]

Even in the third or fourth versions of the PRSP, some governments would often write, "what they thought the donors wanted to hear":

> You know this whole business of the PRSP, country-driven, the country in the driver's seat and all these things. It's still the fact that they knew that they had to produce a PRSP that would pass muster with the donor. Otherwise, they weren't going to get debt relief. There was conditionality here. So they wrote these things with all the right buzzwords which the donors wanted to hear.[121]

In the end, the PRSP was the first attempt to decentralize policymaking at the Bank, even if the extent of ownership varied. The PRSPs acted as an anchoring practice: they rendered other practices possible and accelerated the adoption of consultative mechanisms, tools, and concepts that endured beyond the PRSP. Even if later generations of PRSPs partly responded to criticisms of being one-size-fits-all or rushed participation processes, they encouraged a certain adherence to a previously imposed model. This is so because as pro forma conditionalities, the PRSPs had to be written and accepted to access new loans. In the 1990s and 2000s, many civil society observers hoped for a fundamental change in the Bank's orientation and modus operandi, only to be disappointed later on as to the extent of inclusion that donors and Bank officials favored.[122] Participation was "domesticated away from its radical roots," and considerations of power were put aside.[123] The PRSP, especially, did not open a real space for discussing alternative political options but ended up being substantively similar to the previous structural adjustment programs.

Uma Kothari argues that development experts integrated new ideas in a way that furthers a particular view of social change and the practice of development.[124] Ilan Kapoor also argues that radical participation practices, once integrated into the mainstream, became quantifiable and measurable tools to attain specific goals. According to many observers in borrowing countries, participatory projects simply became tools for achieving better, measurable project outcomes.[125] Participation, according to these scholars, was thus

> molded to fit bureaucratic or organizational needs: people can meet, but decisions have to be taken quickly to obey budgetary or reporting deadlines; community input is good, but quantitative information (e.g., counting votes) is privileged over qualitative information (e.g., women's narratives).[126]

While some observers argue that there is a potential window of opportunity for Global South people to gain power or to learn through inclusion, most conclude that participatory development at the Bank was limited and subject to a technocratic logic. Most terms associated with inclusive development, such as empowerment, have been stripped from their original radical meanings to represent a less contentious "delegation from above."[127] Many participatory processes were eventually implemented to achieve project goals or to gain legitimacy for the Bank instead of giving value to context-specific knowledge (e.g., women's knowledge or Indigenous concerns) per se. This was especially the case for broad-based participation under the PRSP. Because of short delays or pressure to implement an effective process, participants in participatory workshops or projects often ended up supporting an official story: "Rather than fostering information exchange and free debate, then, participation in this case stifles, censors, disciplines or silences participants, particularly those who are already disadvantaged."[128]

The process of translation through neoliberal/technocratic rationality has depoliticized ideas of ownership and participation into more technical practices of consultation and inclusion. As James Ferguson describes, the development industry became an "anti-politics machine."[129] Development experts' objective of transcending ideological and political divides derives directly from the technocratic bias of those in power.[130] The fact that participatory development can now be learned in mainstream university departments and through specialized training has contributed to this depoliticization to such an extent that participatory development is no longer associated with communities in the Global South where the concept originated, but instead with development experts who professionalized participatory techniques in international agencies.

Joint staff assessments, established to evaluate the content of the PRSP periodically, also undermined country ownership. These assessments were written after rounds of negotiations between a Bank team and the borrowing government. While the government could always refuse to endorse the assessment, refusal would often lead to their inability to access funds. One Bank official recalled that discussions could sometimes be harsh, and that if government officials said "no, that's it, that's what we want," they would do their due diligence and "let our boards know that we did not find this program to be completely satisfactory, but overall it's a good basis."[131] He adds that the joint staff assessments had to be diplomatically written in order "not to upset the governments about something they had ownership over."[132] Bank teams still maintained an expert relationship with borrowing governments but were changing the way they approached them. Even if some Bank economists still did not believe borrowing governments had sufficient capacity to influence the policy process, the relationship evolved to a more respectful one, and policies were better implemented according to Bank measurement.

The structural adjustment loans were simultaneously replaced by development policy loans—quickly disbursed financing instruments for policy and institutional reforms. Based on a new vision of conditionalities, this lending usually amounted annually to around 30 to 40 percent of the Bank's new commitments.[133] There are many differences between the two eras. First, after fulfilling prior macroeconomic conditions determined by the board of directors, loans were granted and became part of the government's budget. They were not earmarked as they were not linked to specific investment projects. Second, in addition to macroeconomic stability, the conditions, targets, and objectives were drawn from the country's development plan.[134] In 2014, this type of lending was renamed "development policy financing." In the 1980s, this sort of lending, then called adjustment lending, was mainly meant to support macroeconomic stability. It then evolved to support the "promotion of competitive market structures, the correction of distortions in incentive regimes, appropriate monitoring and safeguards, the institutional environment needed to attract private sector investment, the promotion of private sector activity, and good governance."[135]

The emergence of the development policy loans (renamed development policy financing in 2014) was a significant part of the shift in the relationship between borrowing governments and the Bank. More rapidly disbursed, these loans needed the fulfillment of certain pro forma macroeconomic conditions decided by the board of directors *before* being granted, instead of attributing multiple tranches with conditionalities at each stage as it had been for structural adjustment programs. In other words, governments had to fulfill certain obligations up front but then had better control over the use of the funds. The conditions, targets, and objectives to be fulfilled *a priori* are supposed to be drawn from the country's development plan.[136]

Another practical change was that once granted by the board, the loan became an integral part of the government's budget, which rendered the attribution of public funds much more effective. One example of development policy financing was the Poverty Reduction Support Credit, a development policy loan meant to support a country's PRSP, similar to how structural adjustment programs supported the policy framework papers. A senior Bank economist stressed that this new openness eventually became part of the general attitude with borrowing governments:

> We wouldn't go to Zambia, give them a [development policy financing], and say: "look, reduce your interest rate from 100 down to 90 percent. We will play along, we will play ball until you privatize [national industries]." We cannot do that. But more than that, we wouldn't *want* to do that.[137]

The experience of the PRSP and the Highly Indebted Poor Countries initiative officially ended in 2014. While the data and the critical development literature on the PRSP show that the inclusion of borrowing governments did not represent a full transfer of power, relationships between borrowers and lenders during that period changed, as did Bank employees' readiness to work in partnership. Many Bank employees mentioned the growing commitment of borrowing governments to implement reforms, partly because the relationship was "on a better base."[138] Accordingly, despite the similarities in content, the success of the policies changed dramatically from the 1980s onward. Despite all these caveats, the PRSP is still considered by many observers and a majority of people working at the Bank as a "tipping point" in multilateral development policy.[139]

Many Bank employees also qualify the PRSPs as a significant benchmark in the evolution of Bank relationships with borrowing governments, or an anchoring practice. Changes in practices are made of fluctuations instead of linear progress. Major changes are attempted, last for a while, and may disappear, without negating the change. The PRSP acted as an anchoring practice to many others, albeit smaller-scale inclusive practices. This case is similar to how global benchmarks, environmental or otherwise, reshaped political conversations and institutionalized authoritative language but did not exert a lasting influence over policies.[140] Communities of practice are constantly trying new tools and avenues that will only sometimes be institutionalized. The PRSP can still be considered to have had an influence as an anchoring practice.

Senior officials who worked for decades at the Bank recalled that in the 1990s, a particular type of relationship between the Bank and aid-targeted communities emerged. In the 1980s, Bank employees felt they were superior to and had more expertise than borrowing governments, populations, and NGOs, and often imposed policies without any feedback from project participants. While this attitude has continued in many quarters of the Bank, especially among some senior economists, the relationship with all stakeholders has changed since the adoption of inclusive policymaking practices. According to many Bank employees and officials, the slow adoption of new policymaking practices created a "big change in attitude" because many Bank employees opened up to new perspectives.[141] According to one senior Bank economist, while it did not necessarily change the substance of the policies advocated by the Bank, it created an atmosphere of openness that allowed internal debates.[142] In 1987, *World Development* published a special issue on the "Challenge of NGOs" to mainstream development organizations.[143]

At the beginning of the 1990s, Conable's successor, Lewis T. Preston, attributed the success (or lack thereof) of Bank projects to the "quality of its staff and its constantly accumulating knowledge," instead of, for example, its capacity to listen, accumulate specific knowledge, develop country-sensitive projects, or integrate dissenting views.[144] Yet, the narrative about the purpose of the Bank evolved during his tenure. Preston's first address to the board of governors that year acknowledged the Bank's need to engage in consultation and seek broader participation in all development projects.[145] Before that, from 1981 to 1991, Preston's predecessors, Alden W. Clausen and Barber Conable, seldom made public references to the fact that borrowing governments or their citizens had something to contribute to development policymaking and rarely (if ever) mentioned a role or "agency" for disadvantaged populations in the development process.

The "need" to include project participants thus already existed in 1985 when the report *Putting People First. Sociological Variables in Rural Development* was first published, but what evolved was the broader recognition of the need for public participation by a wider variety of CoPs. In the second edition in 1991, one of the first social scientists to become manager at the Bank, Michael Cernea, stated that the Bank is now taking a "firm stand against the technocratic and econocratic biases in development work."[146] In the foreword of this second edition, Cernea stated that including people targeted by development projects in policymaking processes is "no less an imperative now than before: in fact, it is even more readily recognized as the crucial requirement for inducing accelerated development."[147] He mentioned that the development paradigm is "gradually modifying" toward "new themes" that were already included in the first edition but not in official discourse and practices.

Many development practitioners recognized the effectiveness of including borrowing governments and populations in the early 1990s, but practices began to fluctuate. In the foreword of a book on participatory poverty assessments, entitled *Can the Poor Influence Policy? Participatory Poverty Assessments in the Developing World*, the Bank's ninth president, James Wolfensohn, and then managing director Horst Kohler acknowledged the role of local input in determining specific development paths. The "poor," they say, "are able to analyze their poverty, suggest solutions, and prioritize policies. Poor people want a chance and they want an opportunity to transform their lives."[148] This statement was not made in a vacuum; it was part of a constant fluctuation and evolution of narrative.

The adoption of inclusive practices was not only happening on normative grounds, that is, because it was the "right thing to do." From the 1980s to the 1990s, Bank employees learned about the effectiveness of inclusive practices in achieving their goals. In 1995, participatory poverty assessments started to be undertaken to create comprehensive localized analyses of poverty. The participatory poverty assessments had three major impacts: deepening the Bank's understanding of poverty (as multidimensional); influencing attitudes and policy (multilaterally and nationally; e.g., with the PRSP); and strengthening the policy delivery framework (increasing the policy impact for sustainable poverty reduction).[149] On the basis of participatory methods such as household surveys, the assessments were meant to include the complex reality of poor people in order to formulate better policies, as well as underline the idea that the poor are disadvantaged not only regarding resources but also overall "power."[150]

Discussions with governments, consultations with civil society organizations, and the participation of populations came to be understood as improving the acceptability, quality, effectiveness, and sustainability of projects, according to Bank standards. Consultative and participatory mechanisms enabled the collection of more accurate and comprehensive data as well as a better technical determination of poverty, which often led to the better design and implementation of solutions.[151] Even if they did not consistently influence policymaking or "empower" targeted populations in the sense that earlier proponents of the practice intended, the participatory poverty assessments developed in the 1990s better reflected the socio-economic situation of countries than the previous top-down poverty assessments made by Bank employees with no input from people it intended to work for. They became a more effective means of informing and guiding policy.

In some cases, the inclusion of populations in project elaboration led to decreased operational costs. For example, a water supply project in Côte d'Ivoire gave water committees in each village responsible for water pump maintenance.

The construction of water pumps in the 1980s often failed due to a lack of proper care and maintenance of the pump equipment or to their installation in locations that did not serve the women who had to fetch water. While complicating the project's oversight by the Bank's country team, including water committees in the design and maintenance of those projects, in some instances, reduced by half the costs for annual maintenance as compared to a centralized system and lessened the breakdown of hand pumps to 11 percent from 50 percent in previous projects.[152] A comparative evaluation report by the Bank stated that in an irrigation system project managed by a farmers' association, costs of operation and maintenance were "significantly lower" than a centrally managed system, due to "cost-sharing contributions and policing by the associations."[153]

As epistemic boundary objects, reports and evaluations regularly encouraged Bank employees to integrate participatory mechanisms in their practice. For example, a 1994 background paper for the *World Development Report* argued that public participation led to improved performance in the 121 rural water supply projects evaluated. The report found that 68 percent of projects with high levels of participation qualified as "highly successful," compared to only 12 percent of projects without participation.[154] The Operations Policy Department also published an action plan on promoting participation at the Bank and devised many mechanisms and small grants to promote participation, such as field-based learning opportunities and training programs for employees and managers, learning and innovation loans, flexible program lending, and social funds oriented toward community development projects. The Bank approved 51 such social funds in 32 countries before the end of 1996, totaling approximately US$1 billion.[155]

Frannie Leautier, a former director in the Office of the President, noted that after the 1997 decentralization, employees from borrowing countries were increasingly hired in country offices. Because they had sectoral knowledge of their country, these employees offered "a different perspective than the people we could have brought from Washington."[156] These new hires provided Bank teams insights that were more attuned to aid-targeted populations. A Bank official interviewed for this research agreed that country offices became more central in implementing policies, producing knowledge, and making decisions. The goal was to get country directors to focus more on the specificities of their countries rather than on "Bank bureaucracy."[157]

For these reasons, the inclusion of more stakeholders came to matter a great deal for policymakers at the Bank. This inclusivity rendered Bank projects more effective by increasing social acceptability and commitment and led to better overall outcomes according to the Bank's measures of success. For example, the projects deemed satisfactory by Bank evaluation criteria went from 64 to 77 percent in Africa and from 79 to 89 percent in East Asia.[158] While the poverty reduction strategy did not lead to great results everywhere, an analysis done on countries that adopted poverty reduction strategies and a control group did not find that the first group saw a more significant reduction in headcount poverty, infant mortality, and HIV prevalence, as well as better access to sanitation, higher primary school enrollments, and a better ratio of girls to boys in this enrollment.[159]

Conclusion

It is important to examine procedural changes in policymaking practices in this specific case because such practices modified how the Bank does business with borrowing countries and their populations. If they are being honest, even the most critical observers must admit that the ideas revolving around partnership and inclusion have, if not "profoundly altered" the relationship between donor institutions and borrowing governments, at least slightly modified how they interact and how policies are developed, implemented, and evaluated.[160] Inclusive practices changed how the Bank perceives and works with borrowing governments and civil society actors. While inclusive practices did not challenge the asymmetry of global power relations (arguably still influenced by a colonial legacy), because the Bank still has financial leverage, they changed the relationships between countries of the Global South and the Bank as a lending institution. According to many Bank economists I spoke with, the attitude of borrowing governments has also changed, rendering the relationship more, in their words, "productive."[161]

Including more government officials in policymaking and the greater participation of civil societies led Bank CoPs to redefine what being a stakeholder meant and, more importantly, how to effectively implement projects after past failures. While many scholars and Bank officials disagree about the extent of this change, the classic top-down and one-size-fits-all structural adjustment programs ended. This is not to say that the macroeconomic policies that are conditions of Bank loans are *substantively different* today than the ones promoted in the 1980s, but that the procedure to devise them changed.

I thus argue that it would be unfair to state that the institution has not changed since the infamous structural adjustment period. If many participatory methods did not directly trigger a policy change and if they were sometimes implemented with the intention of coopting local populations, it often changed the attitudes of Bank employees toward aid-targeted communities and governments. Inclusive practices also sometimes changed policy content in areas such as gender, social safety nets, or water and land access, if not in macroeconomic prescriptions. While inclusion did not suppress the international system of power inequalities between the borrowing and borrowers, civil society actors and borrowing governments now have a voice to influence what the Bank does, and have access to internal documents in an unprecedented manner. One proof is that global criticisms of the Bank's actions have somehow tamed over time. Many new governance strategies for how the Bank goes about its work have changed.[162] If the trigger for this change and the intentionality behind it are contested, and if a discrepancy between talks and practices is still visible,[163] it would be unfair to deny the very existence of a change in procedural practices at the World Bank.

Notes

1 Pailey, "De-centring the 'White Gaze' of Development"; Shallwani and Dossa, "Evaluation and the White Gaze in International Development"; Khan, Dickson, and Sondarjee, *White Saviorism in International Development*.

2 Wolfensohn, *A Global Life*.
3 Chambers, "The Origins and Practice of Participatory Rural Appraisal."
4 (1) *Can anyone hear us?* (2000); (2) *Crying out for change* (2000); and (3) *From many lands* (2002).
5 Narayan, *Voices of the Poor. Can Anyone Hear Us?*, 68.
6 Phillips, *Reforming the World Bank*, 158.
7 Operations Policy Department, 14.
8 Operations Evaluations Department, *Annual Review of Evaluation Results*.
9 Narayan, *The Contribution of People's Participation*.
10 McIntosh et al., *The Global Poll*.
11 Interview 28, August 15, 2017.
12 Interview OHP Willi Wapenhans, July 21 and August 19, 1993, 36.
13 Hentschel.
14 Operations Policy Department, 22.
15 NGO and Civil Society Unit, *Consultations with Civil Society Organizations*, 3.
16 Best, "Legitimacy Dilemmas," 472.
17 Interview 10, June 13, 2017; Interview 21, July 19, 2017; Interview 26, July 24, 2017; Interview 36, November 10, 2017.
18 Drabek, "Development Alternatives."
19 Danaher, *50 Years Is Enough*, 4.
20 Interview 20, July 17, 2017.
21 Interview OHP Ismail Serageldin, October 25–26, 2000.
22 Driscoll and Evans, "Second-Generation Poverty Reduction Strategies."
23 Elkins, Feeny, and Prentice, "Do Poverty Reduction Strategy Papers Reduce Poverty and Improve Well-Being."
24 Lazarus, "Participation in Poverty Reduction Strategy Papers."
25 Rodrik, "Goodbye Washington Consensus, Hello Washington Confusion?" 973.
26 Nankani, "Foreword."
27 Cling, Razafindrakoto, and Roubaud, *Les Nouvelles Stratégies Internationales de Lutte Contre La Pauvreté*; Momani, "IMF Rhetoric on Reducing Poverty and Inequality."
28 Campbell and Losch, "Les Pauvres, Bénéficiaires Ou Otages Des Stratégies de Réduction de La Pauvreté?"
29 Paul, "Le Document de Strategie de Réduction de La Pauvreté (DSRP)."
30 Weber, "A Political Analysis of the PRSP Initiative."
31 Woods, *The Globalizers*; Ruckert, "The Forgotten Dimension of Social Reproduction"; Dutta and Rastogi, "Deconstructing PRSP Measurement."
32 Campbell and Losch, 176.
33 Wood, "The ABC of the PRSP," 9.
34 Stewart and Wang, "Do PRSPs Empower Poor Countries and Disempower the World Bank"; Gottschalk, "The Macro Content of PRSPs"; Sumner, "In Search of the Post-Washington (Dis)Consensus."
35 Ansoms, "How Successful is the Rwandan PRSP?"; Dijkstra, "The PRSP Approach and the Illusion of Improved Aid Effectiveness."
36 Sondarjee, "Change and Stability at the World Bank."
37 Vetterlein, "Seeing Like the World Bank on Poverty," 53.
38 Levy, "Learning and Foreign Policy," 286.
39 Babb, "The Social Consequences of Structural Adjustment," 200.
40 Jaycox, "Structural Adjustment in Sub-Saharan Africa," 40.
41 World Bank, *Adjustment Lending Retrospective. Final Report*.
42 Williamson, *A Short History of the Washington Consensus*.
43 Stiglitz and Chemla, *La grande désillusion*.
44 World Bank, "World Bank Group Archivists' Chronology 1944–2013," 210–11.
45 Mallaby, *The World's Banker*, 46.

46 World Bank, *The World Bank Participation Sourcebook*, 4.
47 (Collier and Gunning 1999, 634; Shams 1988, 209).
48 Interview 26, July 24, 2017.
49 Conable, "To the Board of Governors," 68.
50 Interview 20, July 17, 2017.
51 Sending, *The Politics of Expertise*, 20.
52 Interview 21, July 19, 2017; Interview 26, July 24, 2017; Interview 36, November 10, 2017.
53 Interview 18, July 16, 2017.
54 Krugman, "The Good News."
55 Interview 20, July 17, 2017.
56 Interview 20, July 17, 2017.
57 Interview OHP Shahid Husain, July 5, 1991.
58 Interview 35, November 9, 2017.
59 Interview 28, August 15, 2017.
60 Interview 20, July 17, 2017.
61 Interview 36, November 10, 2017.
62 Interview 36, November 10, 2017.
63 Mallaby, 448.
64 Interview 35, November 9, 2017.
65 Interview OHP Robert Goodland, January 26, 2005.
66 Interview 26, July 24, 2017.
67 Interview 10, June 13, 2017.
68 Interview 14, June 26, 2017; Interview 15, July 16, 2017.
69 Interview 31, November 6, 2017.
70 Miller-Adams, *The World Bank*, 73.
71 Miller-Adams, 73.
72 Interview OHP Gloria Davis, June 28–29, 2004.
73 World Bank, *The World Bank Policy on Disclosure of Information, 2002*.
74 Aycrigg, "Participation and the World Bank Success, Constraints, and Responses," 25.
75 Killick, Gunatilaka, and Marr, *Aid and the Political Economy of Policy Change*.
76 Interview 35, November 9, 2017.
77 Mallaby, 101.
78 Letter to Employees, April 22, 1994, cited in Operations Policy Department 1994.
79 World Bank, International Monetary Fund, and Development Committee, *Problems and Issues in Structural Adjustment*, 45.
80 World Bank, International Monetary Fund, and Development Committee, 45.
81 World Bank, 4.
82 NGO and Civil Society Unit, *Consultations with Civil Society Organizations*, 4.
83 Garrison and Monico, "World Bank — Civil Society Engagement," xiii.
84 Zoellick, "From Hubris to Humility."
85 Interview 41, November 21, 2017.
86 www.worldbank.org/en/about/partners/civil-society#2, Consulted May 10, 2020.
87 NGO and Civil Society Unit, 3.
88 Miller-Adams, 72.
89 Garrison and Monico, xiii.
90 Malena and World Bank, "Working with NGOs"; NGO and Civil Society Unit; Civil Society Team, *Consultations with Civil Society*.
91 Aycrigg, 4.
92 Aycrigg, 15.
93 Tenney and Salda, *Historical Dictionary of the World Bank*, 81.
94 Civil Society Team, 5.
95 Civil Society Team.
96 Kapur, Lewis, and Webb, *The World Bank*, 501.

97 Interview 26, July 24, 2017; Interview 34, November 8, 2017; Interview OHP Winston Temple, October 25–26, 2000.
98 Interview 20, July 17, 2017.
99 Interview 26, July 24, 2017; Interview 34, November 8, 2017; Interview OHP Winston Temple, October 25–26, 2000.
100 Interview 26, July 24, 2017; Interview OHP Paul Cadario, April 4–17–22–30, 2013.
101 Interview 26, July 24, 2017.
102 Collier and Gunning, "The IMF's Role in Structural Adjustment," 645.
103 Interview OHP Paul Cadario, April 4–17–22–30, 2013.
104 Bajaj and Panchamukhi, "Aid in the 1990's with Special Reference to World Bank and IDA," 61.
105 Bajaj and Panchamukhi.
106 Interview 28, August 15, 2017.
107 Interview 20, July 17, 2017.
108 Interview 26, July 24, 2017.
109 Board Discussion Paper, R99–241, December 10, 1999.
110 Minutes of Meeting, December 20, 1999.
111 Board Discussion Paper, R99–241, December 10, 1999.
112 Minutes of Meeting, Executive Board, December 20, 1999.
113 IMF and World Bank Group, *Review of the Poverty Reduction Strategy Paper (PRSP) Approach*; Cling, Razafindrakoto, and Roubaud, "Introduction."
114 (Craig and Porter 2001).
115 Interview 20, July 17, 2017.
116 Interview 33, November 7, 2017.
117 Interview 33, November 7, 2017, 13.
118 Board Discussion Paper, R99–241, December 10, 1999, 10.
119 Interview 28, August 15, 2017.
120 Interview 28, August 15, 2017.
121 Interview 28, August 15, 2017.
122 Rowden and Irama, "Rethinking Participation."
123 Cleaver, "Paradoxes of Development," 608.
124 Kothari, "Authority and Expertise," 437.
125 Makuwira, "Non-Governmental Organizations (NGOs) and Participatory Development in Basic Education in Malawi."
126 Kapoor, "Concluding Remarks," 126–27.
127 James, "The Anthropology of Power: Empowerment and Disempowerment in Changing Structures," 14.
128 Kapoor, 127.
129 Ferguson, *The Anti-Politics Machine*.
130 Pierre de Senarclens, "How the United Nations Promotes Development through Technical Assistance," 195.
131 Interview 21, July 19, 2017.
132 Interview 21, July 19, 2017.
133 Tenney and Salda, 87; Moll, Geli, and Saavedra, "Correlates of Success in World Bank Development Policy Lending," 2.
134 Moll, Geli, and Saavedra, 2.
135 {Citation}.
136 Moll, Geli, and Saavedra, 2.
137 Interview 26, July 24, 2017.
138 Interview 26, July 24, 2017.
139 Christiansen and Hovland, "The PRSP Initiative."
140 Sending and Lie, "The Limits of Global Authority."
141 Interview 26, July 24, 2017; Interview 41, November 21, 2017.

142 Interview 26, July 24, 2017.
143 Drabek, "Development Alternatives."
144 Preston, "Opening Remarks," 8.
145 Sandstrom, "Foreword," xiii.
146 Cernea, *Putting People First*, xii.
147 Cernea, xii.
148 Robb, *Can the Poor Influence Policy?* vii.
149 Robb, 17.
150 Salmen, "Participatory Poverty Assessment," 1.
151 Robb, 104.
152 Operations Policy Department, *The World Bank and Participation*, 23.
153 Operations Policy Department, 23.
154 Isham, Narayan, and Pritchett, "Does Participation Improve Project Performance?"
155 Aycrigg, 15.
156 Interview OHP Frannie Leautier, May 16–18, 2007.
157 Interview OHP Mark Baird, May 5–6, 2002.
158 Phillips, *Reforming the World Bank*, 158.
159 Elkins, Feeny, and Prentice.
160 Lie, "Developmentality," 734.
161 Interview 21, July 19, 2017; Interview 28, August 15, 2017.
162 Best, *Governing Failure*.
163 Bebbington et al., "Of Texts and Practices"; Weaver, *Hypocrisy Trap*; Wade, "US Hegemony and the World Bank."

References

Ansoms, An. "How Successful Is the Rwandan PRSP? Growth, Poverty & Inequality." *Review of African Political Economy* 34, no. 112 (2007): 371–79.

Aycrigg, Maria. "Participation and the World Bank Success, Constraints, and Responses." In *Draft for Discussion at the International Conference on Upscaling and Mainstreaming Participation: Lessons Learned and Ways Forward*. Washington, DC: The World Bank, 1998.

Babb, Sarah. "The Social Consequences of Structural Adjustment: Recent Evidence and Current Debates." *Annual Review of Sociology* 31 (2005): 199–222.

Bajaj, J. L., and V. R. Panchamukhi. *Aid in the 1990's with Special Reference to World Bank and IDA*. New Delhi, India: Research and Information System for the Non-Aligned and Other Developing Countries (RIS), 1990.

Bebbington, Anthony, David Lewis, Simon Batterbury, Elizabeth Olson, and M. Shameem Siddiqi. "Of Texts and Practices: Empowerment and Organisational Cultures in World Bank-Funded Rural Development Programmes." *The Journal of Development Studies* 43, no. 4 (May 2007): 597–621.

Best, Jacqueline. *Governing Failure: Provisional Expertise and the Transformation of Global Development Finance*. Cambridge and New York: Cambridge University Press, 2014.

Campbell, Bonnie, and Bruno Losch. "Les Pauvres, Bénéficiaires Ou Otages Des Stratégies de Réduction de La Pauvreté?" *Politique Africaine*, no. 87 (2002): 175–84.

Cernea, Michael M., ed. *Putting People First: Sociological Variables in Rural Development*. New York: Published for the World Bank [by] Oxford University Press, 1991.

Chambers, Robert. "The Origins and Practice of Participatory Rural Appraisal." *World Development* 22, no. 7 (July 1994): 953–69.

Christiansen, Karin, and Ingie Hovland. *The PRSP Initiative: Multilateral Policy Change and the Role of Research*. London: Overseas Development Institute, 2003.

Civil Society Team. *Consultations with Civil Society. A Sourcebook*. Washington, DC: World Bank, 2007.

Cleaver, F. "Paradoxes of Development: Questioning Participatory Approaches to Development." *Journal of International Development* 11, no. 4 (1999): 597–612.
Cling, Jean-Pierre, Mireille Razafindrakoto, and François Roubaud. "Introduction. Tout Changer Pour Que Tout Reste Pareil?" In *Les Nouvelles Stratégies Internationales de Lutte Contre La Pauvreté*, edited by Jean-Pierre Cling, Mireille Razafindrakoto, and François Roubaud. Paris: DIAL/Economica, 2002a.
Cling, Jean-Pierre, Mireille Razafindrakoto, and François Roubaud. *Les Nouvelles Stratégies Internationales de Lutte Contre La Pauvreté*. Paris: DIAL/Economica, 2002b.
Collier, Paul, and Jan Willem Gunning. "The IMF's Role in Structural Adjustment." *The Economic Journal* 109 (1999): F634–51.
Conable, Barber. "To the Board of Governors." Address to the Board of Governors at the Annual Meetings of the World Bank and IMF, Berlin, September 27, 1988, 68.
Craig, David and Doug Porter. 2001. "Poverty Reduction Strategy Papers: A new convergence. What does it miss, and what can be done about it?" Proceedings called *Theme 1: Governance and Participation in Developing and Implementing Poverty Reduction Strategies,* from conference *Regional Conference on National Poverty Reduction Strategies* in Hanoi, Vietnam.
Dijkstra, Geske. "The PRSP Approach and the Illusion of Improved Aid Effectiveness: Lessons from Bolivia, Honduras and Nicaragua." *Development Policy Review* 29, no. s1 (2011): s111–33.
Drabek, A. G. "Development Alternatives: The Challenge of NGOs." *World Development* 15 (1987): ix–xv.
Driscoll, Ruth, and Alison Evans. "Second-Generation Poverty Reduction Strategies: New Opportunities and Emerging Issues." *Development Policy Review* 23, no. 1 (January 2005): 5–25.
Dutta, Mohan, and Rahul Rastogi. "Deconstructing PRSP Measurement: Participation as Neoliberal Colonization." *Journal of Creative Communications* 11, no. 3 (2016): 211–26.
Elkins, Meg, Simon Feeny, and David Prentice. *Do Poverty Reduction Strategy Papers Reduce Poverty and Improve Well-Being. Discussion Paper in Economics*. UK, China and Malaysia: University of Nottingham, 2015.
Ferguson, James. *The Anti-Politics Machine: "Development," Depoliticization, and Bureaucratic Power in Lesotho*. Cambridge, England and New York: Cambridge University Press, 1990.
Garrison, John, and Carmen Monico. *World Bank – Civil Society Engagement. Review of Fiscal Years 2002–2004*. Washington, DC: World Bank, 2005.
Gottschalk, Ricardo. "The Macro Content of PRSPs: Assessing the Need for a More Flexible Macroeconomic Policy Framework." *Development Policy Review* 23, no. 4 (July 2005): 419–42.
IMF and World Bank Group. *Review of the Poverty Reduction Strategy Paper (PRSP) Approach: Early Experience with Interim PRSPs and Full PRSPs*. Washington, DC: International Monetary Fund and International Development Association, 2002.
Isham, Jonathan, Deepa Narayan, and Lant Pritchett. *Does Participation Improve Project Performance? Establishing Causality with Subjective Data. Background paper for the World Development Report*. Washington, DC: World Bank, 1994.
James, Wendy. *The Anthropology of Power: Empowerment and Disempowerment in Changing Structures*. Edited by Angela P. Cheater, 13–27. London: Routledge, 1999.
Jaycox, Edward V. K. "Structural Adjustment in Sub-Saharan Africa: The World Bank's Perspective." *Issue: A Journal of Opinion* 18, no. 1 (1989): 36–40.
Kapoor, Ilan. "Concluding Remarks: The Power of Participation." *Current Issues in Comparative Education* 6, no. 2 (2004): 125–29.
Kapur, Devesh, John P. Lewis, and Richard Charles Webb. *The World Bank: Its First Half Century*. Washington, DC: Brookings Institution, 1997.

Khan, Themrise, Kanakulya Dickson, and Maïka Sondarjee, eds. *White Saviorism in International Development: Theories, Practices and Lived Experiences*. Cantley, Quebec: Daraja Press, 2023.

Kothari, Uma. "Authority and Expertise: The Professionalisation of International Development and the Ordering of Dissent." *Antipode* 37, no. 3 (June 2005): 425–46.

Krugman, Paul. "The Good News." *The New York Times*, November 29, 2003.

Lazarus, Joel. "Participation in Poverty Reduction Strategy Papers: Reviewing the Past, Assessing the Present and Predicting the Future." *Third World Quarterly* 29, no. 6 (2008): 1205–21. https://doi.org/10.1080/01436590802201188.

Levy, Jack S. "Learning and Foreign Policy: Sweeping a Conceptual Minefield." *International Organization*, no. 48 (1994): 279–312.

Lie, Jon Harald Sande. "Developmentality: Indirect Governance in the World Bank–Uganda Partnership." *Third World Quarterly* 36, no. 4 (April 3, 2015): 723–40.

Makuwira, Jonathan. "Non-Governmental Organizations (NGOs) and Participatory Development in Basic Education in Malawi." *Current Issues in Comparative Education* 6, no. 2 (2004): 113–24.

Malena, Carmen, and World Bank. *Working with NGOs. A Practical Guide to Operational Collaboration between the World Bank and Non-Governmental Organization*. Washington, DC: World Bank Operations Policy Department, 1995.

Mallaby, Sebastian. *The World's Banker: A Story of Failed States, Financial Crises, and the Wealth and Poverty of Nations. A Council on Foreign Relations Book*. London, UK: The Penguin Press, 2006.

Miller-Adams, Michelle. *The World Bank: New Agendas in a Changing World*. London: Routledge, 1999.

Moll, Peter G., Patricia Geli, and Pablo Saavedra. *Correlates of Success in World Bank Development Policy Lending. World Bank Policy Research Working Paper*. Washington, DC: World Bank, 2015.

Momani, Bessma. "IMF Rhetoric on Reducing Poverty and Inequality." In *Global Governance, Poverty and Inequality*, edited by Jennifer Clapp and Rorden Wilkinson, 71–90. New York: Routledge, 2010.

Moore, Mick. "Empowerment at Last?" *Journal of International Development* 13, no. 3 (April 2001): 321–29.

Nankani, Gobind. "Foreword." In *Economic Growth in the 1990s Learning from a Decade of Reform*. Washington, DC: The World Bank, 2005.

Narayan, Deepa, ed. *Voices of the Poor. Can Anyone Hear Us? Voices of the Poor*. New York: Published by Oxford University Press for the World Bank, 2000.

Narayan, Deepa, Robert Chambers, Meera K. Shah, and Patti L. Petesch, eds. *Voices of the Poor. Crying Out for Change. Voices of the Poor*. Washington, DC: A Copublication of Oxford University Press and the World Bank, 2000.

Narayan, Deepa, and Patti L. Petesch, eds. *Voices of the Poor. From Many Lands. Voices of the Poor*. Washington, DC: A Copublication of Oxford University Press and the World Bank, 2002.

NGO and Civil Society Unit. *Consultations with Civil Society Organizations. General Guidelines for the World Bank Staff*. Washington, DC: World Bank Social Development Department, 2000.

Operations Policy Department. *The World Bank and Participation*. Washington, DC: The World Bank, 1994.

Pailey, Robtel Neajai. "De-centring the 'White Gaze' of Development." *Development and Change* 51, no. 3 (May 2020): 729–45.

Paul, Elizabeth. "Le Document de Strategie de Réduction de La Pauvreté (DSRP): Du Neuf à l'Horizon de l'Aide Au Développement?" In *Pauvreté et hégémonismes: Les sociétés civiles africaines face aux ajustements structurels de type nouveau*, edited by Jacques Habib, 221–64. Dakar, Senegal: Aid Transparency/Oxfam America, 2002.

Phillips, David A. *Reforming the World Bank: Twenty Years of Trial -- and Error*. New York: Cambridge University Press, 2009.
Preston, Lewis. "Opening Remarks." Address to the Board of Governors at the Annual Meetings of the World Bank and IMF, Washington, DC, October 15, 1991, 8.
Robb, Caroline M. *Can the Poor Influence Policy? Participatory Poverty Assessments in the Developing World*. 2nd ed. Washington, DC: International Monetary Fund, World Bank, 2002.
Rodrik, Dani. "Goodbye Washington Consensus, Hello Washington Confusion? A Review of the World Bank's 'Economic Growth in the 1990s: Learning from a Decade of Reform." *Journal of Economic Literature* 44, no. 4 (2006): 973–87.
Rowden, Rick, and Jane Ocaya Irama. *Rethinking Participation. Questions for Civil Society about the Limits of Participation in PRSPs. Discussion Paper*. Washington, DC: Action Aid, 2004.
Ruckert, Arne. "The Forgotten Dimension of Social Reproduction: The World Bank and the Poverty Reduction Strategy Paradigm." *Review of International Political Economy* 17, no. 5 (2010): 816–39.
Salmen, Lawrence F. *Participatory Poverty Assessment. Incorporating Poor People's Perspectives into Poverty Assessment Work. Environment Department Papers. Social Assessment*. Washington, DC: World Bank, 1995.
Sandstrom, Sven. "Foreword." In *Participatory Development and the World Bank: Potential Directions for Change*, *World Bank Discussion Papers 183*, edited by Bhuvan Bhatnagar and Aubrey C. Williams. Washington, DC: The World Bank, 1992.
Senarclens, Pierre de. "How the United Nations Promotes Development through Technical Assistance." In *The Post-Development Reader*, edited by Majid Rahnema and Victoria Bawtree. London, Atlantic Highlands, NJ, Dhaka, Halifax, NS and Cape Town: Zed Books, University Press, Fernwood Publishing and David Philip, 1997.
Sending, Ole Jacob. *The Politics of Expertise: Competing for Authority in Global Governance. Configurations: Critical Studies of World Politics*. Ann Arbor: University of Michigan Press, 2015.
Sending, Ole Jacob, and Jon Harald Sande Lie. "The Limits of Global Authority: World Bank Benchmarks in Ethiopia and Malawi." *Review of International Studies* 41, no. 05 (December 2015): 993–1010.
Shallwani, Sadaf, and Shama Dossa. "Evaluation and the White Gaze in International Development." In *White Saviorism in International Development. Theories, Practices and Lived Experiences*, edited by Themrise Khan, Kanakulya Dickson, and Maïka Sondarjee, 42–62. Ottawa: Daraja Press, 2023.
Shams, Rasul. "The World Bank's Structural Adjustment Loans: A Critique." *Intereconomics* (1988): 208–11.
Sondarjee, Maïka. "Change and Stability at the World Bank: Inclusive Practices and Neoliberal Technocratic Rationality." *Third World Quarterly* 42, no. 2 (2021): 348–65.
Stewart, Frances, and Michael Wang. "Do PRSPs Empower Poor Countries and Disempower the World Bank, or is It the Other Way Round?" In *Globalization and the Nation State: The Impact of the IMF and World Bank*, edited by G. Ranis, James Raymond Vreeland, and S. Kosack, New York: Routledge, 2004.
Stiglitz, Joseph E., and Paul Chemla. *La grande désillusion*. Paris: Fayard, 2002.
Sumner, Andy. "In Search of the Post-Washington (Dis)Consensus: The 'Missing' Content of PRSPS." *Third World Quarterly* 27, no. 8 (2006): 1401–12.
Tenney, Sarah, and Anne C. M. Salda. *Historical Dictionary of the World Bank. Historical Dictionaries of International Organizations*. 2nd ed. Lanham: The Scarecrow Press, Inc., 2014.
Vetterlein, Antje. "Seeing Like the World Bank on Poverty." *New Political Economy* 17, no. 1 (2012): 35–58.

Wade, Robert. "US Hegemony and the World Bank: The Fight Over People and Ideas." *Review of International Political Economy* 9, no. 2 (2002): 215–43.
Weaver, Catherine. *Hypocrisy Trap: The World Bank and the Poverty of Reform*. Princeton: Princeton University Press, 2008.
Weber, Heloise. "A Political Analysis of the PRSP Initiative: Social Struggles and the Organization of Persistent Relations of Inequality." *Globalizations* 3, no. 2 (2006): 187–206.
Williamson, John. *A Short History of the Washington Consensus*. Barcelona: Fundación CIDOB, 2004.
Wolfensohn, James D. *A Global Life: My Journey among Rich and Poor, from Sydney to Wall Street to the World Bank*. 1st ed. New York: Public Affairs, 2010.
Wood, Angela. "The ABC of the PRSP. An Introduction to the New Bank and Fund Poverty Reduction Strategy Papers." *Bretton Woods Projects. Critical Voices on the World Bank and the IMF* (blog), June 14, 2000.
Woods, Ngaire. *The Globalizers. The IMF, the World Bank and Their Borrowers*. Ithaca and London: Cornell University Press, 2006.
World Bank, ed. *The World Bank Participation Sourcebook*. Washington, DC: The World Bank, 1996.
World Bank. *Adjustment Lending Retrospective. Final Report*. Washington, DC: The World Bank, June 15, 2001.
World Bank, ed. *The World Bank Policy on Disclosure of Information, 2002*. Washington, DC: World Bank, 2002.
World Bank. *World Bank Group Archivists' Chronology 1944–2013*. Washington, DC: The World Bank, 2014.
World Bank, International Monetary Fund, and Development Committee, eds. *Problems and Issues in Structural Adjustment: Papers. Development Committee, No. 23*. Washington, DC, USA: Joint Ministerial Committee of the Boards of Governors of the World Bank and the International Monetary Fund on the Transfer of Real Resources to Developing Countries (Development Committee), 1990.
Yi-Chong, Xu, and Patrick Weller. *Inside the World Bank: Exploding the Myth of the Monolithic Bank*. New York: Palgrave Macmillan, 2009.
Zoellick, Robert. "From Hubris to Humility." Speech at Georgetown University, 2010.

5 Boundaries as sites for collective learning

Including borrowing government officials and their populations increased the effectiveness of aid projects and policies, according to Bank employees I spoke to. It increased effectiveness according to their own evaluation standards. More inclusive procedural practices allowed Bank employees gain more accurate and comprehensive data on poverty; eventually decreased the need for supervision; led to better measurable outcomes; and decreased operational costs, even if it often increased elaboration costs. Many communities of practice in (and outside) the Bank learned to adopt inclusive practices because they interacted with more inclusive communities who successfully implemented policies and projects. Multiplication of these encounters, reports, and contestation claims at the boundaries between CoPs, encouraged by a change in narrative at the managerial level, led to a scaling up of participatory tools and mechanisms.

The atmosphere of secrecy at the Bank partly waned, and the organization became somewhat more open (again: at least in the procedures, if not in the policies). This shift was accompanied by the arrival of non-economists in internal Bank CoPs, the creation of new CoPs inside and outside the organization, and the growing pressure from outside ones. Because of these environmental and internal changes, the organization started to open communication channels with civil society and borrowing governments. Many Bank employees suspicious of civil society organizations and NGOs began to acknowledge that their direct ties with populations could be an asset in collecting data or implementing small-scale projects. This chapter explores how the use of epistemic boundary objects, boundary encounters, and boundary brokering participated in institutionalizing inclusive practices.

Adopting other CoPs' inclusive practices

The expert-based knowledge promoted by Bank employees did not wholly vanish but was coupled with a recognition of the need for context-specific knowledge to access more comprehensive data about poverty in each setting. For example, the 1996 Bank report *Participation Sourcebook* (a major epistemic boundary object traveling from one CoP to others in the Bank) states that what "development experts have to offer [in participatory projects] has a much better chance of being accepted and used than when they rely on reports and briefings to share their expertise" with

DOI: 10.4324/9781003529279-5

populations.[1] According to the then director of the Social Development Department, Gloria Davis, this change was more of an evolution than a revolution:

> In the earliest stages, participation meant consultation; . . . if you were trying to figure out what was going on, you would ask people. Now, they didn't get a say in the outcome but they could provide important feedback, and that was institutionalized both in the social impact assessment process and also in the environmental impact assessment process, which became much more "participatory," in quotation marks, over time.[2]

Social scientists Michael Cernea and Robert Chambers became some of the most mentioned people who participated in boundary brokering of inclusive procedural tools between Bank CoPs, like participatory rural appraisal techniques designed for learning about rural life "with and by rural people."[3] These participatory analyses encompassed a variety of mechanisms to enable aid-targeted people to "express, enhance, share and analyze their knowledge of life and conditions, to plan and to act."[4] Methods to consult the most disadvantaged groups included translating information into local languages, mapping, modeling, as well as using visual representations, collective walks, or group-based planning. Not only through discursive interventions but also by simply developing these new tools, Cernea and Chambers initiated brokering processes to set an example of what was possible in terms of inclusion. If former Bank president James Wolfensohn was able to change the narrative in the 1990s, many brokering processes happened in the Bank before his tenure, in domains of knowledge where new tools were devised for inclusiveness. Cernea and Chambers, for example, did not intend to promote a whole new set of practices or normative structure; they only wanted an alternative to "rapid rural assessments," whose goals were solely to extract information from the community level.

In December 1990, the Central Operations Department and the External Affairs Department launched a new CoP made mainly of social scientists: the Bank-wide Learning Group on Participatory Development. Their goal was to broker new mainstream participatory approaches among Bank practices by organizing boundary encounters between CoPs. The Swedish government financed the group with a trust of $1.3 million, an example highlighting the importance of having allies to support epistemic power with financial leverage and the possibility for smaller states to influence policymaking at the Bank. Fifteen people, in majority from the NGO Unit and the Social Policy Division, constituted the group and secured funding to finance its research activities for the first three years. The CoP was meant to document 20 Bank operations that used participatory approaches (a boundary object then shared with other Bank CoPs), accelerate Bank learning on those issues based on initiatives taking place inside and outside the Bank, as well as examine how to modify the Bank's operational practices to encourage public participation.[5]

In 1992, the Social Policy and Resettlement Division was also created and placed under the authority of the Vice Presidency for Environmentally and Socially Sustainable Development. A CoP within this division was established to develop brief guidelines for incorporating social analysis and participation into project design and implementation. The social assessments now required thus went beyond simply determining whether projects would harm populations they aimed to help; they stressed how World Bank projects could have a positive social impact if populations and institutions participated in project development.[6] In addition, the CoP started to offer training courses for Bank employees on participation and consultation at Bank headquarters in Washington, D.C., and in country offices. They also set up an intranet and an electronic guidebook on social assessment to share best practices in social assessment, including the contact information of specialists in this domain.[7]

In February 1992, the Learning Group organized a boundary encounter in the form of a workshop on participatory development with 80 participants from CoPs inside and outside the Bank. In the epistemic boundary object resulting from this encounter, entitled *Participatory Development and the World Bank*, the policy recommendations to mainstream participation were threefold: the Bank should provide operational support for participatory projects; set up participation-related training; and have better mechanisms of information-sharing within the Bank.[8] These recommendations were meant to promote best practices from successful projects the group observed in various countries and by other organizations. The encounter itself enabled the sharing of best participatory practices and served as an incubator for inclusive practices.

Four years later, after many boundary encounters in the forms of workshops and conferences, the *Participation Sourcebook* was put together by David Beckmann and Aubrey Williams. The *Sourcebook*, which rapidly became a epistemic boundary object, was meant as a toolbox to help managers implement participatory methods to include borrowers, affected populations, and civil society organizations.[9] The document presented Bank employees' experience in borrowing countries and contained in-depth case studies of successful participatory projects or projects modified midway to include targeted populations. During this period, the group published five other reports on various topics and regions, all realized with a participatory approach and underlining the input of all stakeholders.

Joint workshops and meetings also led Bank employees to learn from outside communities about the effectiveness of consulting with aid-targeted populations. Informal boundary encounters with members of other CoPs often tacitly influenced employees to adopt inclusive practices. Many Bank employees recalled informal lunches and end-of-the-day drinks with employees of Global South NGOs, the United Nations Children's Fund (UNICEF), or the United Nations Development Program (UNDP). Despite rare mentions of such encounters in the academic literature on the Bank, these were repeatedly mentioned by interviewees as important in day-to-day work.[10] This type of "sociability" in boundary encounters has a great impact on the evolution of practices, even if power structures like gender, race, coloniality, or class are often reproduced in those encounters.[11]

Boundary encounters are often informal. Sunita Gandhi, task manager for the Bank team working in Morocco, remembered that in 1996, for a women's development project, she sought to convince her superiors to give her funds to consult with Moroccan women. However, when she eventually accessed that funding, she had no idea how to proceed regarding consultation methods. She recalled learning about participatory methods during an informal boundary encounter with a colleague from another community of practice: "I mentioned this to a Bank colleague one afternoon over a cup of tea. He suggested that I consider using participatory rural appraisal methodologies. This was completely new to me, but I decided to look into it."[12]

Learning about the impact of inclusive practices on a project's effectiveness also happened in boundary encounters when Bank employees visited other country teams' work sites or vice versa. Among others, the anthropologist Gloria Davis, director of the Bank's Social Development Department from 1997 to 2000, reinforced the custom of knowledge sharing between the teams who supported community-level projects and others who didn't.[13] She invited various teams to visit countries where successful consultations were in place, and participatory and consultative tools and mechanisms then spread from one team to another, from one country to another, from one CoP to another.

A senior Bank employee also remembered learning the value of participatory approaches from a poverty expert from the United Kingdom whom she worked with during the 1990s, who was unknowingly doing boundary brokering. The UK constituency at the Bank paid for the expert to be included in her team, so she accepted but with "very low expectations."[14] She was subsequently impressed by his ability to connect with aid-targeted people, which led her to a different understanding of the concept of basic needs. Boundary brokering in this case encountered resistance but was then successful in challenging existing practice. The Bank employee recalled that the poverty expert would sit with heads of households to understand their specific conditions, something she had never done before. His addition to the report was "immense," as her team "started looking at things differently."[15] While making the process of data collection more inclusive, she realized that having a wider variety of data would improve the effectiveness of her project.

These boundary encounters with people from other CoPs accelerated the pace of collective learning about the effectiveness of inclusive procedural practices. Through encounters like joint practices and projects, longer-term employees in country offices or evaluation departments were confronted with new employees' routines, day-to-day tools to deal with problems, and practical skills, which they eventually added to their toolkit. It was because of new hires and the change in mentality, one Bank economist recalled, that the restructuring process toward more inclusiveness and openness eventually became entrenched in the Bank's culture.[16]

Following boundary encounters, practices were imported and exported from one CoP to another. In the early 2000s, the Bank's country director in Kyrgyzstan, Dennis De Tray, imported the idea for the Village Investment Project after visiting a similar village infrastructure project by a Bank CoP based in Indonesia. Pioneered by the former lead social scientist for East Asia Pacific, Scott Guggenheim, the project (which became the Kecamatan Development Project) aimed to promote ownership of programs at the village level in Indonesia. First developed as a pilot project in 1998, it was implemented in 28 villages in one sub-district. However, with the departure of the military leader Suharto after 31 years in power, corruption was widespread in national and lower-level government offices, which affected the Bank's delivery of funds. To bypass this problem, Guggenheim developed a transparent method of sending money directly to the villagers. According to World Bank documents, the project eventually channeled $50,000–$150,000 to each subdistrict, creating 31,000 roads, 8,000 bridges, 9,000 clean water supply units, 9,000 irrigation systems, and 5,000 new or rehabilitated schools.[17] The project closed officially on December 31, 2002, and was transferred to the Indonesian government. The government of Indonesia expanded the Kecamatan Project to all rural communities from 2006 to 2009, with financial support from the World Bank, the Asian Development Bank, and the Japanese development agency. De Tray witnessed the successes of this project when he visited Indonesia and met with Guggenheim's team. He then decided to implement similar mechanisms in Kyrgyzstan. Like in the original project, he decided to include villagers in the allocation of funds for infrastructure projects and promoted capacity building at the lower level:

> Both projects had the same general characteristic . . . to try to bring more accountability into the system and hopefully less leakage and less corruption. Decision-making took place at [the] village or Kacamatan level. Local people decided how to spend the money, within some bounds. They were supported by village engineers who could advise them on whether the bridge was going to stay up or not, if they wanted a bridge. They had to account for the money. These were fairly large projects, in the $70,000 to $100,000 range.[18]

These participatory projects changed the relationship between Bank employees and borrowing governments and allowed the latter to influence the use of funds and the implementation of projects. The Indonesian project went from $20–$25 million to about $6.5 billion and now covers 34,000 villages in Indonesia; the cost was eventually transferred from the Bank to the government.[19] Guggenheim's impact on the emergence of inclusive practices and his influence on other internal disrupters thus cannot be considered as the effect of a lone boundary broker, but a social process of contestation whereby many brokers promote new practices or contest existing practices.

A similar process happened in Bolivia, where the Bank's country team learned from Bolivian government participation experts in the late 1990s in various boundary encounters and brokering, as well as through epistemic boundary objects. In 1997, Bolivian Vice President Jorge Quiroga launched three weeks of broad consultations with NGOs, trade unions, academics, and journalists to discuss Bolivia's development plan. Witnessing the growing popular support of Quiroga's techniques, the Bank's country director, Isabel Guerrero, granted the Bank support for similar consultations. Guerrero and her team eventually prioritized consultation with Bolivian populations in the Bank's policymaking practices in Bolivia.

This encounter between Quiroga's participatory team and the Bank's country team departed from routinized relations between Bank employees and borrowing governments. Instead, their interaction not only promoted a sharing of tools or methods but also showed how inclusive practices could increase social acceptability and thus the effectiveness of policies. Apparently, the "buzz" from Bolivia was soon all over the Bank: "By backing (such a) model development plan, the Bank was shifting its sights . . . it was moving from rules to results, from centralization to empowered teams."[20] In line with the broad decentralization of the Bank under the 1997 Strategic Compact, Guerrero eventually moved to Bolivia to support Quiroga's efforts. Following this successful experience of including Bolivian people in policymaking, Guerrero participated in boundary brokering for participatory development in various CoPs inside the Bank. Practitioners in other CoPs invited her to write memos and speak about the participatory experience in Bolivia at many events and conferences, including at the senior managers' annual strategy meeting in 1998. At that meeting, she promoted broad-based participation as a helpful tool to encourage populations to support development reforms.

In 1999, the team in charge of poverty reduction presented an official paper defining the poverty reduction strategy to the board of governors for approval. Then vice president for Poverty Reduction and Economic Management, Masood Ahmed, led the team that wrote the paper; he then found himself in conflict with then President James Wolfensohn, who believed the poverty reduction strategy was given priority over the comprehensive development framework he wrote to reorient the overall Bank strategy. The paper presented to the board cites Bolivia as an example to follow for a successful development plan based on extensive consultations with populations.[21] This internal document shows that Bolivia was not the *only* example of exemplary inclusive practices and that this change was part of a continuous and multi-location change:

> Varying degrees of participatory involvement . . . already take place in many low-income countries. Bolivia is one recent example of extensive consultation. Another is in Guinea, where a National Strategic Vision was developed through a stakeholders' consultation exercise, which engaged citizens from across the country to discuss key questions: Where are we now? Where do we want to go? How do we get there? And, how do we know we are getting there?[22]

Epistemic boundary objects

Research entrenched in epistemic boundary objects is a seemingly straightforward way to influence learning processes in CoPs, but this variable is seldom acknowledged in IR. Most officials I spoke with noted the importance of internal research as a catalyst for the shift in the Bank's practices toward more inclusiveness.[23] Yet, *how* research influences practices is often associated with a spectator theory of knowledge, that is, that arguments contained in documents are unproblematically transferred to readers. What is often undertheorized is how shared documents are transformed instead of transferred in the process. Epistemic boundary objects are pieces of research written by a given community, then read, interpreted, and translated in activities by another community.

As such, epistemic boundary objects are not finite "things" but are infused with interpretive flexibility. Their interpretation and translation will depend on who reads them and for what purpose. Even reports using different quantitative methods on the same issue can reach very different conclusions. As William Easterly, senior advisor in the Macroeconomics and Growth Division in the 1990s, noted, studies on the structural adjustment period, both internal and external, to the Bank have been "all over the map, with positive, zero, or negative effects of adjustment lending on growth."[24] Which research becomes an epistemic boundary object depends on many factors, such as its assumed epistemic strength, perceived methodological rigor, promotion by a powerful broker, timeliness, or fit with previous normative structures or narrative.

However, not all reports or research notes are used as boundary objects. Many reports can fail to travel from one CoP to another or may be known by more than one group inside the Bank but are not actively considered or used in situated activity. Therefore, only some documents produced by communities associated with the UN, non-governmental organizations (NGOs), or think tanks become epistemic boundary objects for a Bank community of practice. As one young Bank employee noted, "it depends on who writes the report."[25] For example, many Bank employees mentioned having had disdain for NGO reports in the 1980s because they considered them "anecdotal evidence" lacking "empirical evidence."[26] This is not only because qualitative single-case or comparative studies were unfamiliar to most of the Bank employees trained in macroeconomics in the United States, but also because reports coming from the Global South in general were devalued in comparison to those produced by bigger NGOs based in the West. The coloniality of epistemic power in research documents will be explored in more depth in Chapter 8.

In the late 1990s, a team of researchers led by Deepa Narayan, and including Robert Chambers, consulted around 60,000 individual recipients of aid in 60 countries to write the report *Voices of the Poor*. They both participated in boundary brokering because they were socially recognized as competent due to their professional expertise. Their capacity to influence meaning-making processes is a testament to the epistemic power they were able to generate in their brokering. This research was published in three reports.[27] These epistemic boundary objects informed the writing of the 2000–2001 *World Development Report: Attacking Poverty*, which mentions words in the lexicon of inclusion 286 times, compared to 30 times only ten years earlier. As previously mentioned, in the 2000s and 2010s, the various teams in charge of writing this flagship Bank publication started to acknowledge citizens' voices as crucial. They started to include consultations in their methodology and began to underline the need for inclusiveness. The fact that Narayan and Chambers were recognized experts in many different communities is a testament to how epistemic power functions: multi-membership is more a strength than an impediment to collective learning processes. Boundary brokering was reinforced by their recognized expertise.

Narayan's boundary brokering revolved around promoting community-driven approaches and consultation with affected populations in Bank projects and research. In addition to being the editor of the series *Voices of the Poor*, she was a senior advisor in the Vice President's Office of the Bank's Poverty Reduction Group. She wrote multiple reports, presented at conferences, and trained Bank employees to include various stakeholders in research and project elaboration. In 2002, she wrote and promoted the *Sourcebook on Empowerment and Poverty Reduction*,[28] used for the writing of the 1999 poverty reduction strategy.

In 1996, the Learning Group on Participatory Development, another *ad hoc* CoP, published the *Participation in Practice* handbook to review how various country CoPs adopted participation tools and mechanisms. The epistemic boundary object details 15 cases of Bank projects in Africa, Asia, and Latin America that integrated participatory practices to render their projects more in tune with targeted populations, and thus more effective.[29] The Bank published its official *Sourcebook on Participation* that same year. After reviewing 16 cases of participation, the *Sourcebook* gives guidelines and "practice pointers" to enable citizens to participate in Bank projects.[30] The practical advice, tools, and formal techniques were designed to help Bank employees implement step-by-step participatory approaches and decide which ones were most useful to their situation. Two years later, the Bank published a set of tools and techniques to realize participatory social assessments.[31].

Many reports by the Operations Evaluation Department also became epistemic boundary objects and influenced the learning process toward more participation. For instance, a 1985 report evaluating the impact of grassroots participation on project sustainability concluded that only 12 out of the 25 projects analyzed reported long-term sustainability, and the main causal factor was the inclusion of grassroots institutions and aid-targeted communities in various stages of policymaking.[32] Two years later, the same department published a review of 42 irrigation projects led by the Bank and similarly found that the involvement of all stakeholders in planning and management was crucial for project sustainability.[33] This internally created knowledge contributed to a growing understanding in other communities of practice at the Bank that the inclusion of populations in developing projects could increase their sustainability.

In the 1980s, the *World Development Report* (WDR), the Bank's flagship publication, never elaborated on the possibility or need to include borrowing governments, NGOs, or citizens in Bank practices. The WDR is one of the main epistemic boundary objects circulating between CoPs at the Bank and is cited not only for its conclusions but also for its methodology. They give a certain orientation to Bank practitioners as to what the cutting-edge development topics and methodologies are. The 1980 WDR on *Poverty and Human Development* mentioned the concept of public or citizens' participation four times and the word NGO only once, in a document of 178 pages (Figure 5.1). Ten years later, the 1990 WDR on Poverty shows slightly more openness, with nine mentions of "participation" and 21 mentions of "NGO" over 276 pages. While focusing on "poverty," none of the WDR associated poverty with a lack of empowerment or defined poverty using the voices of those suffering from it. None of the reports from 1980 to 1990 used concepts of

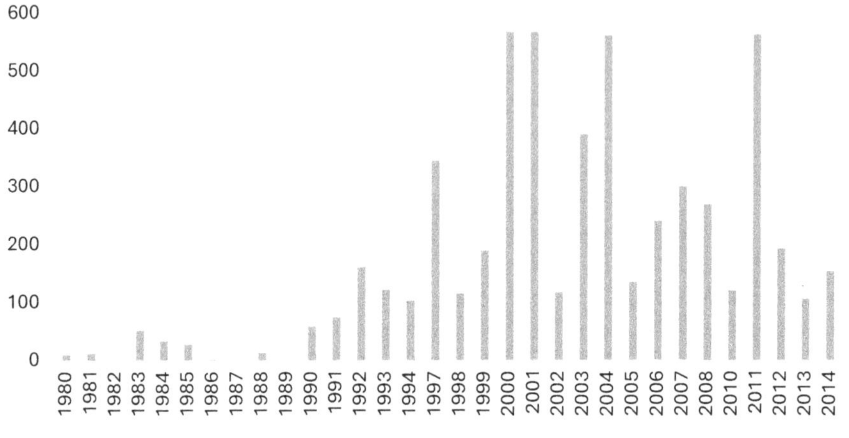

Figure 5.1 Mentions of Words Relating to Inclusion, Consultation, and Participation in *World Development Reports* (number of instances/year)[34]

"empowerment," "inclusion," or "civil society," and only half of them briefly mentioned anything relating to consultation with targeted populations or civil society organizations.

In 1992, the annual WDR mentioned for the first time the correlation between participation and project success. There was a sharp increase in words associated with participation, consultation, empowerment, NGO, and civil society in WDRs. The specific topics in each WDR influenced the integration of some ideas around inclusive development. However, there is an apparent increase in the use of words in the realm of inclusive practices. If in 1980 there were five mentions of words associated with inclusion ("inclu-," "consult-," "empower-," "participat-," "NGO," and "civil society"), 20 years later, in 2000, there were 286 instances. Despite variations throughout the years, there were on average eight mentions of words related to inclusion in WDRs in the 1980s, 61 in the 1990s, and 136 from 2000 to 2014.

According to senior Bank managers, the 2000–2001 *World Development Report* on poverty was the Bank's "first and most high-profile (if necessarily incomplete) attempt to engage with political issues such as 'empowerment,' it is important to note that this effort nonetheless provided a foundation on which subsequent operational and programmatic work has built."[35] Led by the development economist Ravi Kanbur, who worked at the Bank for two decades, the report was the product of a year of consultations worldwide. One of the Bank officials who organized some of these consultations and participated in the writing of the report recalled that, because of the lack of online technology, there were a lot of "face-to-face" consultations, which culminated in large workshops or conferences.[36] Confirming that procedures can change without major change in the content, he concluded that "it was not terribly different from the one in 1990. It was consistent but I think that the framework was more complex and comprehensive."[37] Nonetheless, it is still important to note that the 2000–2001 WDR mentions words in the inclusion lexicon ten times more often than a decade earlier (from 30 in 1990 to close to 300 in 2001).

Many reports, memos, and internal communications becoming epistemic boundary objects point to the need for more involvement of borrowing governments in writing macroeconomic policies and designing Bank projects. The 1998 Bank report *Assessing Aid: What Works, What Doesn't, and Why,* directed by David Dollar and Lant Pritchett, argues that the quality of any recommended reforms is less a factor of success than the commitment of all levels of governments to them. Based on internal evaluations of rural water supply projects, the report states that governments must be involved to ensure project sustainability.[38] They note that the lack of powerful political constituencies in favor of reforms did not affect the approval of the reforms but slowed their effective completion.[39] This report slowly made its way into various Bank CoPs as an epistemic boundary object.

Many other epistemic boundary objects (external reports, research notes, and news articles) informed Bank employees about the effectiveness of inclusive practices; for example, sometimes a chapter about or written by an external institution is included in a Bank-edited volume or reference book and then influenced country teams' practice. For example, this was the case in the 1992 report on participatory development by the Learning Group on Participatory Development, in which the editors included a chapter on UNICEF's experiences with participation.[40] Often, Bank documents mention external sources as having impacted its reports on participation or consultation, or explicitly compare the Bank's practice to that of other agencies, using documents as proof; for instance, in the Operations Policy Department report *The World Bank and Participation*, the authors compare various bilateral agencies' understandings and practices of participation with those of the Bank.[41]

Many Bank employees interviewed for this research emphasized the importance of new information from outside reports and how these reports (as epistemic boundary objects) influenced their thinking on a variety of issues.[42] In many reports, sourcebooks, or internal documents, Bank employees used examples from other institutions to explain the pros and cons of a participatory approach. In the 1992 report on participation, Bhuvan Bhatnagar and Aubrey C. Williams mention best practices by UNICEF and the Organization for Economic Cooperation and Development; the UNDP 1993 *Human Development Report* on people's participation and the Asian Development Bank's *Guidelines for Social Analysis of Development Project*; and the Food and Agriculture Organization's People's Participation Program.[43]

The data-driven reports on the PRSPs prepared by international and national NGOs eventually penetrated the Bank's CoPs, even up to higher management levels; these later reports thus had more impact as epistemic boundary objects than reports by the same organizations in the structural adjustment period. When these external reports started to be used to improve projects' effectiveness, they became an example of how useful interaction with NGOs could be. For example, one senior Bank manager working for the Africa region expressed how he became more receptive to consider NGO criticisms:

> [T]he NGO would ask: "Are you guys using a cross-cutter approach to the PRSP because there are a lot of similarities in the language used in the PRSP in Bosnia, in Uganda, in Bangladesh." So I would say that *because that evidence was brought up*, it is a fair question to ask.[44]

The size of the NGO did not matter as much to the Bank as the documents and evidence they would bring, according to a former employee of the UN who interacted with the Bank for over 30 years. If the documents were recognized as embodying a specific set of expertise, they could be translated and become epistemic boundary objects. This obviously comes from a judgment about what data is valuable, which is influenced by professional standards of evaluation but also by the coloniality of epistemic knowledge. In that sense, some types of reports by some types of organizations have greater chance of becoming epistemic boundary objects. In the end, if research is done using Bank standards and, if useful for Bank projects, would be used and would trickle up within the organization:

> There are a lot of organizations on the ground that are often doing outstanding work. But they often do not have the empirical evidence in support of what they are doing. They do not have the resources to do that kind of additional investigative work. But the result is sometimes that they are not listened to because they . . . seem to be standing in a whole set of values but not always with a lot of evidence into how what they are doing could be taken to scale. And the problem for the Bank is that they are expecting to deliver at a level of scale.[45]

Epistemic boundary objects written by internal Bank CoPs have always had more impact on other Bank CoPs practices than external ones. For example, the 1994 report *The World Bank and Participation* laid out an action plan for greater participation in policy dialogue and public-sector management activities.[46] It suggested that people working in lending operations in sectoral work should ensure that all relevant stakeholders are involved and that all economic and sectoral work projects include brief descriptions of the participatory process.[47] A group of senior managers was appointed to oversee the introduction of participatory practices. However, it was dismantled in 1997 because, according to its evaluators, "the Bank declared victory and moved on."[48] This example shows that collective learning is not a one-way highway; it is made of fluctuation and contestation from both those who champion new practices and those who oppose them. Collective learning is not a linear, uninterrupted cycle; it is a constantly interrupted one.

Another important epistemic boundary object that many interviewees mentioned as crucial to promoting consultation guidelines is the *Sourcebook on Civil Society Consultation* (2007, or its predecessor in 2001), which laid out best practices for the participation of civil society organizations in global, national, and village-based projects.[49] The *Sourcebook* represented a shift from the Bank's focus on empowerment to consultative processes with various stakeholders.

From the mid-1990s to the mid-2000s, the number of projects involving NGOs increased tremendously. From 3–4 percent of projects approved by the executive board in the mid-1990s, including NGOs, the proportion had reached about 40 percent in 2002, and these numbers were shared in internal reports.[50] In April 2010, the Open Data Initiative was launched to increase transparency and legitimacy. It provided free and public access in Arabic, English, French, and Spanish to around 2,000 financial, business, and human-development indicators for over 200 economies and a variety of sets of Bank data, namely those that informed the writing of the annual *World Development Report*. It was former Bank president Zoellick's intention, as he noted in a speech at Georgetown University in 2010, to "open the treasure chest of the World Bank's data and knowledge to every village health care worker, every researcher, everyone."[51] He added that the organization needed to "listen and democratize development economics."[52]

The evaluation reports of Bank projects, which often embodied contestation of existing practices, are an excellent example of epistemic boundary objects used and interpreted between various communities in the Bank. For example, the Independent Evaluation Group, previously the Operations Evaluation Department, may write a draft evaluation report that will be sent to Operations Policy and Country Services. The department then sends the draft to relevant reviewers inside the Bank to collect and synthesize comments that they send back to the Independent Evaluation Group to amend the draft. The former chief of the Debt and Macroeconomic Adjustment Division and lead evaluation officer Guy Pfeffermann explained:

> We will respond back to them and say, "This is good comment. You're right. We need (to) adjust the facts" or "We don't agree with that. The facts speak otherwise and we won't change that." They have the opportunity at that point to say, "If you don't change that, we will write a footnote saying management disagrees with this point." . . . I'll bet you almost every evaluation has at least one footnote.[53]

This knowledge-creating process is inherently social and fluctuating. These evaluations are used by managers and the teams operating the evaluated projects and other communities inside the Bank as well. For example, the writers of the *Annual Review on Development Effectiveness* acknowledged using the data and evaluations realized by the Operations Evaluation Department to produce their annual report.[54] The 2002 report made six main claims on the importance of projects' "ownership" compared to top-down practices, in an implicit contestation of previous practices.[55] First, speed should not be privileged over broad-based ownership. The report acknowledged that governance reforms based on participation may require a long-term investment. Second, the report claims that new forms of conditionality should be established to favor ownership over blueprint solutions. Third, there is a need to balance partnership and country capacity, whereby the more partners you involve, the more difficult it is to coordinate the different views. Fourth, country-led partnerships should not impede donor accountability and vice versa. Fifth, results-based management should be instituted to create stronger monitoring and evaluation capacity. Finally, national and multilateral development solutions should be better articulated.

In an interview with Bank archivists, Pfeffermann also explained how he was influenced by a document produced by the Operations Evaluation Department about the failures of the Bank's rural development projects; it made him realize how unfair it was to ask countries to bear half of the cost of projects designed by Bank teams.[56] The report criticized the lack of ownership of the Bank's rural projects. Although the evaluation did not specifically address his work or regional area, reading about the failure of those projects led Pfeffermann to understand that the practice of cost-sharing with lower-level governments on programs they did not own was one of the organization's "crusades":

> I think that one has a special moral responsibility when you're dealing with poor people. It's a bit like the extension officer who comes to see the poor guy, and he says, "You plant this," or "You plant that," and the guy knows perfectly well that if it's wrong, the extension officer is all going to be in his jeep and his family may be dying of hunger.[57]

The Wapenhans report

One period when Bank's CoPs collective learning regarding inclusive practices accelerated was also before and after the 1992 publication of a major report led by former Bank vice president Willi A. Wapenhans and financed by the United States Congress. The Wapenhans report and its advocacy in boundary brokering greatly affected Bank employees' understanding of the failures of many of their projects and the relation between these failures and the lack of constituents' support and appropriate data. The document influenced the 1997 Strategic Compact with respect to decentralization and a reorganization of departments. The report, which became an epistemic boundary object, had "significant repercussions" in Bank practices of evaluation of performance.[58]

Lewis T. Preston, then Bank president, mandated Wapenhans to gather a community of practice to reflect on a potential restructuring of the Bank's Operations Evaluation Department. The task force was composed of Bank employees from various professional backgrounds who met every second day; an advisory committee was also set up, including Bank directors and department heads, former Bank employees, and consultants. Additionally, Wapenhans insisted on consulting external communities of practice such as borrowers, suppliers, contractors, and people in other development institutions in boundary encounters or international workshops.[59] Many bilateral and multilateral actors, such as the Japanese, many European states, the United States Agency for International Development, and regional development banks, were explicitly invited to the first workshop, while borrowers were invited to the second one.

Apart from those internal and external boundary encounters, the task force used, interpreted, and translated various epistemic boundary objects like Operations Evaluation Department reviews to formulate recommendations that went way beyond the Department's own proposals. Wapenhans was particularly surprised that much of the information on failed projects he came across was not acknowledged by the CoP of senior managers or the board of directors. "But, if all that knowledge was there, why didn't management and/or the board use it?"[60] Using the Operations Evaluation Department data that showed the portfolio performance was deteriorating, Wapenhans formulated critiques on the Bank's incentive culture of imposing technical assistance, which prevented borrowing countries from taking responsibility for Bank projects. In an interview with the Bank archivists, Wapenhans stated that the Bank kept pouring money into problematic projects because the Bank's evaluation process was not done properly and because of a bias toward project completion: "It creates a situation in which the owner disowns the project, loses interest and commitment, or worse, blames the Bank for failure. . . . Increasingly, borrowers asserted that these are no longer theirs but World Bank's projects."[61]

Borrowing governments Wapenhans encountered also made their views clear that the Bank was "saddling them with experimental and risky projects they did not really want; and, the Bank was not sharing in the risks."[62] There was also, according to him, a strong tendency to ignore project participants in project design:

> So, when I urge more local and beneficiary participation, it is not that the Bank should have a hundred thousand farmers vote to get a particular irrigation project built. However, a local constituency needs to participate in the process of preparing the project.[63]

In summary, the Wapenhans report made recommendations on the disbursement imperative, which forces Bank teams to spend funds in a pre-established timeline, neglect project evaluation, Bank expert approval culture, and what he qualified as an overly Washington-centralized hierarchical structure.[64] This became one of the most cited epistemic boundary objects mentioned by Bank officials interviewed for this research.

The writing of the report was made possible due to many boundary encounters on the topic of inclusive procedural practices. When the task force had prepared a first draft of the report, they organized a retreat with the advisory committee formed by Bank employees from various CoPs. When the team writing the report presented the 56 recommendations, the committee was reportedly "shocked."[65] Yet, the conversations at the retreat led the members of the committee to agree to most of the recommendations, often corroborating them with examples from their own experience at the Bank. "As we went into the discussions, [participants] proceeded to relate anecdotal information from their own experience that made the picture even bleaker."[66] Wapenhans explained that the resulting report shed new light on information already available in the Bank because the data were presented differently.

In a boundary encounter with Senior Vice President Ernest Stern to approve the conclusions, Wapenhans recalled that Stern told him not to change the report and that he believed the document would have a welcome influence on the Bank.[67] Stern subsequently organized three days of discussion with regional vice presidents, each of which promoted his conclusions to other CoPs. It must be noted that, for a long time, Stern felt like an outsider in the group of young professionals he was hired with, which he called an "incredibly conservative bunch of people."[68] Having participated in various street demonstrations in the 1960s, he was sensitized to issues most of his colleagues were not. As such, he was a more vigorous advocate for the democratization of the Bank and encountered many conflictual relationships with senior Bank employees.

With the Bank president's recommendations, Wapenhans gave a written statement on his main conclusions to the Joint Audit Committee, which was circulated to the board and was even sent to donor governments. After writing the report, Wapenhans, who had worked for the Bank for over 30 years and was close to retirement, was asked to act as a consultant for a few more months to promote the conclusions of his report. His brokering was instrumental in promoting his report, who might have not become a boundary object infused with epistemic power otherwise.

Many new inclusive tools emerged as a response to Wapenhans' recommendations. The executive board of the Bank established an Inspection Panel in August 1994, meant to act as an independent complaint mechanism for stakeholder groups and individuals who "believe they have been, or are likely to be, harmed by a World Bank-funded project."[69] The panel receives and evaluates requests concerning any of the Bank's activities, ranging from cases of environmental harm or degradation of cultural sites due to infrastructure projects to the rights of Indigenous peoples and forced relocation. A similar complaint mechanism for the private sector also exists, the Compliance Advisor/Ombudsman.[70]

From Uganda's Poverty Eradication Action Plan to the PRSP

While thousands of boundary encounters, brokering, and uses of epistemic boundary objects took place between 1980 and 2014, their instantiations in the 1997 Uganda's Poverty Eradication Action Plan on Bank practices usefully illustrates collective learning at the boundaries of CoPs. This plan was not the beginning or the end of the change in the Bank's policymaking practices – it was a long and iterative process – but it contributed to the emergence and institutionalization of many inclusive practices. This illustration of collective learning shows how successful practices can trickle through the Bank and influence employees to adopt new tools, concepts, and mechanisms.

In the late 1990s, participatory practices were standard in Uganda, and the Bank's country team learned from their collaboration with CoPs in the country. With a new constitution in 1995 and the election of a new government under President Yoweri Museveni in 1996, the Ugandan government aimed to decentralize and began to acknowledge the criticisms made by vocal NGOs that the Bank's structural adjustment programs did not address, and even impeded, socio-economic conditions. Between 1995 and 1997, the government developed a Poverty Eradication Action Plan, a comprehensive national poverty reduction plan, after broad-based consultation with various stakeholders. Drafting the plan and subsequent revisions involved boundary encounters between the Bank's country team, elected members of the parliament, lower-level governments, the donor community, NGOs, civil society organizations, and academics.[71] With the involvement of Bank employees, consultations were initially formal and included only the most vocal NGOs, but in the plan's revision in 2000, more civil society organizations were targeted in specific consultations.[72]

The Ugandan Ministry of Finance, Planning and Economic Development used six mechanisms during these consultations; these represent boundary encounters that led Bank employees to learn that participation was an efficient policymaking practice. First, two major consultative workshops were organized, involving a wide range of stakeholders, from government agencies to NGOs, donors, the private sector, and the media, to review and comment on the plan's current draft. Second, regional meetings were held with district officials to explain the plan's content and discuss the findings of Uganda's Participatory Poverty Assessment Plan. Bank teams subsequently used these mechanisms to develop poverty reduction strategy papers in other countries. Third, Ugandan parliamentarians held a meeting followed by briefing sessions for various committees, and donors were consulted at a donor consultative-group meeting in March 2000. Finally, the writers of the plan built on the existing consultative process, hosting sectoral working groups, NGO consultative meetings, and regular donor meetings to finalize the document. This process was not reproduced *precisely* in other countries but was translated by many other country teams using their country-specific background knowledge. Similar mechanisms have been developed and spread by members of the Bank's Uganda country team, who learned from their partnerships with Ugandan communities and then went to work in other communities. As one economist at the Bank described it, the mechanisms developed in Uganda were the "vanguard" of participatory mechanisms.[73]

Despite limited influence on economic policy or military issues, civil society organizations had acquired some influence on public policy in Uganda. The government, especially the Ministry of Finance, argued that the Poverty Eradication Action Plan was a "breakthrough" for its relationships with civil society actors.[74] Without specifically advocating for inclusivity, it became an epistemic boundary object to promote more inclusive practices through example-setting. The president of the Ugandan Local Authorities Association, Kiwanuka Musisi, similarly asserted in a 1999 United Nations report that the process of writing the plan and its implementation was a great step ahead in their relationship with the central government:

> We in the field appreciate the fact that this is the first time that we have projects which are from the people—not imposed. We have actors running up

> and down in the districts and sometimes we don't even know what they are doing. We were involved right from the project design all the way to even the evaluations. This is increasing our own sense of commitment and ownership. . . . It is a great opportunity to promote sustainability as people use language such as "our projects."[75]

This improved relationship between the Ugandan government and civil society organizations inspired members of the Bank's country team in Uganda, who then translated this experience into other settings. According to the members of the country team, the participatory and consultative practices implemented by the government were a major factor in the policies' success and broad acceptance.[76] They could see in their encounters with the government and civil society CoPs that inclusive practices improved the effectiveness of projects.

Among other projects in that period, the Bank team supported the Ugandan government in organizing participatory public expenditure surveys, inspired by the Bank's participatory poverty assessments. In 1995, the Bank's CoP called the participation group and published a methodology to render poverty assessments more participatory, which was subsequently used as an epistemic boundary object by the Bank's country team in their work with the Ugandan government. This paper is one example of a boundary object whose meaning evolved and was used to develop participatory mechanisms. While learning from various Ugandan communities, the Bank's country team also tried to adapt their knowledge to the reality of the country. A revision of an earlier one written by the Operations Policy Department, the document concluded that

> an effective poverty strategy needs to be understood by its intended beneficiaries as their own; this is most likely to occur when the strategy is constructed with the participation of a wide range of people living in poverty and reflects the concerns voiced by the poor themselves.[77]

John Mackinnon, then a Bank consultant in Uganda, spent much time enacting boundary brokering by helping the Ugandan government articulate the Poverty Eradication Action Plan. His multiple encounters with the Ugandan writing team led him to translate their practices into Bank terms for the assessment of the Bank team in Uganda and other Bank teams. According to a Bank employee on his team, he followed the advice of the Bank participation group's paper that "an effective poverty strategy needs to be understood by its intended beneficiaries as their own"[78]:

> [H]e was listening and was able to translate it into a coherent document that people really felt was taking things forward. . . . Then it became the country's document. Many years after, you would see some young person in a conference or a seminar, and their initial thought was that "this is in our program."[79]

Many Bank officials called the Ugandan Poverty Eradication Action Plan a "success story."[80] Many mechanisms developed by the government of Uganda and the Bank's country team were promoted and replicated by boundary brokering in CoPs, initiated by people who had worked in Uganda during that period. Many Bank employees and senior officials recalled that the idea behind the PRSP was influenced by the Ugandan experience and was "picked up" by the Bank as a good way to organize donors and various stakeholders.[81] The Ugandan practices influenced the country team, which then brought this experience inside the Bank. Similarly, the donor community generally acknowledges that the Ugandan Plan was so successful that it became the "inspiration and template for the Bank's PRSP model."[82] The Ugandan Plan and other experiences in Mozambique, Ghana, and Zambia "predated the PRSP" and were revised and rebranded as the first Bank-approved PRSPs.[83]

The country team in Uganda became an example to emulate. After their experience with Ugandan communities, Bank team leaders and country economists in Uganda were frequently asked to talk about the Poverty Eradication Action Plan in conferences and seminars inside the Bank, thereby creating internal boundary encounters. The story of the Ugandan success was "told many times" inside the Bank, and it was often repeated in interviews with Bank employees.[84] John Mackinnon and Ritva Reinikka, who had also worked on the Ugandan Plan, were mainly mobilized in boundary brokering, to talk about the experience in Uganda. They also wrote many working papers that became epistemic boundary objects circulating inside the Bank.[85] In addition, the document describing the Poverty Eradication Action Plan itself was used as an epistemic boundary object, with parts of it being scaled up to frame the PRSP.

In what became boundary encounters, Bank managers sponsored trips to Uganda for members of other Bank country teams so they could learn from the Ugandan experience. In addition, the Bank paid country-level policymakers to go learn from other countries' experiences with participation: "They were told: 'Here's a country in Africa which seems to have done it right, so why don't you go and learn from them?' There was some technology transfer there."[86] Eventually dispersed into various Bank units, employees who worked in Uganda became internal boundary brokers, promoting a different way to organize donors and loan receivers on the ground.

After many reports on the successes of participation in Uganda, the collective learning process from Uganda eventually reached the board of directors. A Bank official recalled that the British executive director used reports on the Ugandan example to advocate for more participation at board meetings. Bank managers reportedly wanted to replicate the Ugandan experience in other borrowing countries:

> It's time to change, they said. We have seen a process. We want this type of process for all poor countries where [poverty assessments] are being done instead of the regular type of doing of the IMF and the Bank. We need more owned process so that the countries have more ownership.[87]

According to a 20-year veteran Bank economist, the idea for the poverty reduction strategy was partly inspired by the Ugandan experience and was presented in the

Bank as a model.[88] The example set by the Poverty Eradication Action Plan became part of a global learning process happening simultaneously in various parts of the Bank. The multiplication of successful cases of inclusive policymaking processes accelerated the adoption of such practices by Bank employees.

Using these examples, a Bank team then drafted the poverty reduction strategy, including a plan for broad national consultations. As a result, the Highly Indebted Poor Countries (HIPC) initiative was officially launched in 1996. Led mainly by the Bank and the International Monetary Fund (IMF), other regional development banks, such as the Asian Development Bank and the African Development Bank, joined the debt reduction effort. The HIPC initiative was a debt restructuring and relief program, whereby parts of these countries' debt would be erased and the residual debt would be rescheduled. It was intended for the most indebted countries, initially 41 countries—mostly in Africa—whose debt totaled close to $200 billion.[89]

In the 2000s, to access debt relief under the HIPC initiative, governments needed to write a PRSP with inputs from various stakeholders in their population. However, because governments needed debt relief quickly and broad-based participation takes time, the Bank established intermediary PRSPs (I-PRSPs) as a condition to accessing the first tranche of debt relief, with an agreement to eventually undertake broader participation and to implement feedback mechanisms with citizens. Most I-PRSPs were written in only a few months, with unequal results. In Malawi, the I-PRSP was written in about four months, leaving only a few weeks for public participation in a society of 15 million people.[90] In Cambodia, the I-PRSP was translated from English to Khmer only in its final version, making it impossible for most of the population and NGOs to read and comment on it.[91] According to a 2005 joint Bank and IMF report, out of ten national governments surveyed, four said Bank employees had rushed them to write their PRSP (Cambodia, Mozambique, Nicaragua, and Tanzania), often forcing them to copy parts of their I-PRSP into their final documents. The first Tanzanian PRSP, for example, was written less than six months after their I-PRSP, while the usual delay is up to 20 months.

Furthermore, many country teams reproduced the techniques laid out in Bank sourcebooks on participation and poverty reduction, making the process and the outcomes very similar from one country to another. The PRSP embodied less conditionality about the content but more conditionality on the process (i.e., the obligation to develop participatory processes), so the public meetings and the types of inputs collected became very much of a "common blend,"[92] which is contrary to a genuine participatory process focused on the empowerment of Global South communities. A 2005 report from the Operations Evaluation Department criticized borrowing countries that saw the PRSP more as a "source of cash" than as a real commitment to participatory development.[93] Furthermore, while some social impacts were debated in these forums, the macroeconomic policies were rarely up for discussion. NGOs were concerned that the following issues were not the subject of public consultation: "industrial policy, trade protection, subsidy support to domestic industries, domestic investment, levels of deficit spending, price supports, regulation on foreign investment, achieving lower interest rates and subsidized credit for domestic industry."[94]

The fact that the board of directors had to sign off on the programs, even if it was sometimes a formality, further undermined "ownership" of the PRSP: "Stakeholders perceive this practice as 'Washington signing off' on a supposedly country-owned strategy."[95] However, these criticisms were more acute on the first PRSP, and civil society reports on the third and fourth versions acknowledged the improving relationship between Bank teams and civil society.

When the PRSP were discontinued with the end of the HIPC initiative in 2014, broad-based participation of citizens as a condition for debt relief vanished. Despite its failure to institutionalize broad participatory processes in policymaking, many Bank CoPs and external CoPs see the PRSP as part of a process that did not start or end with it.[96] According to a former Bank country manager, despite the failure of the PRSP as mandatory programs, "a lot of things did change, in form if not in substance. In the Bank today, there are more internal debates and discussions. It's a lot less monolithic than it used to be when I joined the Bank."[97] The relationship with aid-targeted populations and the value placed by the Bank on context-specific knowledge have greatly evolved since the 1980s. In that sense, many Bank officials believe the PRSP created a "huge shift" in their practices.[98]

In the end, despite all its downfalls, broad-based participation under the PRSPs became an "anchoring practice," in that they made other practices possible.[99] Anchoring practices have the power to structure discourse and patterns of activity because they define rules and entities concerning a domain of action.[100] The PRSP forced many Bank employees to learn about participatory and consultative mechanisms and gave them tools and resources to engage in other consultative practices. Practices such as broad-based participation under the PRSP became influential not because they lasted decades or because all Bank employees and borrowing governments enacted them but because they defined "an infrastructure, a set of tools for actors to use and deploy in their interaction with each other. It follows that some practices are anchoring because they define one set of strategies for action rather than others."[101]

One senior Bank official argued that the PRSP

> catalyzed a concept, which is the broad participation of national stakeholders, and how that affects national development priorities. The PRSP process was an important part of softening the ground and enabling governments to accept the premise that citizens have a much larger role than just being users of services.[102]

According to many Bank employees and officials interviewed for this research, the slow adoption of new policymaking practices created a "big change in attitude" because many Bank employees opened up to new perspectives coming from NGOs.[103] As one senior Bank economist stated, while it did not necessarily change the substance of the policies advocated by the Bank, it created an atmosphere of openness that allowed internal debates.[104] If the discrepancy between talks and practices exists,[105] it would be unfair to deny the existence of a change in procedural practices at the World Bank.

In a larger sense, an anchoring practice can enable other practices that will persist even when the initial practice vanishes. For example, broad-based participation led to constitutive rules about who counts as a stakeholder and who has a right to participate in policymaking processes in multilateral development. By 2015, most countries had reached the completion points of debt relief under the HIPC initiative, putting an end to the formal requirement to produce PRSPs. In April 2015, the last one to qualify for irrevocable debt relief under the HIPC initiative was Chad.[106] However, many countries' formal budgets still involve PRSPs and formal development planning.

Other participatory mechanisms were later adopted regarding development policymaking. In January 2012, the Bank established the Program-for-Results, funds whose disbursements are linked to achieving previously agreed-upon, tangible and verifiable results. Program-for-Results "operations help countries strengthen institutions, build capacity, and enhance partnerships with a variety of stakeholders."[107] Program-for-Results vary in content and scope: some support the coverage of antenatal care for mothers and newborns, while others support the implementation of sustainable water supply and sanitation services. Program-for-Results are designed to support borrowers' programs if results are measurable and tangible. Regional workshops are often held to bring together participants from African countries who are implementing Program-for-Results operations and those who are considering it.[108]

The Program-for-Results were associated with funds available to support countries' programs or projects, based on the attainment of measurable targets. They at least theoretically emphasize ownership and better coordination of lenders and borrowers as they focus on client-determined needs and projects.[109] Since 2012, there has been a steady increase in the allocation of Program-for-Results. In January 2018, there were 77 active Program-for-Results operations approved by the Bank, for a total of $19.9 billion.[110]

Moreover, in 2013, the Bank developed a Strategic Framework for Mainstreaming Citizen Engagement. The framework is supposed to provide the Bank and civil society organizations with "many opportunities to find synergies and collaborate on public campaigns and education efforts."[111] The Bank noted that in 2012, civil society organizations were involved in policymaking in 82 percent of all projects, compared to 21 percent in 1990.[112] A senior official at the Bank mentioned that during that period, grievance mechanisms had become part of the day-to-day routine: "All operations that had identifiable beneficiaries are required to have beneficiary feedback."[113] A Bank employee added that all projects must have at least "some elements of citizens' oriented design or take into account beneficiary feedback" as part of a "steady mainstreaming effort."[114]

Conclusion

In the end, from 1980 to 2014, many Bank CoPs came to see inclusion as increasing the effectiveness of their policies and projects. As a general indicator, from 1980 to 1988, the effectiveness of projects was in constant decline. At that point, only 56 percent of projects were considered satisfactory according to the Bank's own evaluation criteria. The approval rate then rose to 83 percent in 2006.[115] The participation of citizens in policymaking, albeit on a smaller scale, remains part of the practices of Bank employees to this day. Broad-based countrywide participation, as in the case of the Uganda Poverty Eradication Action Plan or the PRSPs, might have disappeared from Bank practices, but Bank employees still consult civil society groups like NGOs as part of their daily practice, and the inclusion of citizens in project development and implementation is common in many CoPs. In the end, this demonstrates the importance of many inclusive practices from that period as anchoring practices for others to emerge.

Notes

1 World Bank, *The World Bank Participation Sourcebook*, 141.
2 Interview OHP Gloria Davis, June 28–29, 2004.
3 Chambers, "The Origins and Practice of Participatory Rural Appraisal," 953; Cernea, *Putting People First*.
4 Chambers, "Participatory Rural Appraisal (PRA): Analysis of Experience," 1253.
5 (Bhatnagar and Williams 1992, 1).
6 Francis and Jacobs, "Institutionalizing Social Analysis at the World Bank," 346.
7 Francis and Jacobs, 347.
8 Bhatnagar and Williams, *Participatory Development and the World Bank*, 9.
9 World Bank, 6.
10 Interview 10, June 13, 2017; Interview 18, July 16, 2017; Interview 35, November 9, 2017; Interview 38, July 21, 2017.
11 Nair, "Sociability in International Politics."
12 World Bank, 76.
13 Interview OHP Gloria Davis, June 28–29, 2004.
14 Interview 35, November 9, 2017.
15 Interview 35, November 9, 2017.
16 Interview 21, July 19, 2017.
17 World Bank, "Across Indonesia, Villagers Invest in Own Infrastructure Needs."
18 Interview OHP, Dennis De Tray, February 13–21 and March 22, 2006, 65.
19 Interview 9, June 9, 2017.
20 Mallaby, *The World's Banker*, 240, 244.
21 World Bank, "Building Poverty Reduction Strategies in Developing Countries — For Approval by the Board of Governors."
22 World Bank, "Chairman's Summing Up of World Bank Board Discussion of Joint Bank-Fund Paper on 'Poverty Reduction Strategy Papers: Operational Issues,'" 12.
23 Interview 21, July 19, 2017.
24 Easterly, "What Did Structural Adjustment Adjust? The Association of Policies and Growth with Repeated IMF and World Bank Adjustment Loans," 4; Killick et al., *Aid and the Political Economy of Policy Change*.
25 Interview 1, February 28, 2017.
26 Interview 5, May 25, 2017; Interview 15, June 27, 2017.
27 (1) *Can Anyone Hear Us?* (2000), (2) *Crying Out for Change* (2000), and (3) *From Many Lands* (2002).
28 Narayan, "Empowerment and Poverty Reduction: A Sourcebook."
29 World Bank and Rietbergen-McCracken, *Participation in Practice*.
30 World Bank.
31 Rietbergen-McCracken and Narayan-Parker, *Participation and Social Assessment*.

32 Operations Evaluations Department, "Sustainability of Projects: First Review of Experiences."
33 (Bhatnagar and Williams 1992, 3).
34 Firsthand data collection.
35 Bebbington et al., "Exploring Social Capital Debates at the World Bank," 50.
36 Interview 21, July 19, 2017.
37 Interview 21, July 19, 2017.
38 Dollar and Pritchett, *Assessing Aid.*
39 Shams, "The World Bank's Structural Adjustment Loans: A Critique," 210.
40 Bhatnagar and Williams, chapter 6.
41 Operations Policy Department, *The World Bank and Participation*, 19.
42 For example, Interview 5, May 25, 2017; Interview 15, June 27, 2017.
43 Bhatnagar and Williams.
44 Interview 15, June 27, 2017.
45 Interview 5, May 25, 2017.
46 Operations Policy Department.
47 Aycrigg, "Participation and the World Bank Success, Constraints, and Responses," 3.
48 Phillips, *Reforming the World Bank*, 126.
49 Civil Society Team, *Consultations with Civil Society. A Sourcebook.*
50 Interview OHP Alexander Shakow, March 19–20, 2002.
51 Zoellick, "From Hubris to Humility," 14.
52 Zoellick, 18.
53 Interview OHP Catherine Gwin, January 20, 2010.
54 World Bank, *1999 Annual Review of Development Effectiveness.*
55 (World Bank 2002, xiv–xv).
56 Interview OHP Guy Pfeffermann, January 14, 1992, 12.
57 Interview OHP Guy Pfeffermann, January 14, 1992, 12.
58 Interview OHP Katherine Marshall, January 30 and 31, 2007, 22.
59 Interview OHP Willi Wapenhans, July 21 and August 19 1993, 9.
60 Interview OHP Willi Wapenhans, July 21 and August 19 1993, 10.
61 Interview OHP Willi Wapenhans, July 21 and August 19, 1993, 13–14.
62 Interview OHP Willi Wapenhans, July 21 and August 19, 1993, 29.
63 Interview OHP Willi Wapenhans, July 21 and August 19, 1993, 36–37.
64 Wapenhans, "Effective Implementation. Key to Development Impact (Wapenhans Report)," 30; Nielson, Tierney, and Weaver, "Bridging the Rationalist–Constructivist Divide," 116.
65 Wapenhans, 19; Nielson et al., 19.
66 Wapenhans, 19; Nielson et al., 19.
67 Wapenhans, 23; Nielson et al., 23.
68 Interview OHP Ernest Stern, January 18–19, 2001.
69 World Bank, "The World Bank Inspection Panel. Where Your Concerns Are Heard," 2.
70 Ebrahim and Herz, "Accountability in Complex Organizations," 9.
71 Republic of Uganda, "Poverty Eradication Action Plan: A National Challenge for Uganda, Volume I."
72 Mackinnon and Reinikka, "Lessons from Uganda on Strategies to Fight Poverty."
73 Interview 19, November 14, 2017.
74 Lister and Nyamugasira, "Design Contradictions in the 'New Architecture of Aid'?" 98.
75 Cited in Craig and Porter, "Poverty Reduction Strategy Papers: A New Convergence," 63.
76 (Mackinnon and Reinikka 2000, 47).
77 Salmen, "Participatory Poverty Assessment. Incorporating Poor People's Perspectives into Poverty Assessment Work," 1.
78 Salmen, 1.
79 Interview 19, November 14, 2017.
80 World Bank and IMF, "Heavily Indebted Poor Countries (HIPC) Initiative— Strengthening the Link between Debt Relief and Poverty Reduction," 11; Mallaby, 228.

81 Interview 9, July 19, 2017; Interview 12, August 15, 2017; Interview 14, November 8, 2017.
82 Lie, "Developmentality," 728.
83 Interview 6, November 8, 2017.
84 Interview 19, November 14, 2017.
85 Mackinnon and Reinikka; Mackinnon and Reinikka, "How Research Can Assist Policy: The Case of Economic Reforms in Uganda."
86 Interview 12, August 15, 2017.
87 Interview 19, November 14, 2017.
88 Interview 9, July 19, 2017.
89 Campbell and Losch, "Les Pauvres, Bénéficiaires Ou Otages Des Stratégies de Réduction de La Pauvreté?" 181.
90 Serieux 2001, 536–537, cited in Campbell and Losch.
91 Whaites 2002, cited in Cling et al., *Les Nouvelles Stratégies Internationales de Lutte Contre La Pauvreté*, 193.
92 Interview 18, July 16, 2017.
93 Phillips, 135.
94 Rowden and Irama, "Rethinking Participation. Questions for Civil Society about the Limits of Participation in PRSPs," 4.
95 World Bank OED, *The Poverty Reduction Strategy Initiative*.
96 Interview 9, June 9, 2017; Interview 10, June 13, 2017.
97 Interview 41, November 21, 2017.
98 Interview 21, July 19, 2017; Interview 28, August 15, 2017.
99 Swidler, "What Anchors Cultural Practices"; Sending and Neumann, "Banking on Power: How Some Practices in an International Organization Anchor Others."
100 Swidler.
101 Sending and Neumann, 238.
102 Interview 15, July 16, 2017.
103 Interview 26, July 24, 2017; Interview 41, November 21, 2017.
104 Interview 26, July 24, 2017.
105 Wade, "US Hegemony and the World Bank: The Fight over People and Ideas"; Bebbington et al., "Of Texts and Practices: Empowerment and Organisational Cultures in World Bank-Funded Rural Development Programmes"; Weaver, *Hypocrisy Trap*.
106 World Bank and IMF, "Heavily Indebted Poor Countries (HIPC) Initiative and Multilateral Debt Relief Initiative (MDRI) — Statistical Update," 1.
107 Tenney and Salda, *Historical Dictionary of the World Bank*, 212.
108 www.worldbank.org/en/events/2016/06/04/regional-workshop-program-for-results-financing-for-sustainable-development-results, Consulted May 10 2020.
109 Cormier, "Empowered Borrowers? Tracking the World Bank's Program-for-Results."
110 www.worldbank.org/en/programs/program-for-results-financing, Consulted May 10, 2020.
111 www.worldbank.org/en/about/partners/civil-society#2, Consulted May 10, 2020.
112 www.worldbank.org/en/about/partners/civil-society#2, Consulted May 10, 2020.
113 Interview 14, June 26, 2017.
114 Interview 19, July 17, 2017.
115 Phillips, 158.

References

Aycrigg, Maria. "Participation and the World Bank Success, Constraints, and Responses." In *Draft for Discussion at the International Conference on Upscaling and Mainstreaming Participation: Lessons Learned and Ways Forward*. Washington, DC: The World Bank, 1998.

Bebbington, Anthony, Scott Guggenheim, Elizabeth Olson, and Michael Woolcock. "Exploring Social Capital Debates at the World Bank." *Journal of Development Studies* 40, no. 5 (June 2004): 33–64.

Bebbington, Anthony, David Lewis, Simon Batterbury, Elizabeth Olson, and M. Shameem Siddiqi. "Of Texts and Practices: Empowerment and Organisational Cultures in World Bank-Funded Rural Development Programmes." *The Journal of Development Studies* 43, no. 4 (May 2007): 597–621.

Bhatnagar, Bhuvan, and Aubrey C. Williams, eds. *Participatory Development and the World Bank: Potential Directions for Change. World Bank Discussion Papers 183*. Washington, DC: The World Bank, 1992.

Campbell, Bonnie, and Bruno Losch. "Les Pauvres, Bénéficiaires Ou Otages Des Stratégies de Réduction de La Pauvreté?" *Politique Africaine*, no. 87 (2002): 175–84.

Cernea, Michael M., ed. *Putting People First: Sociological Variables in Rural Development*. New York: Published for the World Bank [by] Oxford University Press, 1991.

Chambers, Robert. "Participatory Rural Appraisal (PRA): Analysis of Experience." *World Development* 22, no. 9 (1994a): 1253–68.

Chambers, Robert. "The Origins and Practice of Participatory Rural Appraisal." *World Development* 22, no. 7 (July 1994b): 953–69.

Civil Society Team. *Consultations with Civil Society. A Sourcebook*. Washington, DC: World Bank, 2007.

Cling, Jean-Pierre, Mireille Razafindrakoto, and François Roubaud. *Les Nouvelles Stratégies Internationales de Lutte Contre La Pauvreté*. Paris: DIAL/Economica, 2002.

Cormier, Ben. "Empowered Borrowers? Tracking the World Bank's Program-for-Results." *Third World Quarterly* 37 (2016): 209–26.

Craig, David, and Doug Porter. "Poverty Reduction Strategy Papers: A New Convergence." *World Development* 31, no. 1 (January 2003): 53–69.

Dollar, David, and Lant Pritchett. *Assessing Aid: What Works, What Doesn't, and Why*. Washington, DC: World Bank, 1998.

Easterly, William. "What Did Structural Adjustment Adjust? The Association of Policies and Growth with Repeated IMF and World Bank Adjustment Loans." *Journal of Development Economics* 76 (2005): 1–22.

Ebrahim, Alnoor, and Steven Herz. *Accountability in Complex Organizations: World Bank Responses to Civil Society. J.F.K. School of Government Faculty Research Working Paper Series*. Cambridge: Harvard University, 2007.

Francis, Paul, and Susan Jacobs. "Institutionalizing Social Analysis at the World Bank." *Environmental Impact Assessment Review* 19, no. 3 (1999): 341–57.

Killick, Tony, Ramani Gunatilaka, and Ana Marr. *Aid and the Political Economy of Policy Change*. London and New York: Routledge, 1998.

Lie, Jon Harald Sande. "Developmentality: Indirect Governance in the World Bank–Uganda Partnership." *Third World Quarterly* 36, no. 4 (April 3, 2015): 723–40.

Lister, Sarah, and Warren Nyamugasira. "Design Contradictions in the 'New Architecture of Aid'? Reflections from Uganda on the Roles of Civil Society Organisations." *Development Policy Review* 21, no. 1 (January 2003): 93–106.

Mackinnon, John, and Ritva Reinikka. *Lessons from Uganda on Strategies to Fight Poverty. Policy Research Working Paper*. Washington, DC: World Bank Group, 2000.

Mackinnon, John, and Ritva Reinikka. "How Research Can Assist Policy: The Case of Economic Reforms in Uganda." *The World Bank Research Observer* 17, no. 2 (2002): 267–92.

Mallaby, Sebastian. *The World's Banker: A Story of Failed States*, Financial Crises, and the Wealth and Poverty of Nations. A Council on Foreign Relations Book. London, UK: The Penguin Press, 2006.

Nair, Deepak. "Sociability in International Politics: Golf and ASEAN's Cold War Diplomacy." *International Political Sociology* 14, no. 2 (June 1, 2020): 196–214. https://doi.org/10.1093/ips/olz024.

Narayan, Deepa, ed. *Voices of the Poor. Can Anyone Hear Us? Voices of the Poor*. New York: Published by Oxford University Press for the World Bank, 2000.
Narayan, Deepa. *Empowerment and Poverty Reduction: A Sourcebook*. Washington, DC: World Bank Group, 2002.
Narayan, Deepa, Robert Chambers, Meera K. Shah, and Patti L. Petesch, eds. *Voices of the Poor. Crying Out for Change. Voices of the Poor*. Washington, DC: A Copublication of Oxford University Press and the World Bank, 2000.
Narayan, Deepa, and Patti L. Petesch, eds. *Voices of the Poor. From Many Lands. Voices of the Poor*. Washington, DC: A Copublication of Oxford University Press and the World Bank, 2002.
Nielson, Daniel L, Michael J. Tierney, and Catherine E. Weaver. "Bridging the Rationalist–Constructivist Divide: Re-Engineering the Culture of the World Bank." *Journal of International Relations and Development* 9, no. 2 (June 2006): 107–39.
Operations Evaluations Department. *Sustainability of Projects: First Review of Experiences*. Washington, DC: World Bank, 1985.
Operations Policy Department. *The World Bank and Participation*. Washington, DC: The World Bank, 1994.
Phillips, David A. *Reforming the World Bank: Twenty Years of Trial -- and Error*. New York: Cambridge University Press, 2009.
Republic of Uganda. *Poverty Eradication Action Plan: A National Challenge for Uganda*. Vol. I. Kampala: Ministry of Finance, Planning and Economic Development, 1997.
Rietbergen-McCracken, Jennifer, and Deepa Narayan-Parker. *Participation and Social Assessment: Tools and Techniques*. Washington, DC: International Bank for Reconstruction and Development/World Bank, 1998.
Rowden, Rick, and Jane Ocaya Irama. *Rethinking Participation. Questions for Civil Society about the Limits of Participation in PRSPs. Discussion Paper*. Washington, DC: Action Aid, 2004.
Salmen, Lawrence F. *Participatory Poverty Assessment. Incorporating Poor People's Perspectives into Poverty Assessment Work. Environment Department Papers. Social Assessment*. Washington, DC: World Bank, 1995.
Sending, Ole Jacob, and Iver B. Neumann. "Banking on Power: How Some Practices in an International Organization Anchor Others." In *International Practices*, edited by Emanuel Adler and Vincent Pouliot, 231–54, New York: Cambridge University Press, 2011,
Shams, Rasul. "The World Bank's Structural Adjustment Loans: A Critique." *Intereconomics* (1988): 208–11.
Swidler, Ann. "What Anchors Cultural Practices." In *The Practice Turn in Contemporary Theory*, edited by Karin Knorr Cetina, Theodore Richard Schatzki, and Eike Von Savigny. New York: Routledge, 2000.
Tenney, Sarah, and Anne C. M. Salda. *Historical Dictionary of the World Bank. Historical Dictionaries of International Organizations*. 2nd ed. Lanham: The Scarecrow Press, Inc., 2014.
Wade, Robert. "US Hegemony and the World Bank: The Fight Over People and Ideas." *Review of International Political Economy* 9, no. 2 (2002): 215–43.
Wapenhans, W. *Effective Implementation. Key to Development Impact (Wapenhans Report). Report*. Washington, DC: The World Bank, 1992.
Weaver, Catherine. *Hypocrisy Trap: The World Bank and the Poverty of Reform*. Princeton: Princeton University Press, 2008.
World Bank. *The World Bank Inspection Panel. Where Your Concerns Are Heard*. Washington, DC: World Bank, 1993.
World Bank, ed. *The World Bank Participation Sourcebook*. Washington, DC: The World Bank, 1996.
World Bank. *Building Poverty Reduction Strategies in Developing Countries – For Approval by the Board of Governors*. Washington, DC: The World Bank, 1999a.

World Bank. *Chairman's Summing Up of World Bank Board Discussion of Joint Bank-Fund Paper on 'Poverty Reduction Strategy Papers: Operational Issues'*. Washington, DC: World Bank Board of Directors, December 20, 1999b.

World Bank. *1999 Annual Review of Development Effectiveness.* Washington, DC: The World Bank, 2002.

World Bank. *Across Indonesia, Villagers Invest in Own Infrastructure Needs.* Washington, DC: World Bank Group, 2007.

World Bank, and IMF. *Heavily Indebted Poor Countries (HIPC) Initiative – Strengthening the Link between Debt Relief and Poverty Reduction.* Washington, DC: The World Bank and International Monetary Fund, 1999.

World Bank, and IMF. *Heavily Indebted Poor Countries (HIPC) Initiative and Multilateral Debt Relief Initiative (MDRI) – Statistical Update*. Washington, DC: World Bank and IMF, 2016.

World Bank, and Jennifer Rietbergen-McCracken. *Participation in Practice: The Experience of the World Bank and Other Stakeholders. World Bank Discussion Paper, No. 333.* Washington, DC: The World Bank, 1996.

World Bank, and OED, ed. *The Poverty Reduction Strategy Initiative: An Independent Evaluation of the World Bank's Support through 2003. Operations Evaluation Studies.* Washington, DC: The World Bank, 2004.

Zoellick, Robert. "From Hubris to Humility." Speech at Georgetown University, 2010, 14.

6 Boundary brokers are not alone, not even James Wolfensohn

The election of James Wolfensohn as the ninth president of the Bank in 1995 accelerated the inclusion of civil society actors and the delegation to borrowing governments in the organization's practices. In his biography, Wolfensohn criticizes the dismissive attitude of the Bank in the 1980s, and he writes that a generalized defensiveness made the Bank arrogant and elitist: "Instead of engaging in a dialogue with them, the Bank closed in on itself, believing that the soundness of its plans and solutions and its own long experience would suffice."[1] He was one of many who shared that assessment. From a narrative developed around the idea of external expertise as the only way to promote growth, many senior officials also came to view this expert-led strategy as a "complete failure."[2] In the 1980s, Bank employees had started to read external reports by civil society organizations and NGOs more carefully, if only because the contestation was growing louder.

In terms of boundary brokering and epistemic power, Wolfensohn made unprecedented moves in meeting with NGO activists and civil society leaders on his first trip to Africa in 1995. By 2001, he sent 70 NGO liaison officers to work in the Bank's 90 country offices, and there were 120 officers by the end of 2007, which accelerated the pace of the change. Two units in Washington supported these officers: the Civil Society Team (affiliated with the External Affairs Department) and the Participation and Civic Engagement Team (affiliated with the Sustainable Development Network).[3] These teams acted as communities of practice with newly acquired epistemic power, implicitly or explicitly organizing brokering in various country teams. They were also able to share epistemic boundary objects like reports and memos about the effectiveness of country teams' inclusion of non-governmental and civil society organizations.

In 1997, Wolfensohn visited a primary school in the rural regions of Ghana that the Bank's president described as becoming an "empty shell" because of a lack of appropriation of Bank-led education projects. This encounter led him to associate many development failures with lacking community inclusion, who felt disconnected from the project or the physical facilities. Speaking to community leaders and his country team, he suspected that it could have been done otherwise:

> Governments alone cannot create a successful school; parents, teachers, the village council and the local agricultural cooperative must also contribute to

DOI: 10.4324/9781003529279-6

> its planning and administration. . . . The best-intentioned and most brilliant plans drawn in Washington without local support could never have the impact and the traction needed to change lives. If we listened more to the people in the slums and villages, and their leaders as well as their emerging civil societies, we could vastly improve the effectiveness of our interventions.[4]

While the arrival of a new president or managing director can initiate a break with past practices, an individualized and synchronic understanding of change would obscure the fact that change began before the election of James Wolfensohn and continued afterwards, in a decentralized fashion and without direct orders. He might have created anchoring practices and accelerated the speed of the change, but attributing him sole individual agency in this change would be misleading. In addition to coming from a former CoP and bringing with them intersubjective background knowledge and tools, boundary brokers' claims for change will only be effective if they find allies and receptive constituents; the same goes for board members trying to implement a new practice, even the United States. In short, hard power or institutional leverage is not always correlated with epistemic power to influence meaning-making processes. Additionally, other members of the organization will influence the new leader's thinking, making the change process more complex and intersubjective. This chapter explores the role of boundary brokering as a social process, the influence of epistemic power, and the embeddedness of boundary brokers in social relations.

Structural changes

Under Wolfensohn's tenure, further decentralization to increase the effectiveness of policy and project elaboration occurred with the 1997 Strategic Compact. The goal of this initiative, led by the CoP of top senior managers, was not only to gain more legitimacy for the Bank but also for Bank in-country CoPs to achieve greater effectiveness by being physically closer to borrowing countries' officials. As a result, country offices were given more power (e.g., authority over their budget), and transversal communities of practice were created or emerged by themselves. With new powers delegated to country offices, the Strategic Compact was designed to improve the Bank's relationship with borrowing countries' governments by reallocating more resources toward the "front line" of operations.[5] In a speech to the Bank's board of governors in 1997, Wolfensohn asserted that the compact was not about "our organization and internal change" but about "our *clients* and meeting their needs more effectively": "To take this beyond rhetoric, we have decentralized aggressively to the field."[6] In giving Bank teams more autonomy, the 1997 Strategic Compact decentralization modified their interactions with borrowing governments. Members of Bank teams were invited more frequently to in-country meetings and had more direct access to government agencies and ministries. Having larger teams in country offices also gave them more time and resources to meet with country officials.

The Strategic Compact decentralization enabled the creation of localized mechanisms for faster disbursements and procurement for partners, which impacted capacity building and interaction with civil society organizations.[7] Changes in guidelines provided project managers greater flexibility to acquire material, pay partners, and give small grants to civil society associations without waiting for bureaucratic approvals.[8] One senior Bank employee remembered a school plan she was supervising in which teachers would participate in a nationwide training program. A team manager interviewed for this research told me that teachers often skipped training sessions because they would not get reimbursed beforehand for their travels:

> So I went to a disbursement officer who had lived there for many years . . . and I said, "how can we do this?" So we created a system where people who show up, they would sign in and the day they left, they were handed money calculated on local bus fees.[9]

She explained that her team could also contract NGOs and get grants to communities much more quickly after 1997 than before. These mechanisms greatly impacted the relationship with non-state actors on the ground.

Many country office directors previously based in Washington, D.C., were sent to borrowing countries or were replaced by managers living in those countries, which changed the composition of in-country CoPs. About one-third of the employees of the Bank were relocated to field offices, from a total of 1,990 employees located outside Washington, D.C., before 1998 to 2,469 by 2001.[10] According to Wolfensohn, 18 of 48 country directors were based in their country of assignment by 2001, compared to three in 1996.[11] By 2003, three-quarters of the newly created country director jobs were in-country positions.[12] This shift in employees' physical location enabled more encounters with advocates for inclusive practices, and greater epistemic power for brokering from various communities in borrowing countries to influence Bank CoPs in Washington, D.C. With a different set of background knowledge, routines, and practices, brokering involving practitioners from various CoPs could influence their new domain of knowledge through example-setting or advocacy.

The structural reorganization also led to shifts of Bank employees from one community of practice to another inside the Bank. In doing so, boundary brokering took place when new members integrated new CoPs and enabled example-setting about the value of inclusive practices. For example, Mark Baird used his experience as a lead economist in Indonesia when he was promoted to vice president of Strategy and Resource Management in the late 1990s. Coming from a team that developed a very close relationship with the Indonesian government, he asserted in an interview with Bank archivists that the 1997 decentralization followed the Indonesia model:

> Indonesia office had the country director on the field. It had always seemed to me a natural step in this concept of country ownership. Perhaps for [James Wolfensohn] it had the added advantage of downplaying the role of the board, because it shifted power somewhat out, but for me it was much more

> about getting country directors focused on their countries and spending less time on the internal bureaucracy of the Bank.[13]

According to a senior Bank official, this more frequent interaction increased the willingness of country officials to work with Bank teams: "That has changed the dynamic. You are much closer, by definition, to the client. You live there, you talk to them all the time. That is a very big change compared to the Bank before 1997."[14] The Bank employee recalled that his office in Thailand grew from seven or eight people to about 50–60. However, his enthusiasm for decentralization decreased when he realized that, in some cases, being physically close to borrowing country officials did not translate into an equal partnership. Of course, power dynamics still exist between Bank teams and borrowing governments and between the Bank and NGOs and citizens' groups, not the least based on coloniality of power and racial hierarchies.[15]

In 1996, Wolfensohn established channels of dialogue with CoPs outside the Bank and cultivated new trans-organization CoPs, among others, with various advocacy groups on the social impacts of structural adjustment. One of these CoPs was the Structural Adjustment Participatory Review International Network. This organization later published a report on the policy roots of economic crisis and poverty based on a multiple-country participatory assessment of structural adjustment,[16] which became an epistemic boundary object. National steering committees organized an investigation of the effects of structural adjustment through public forums, field research to target specific policy impacts, and literature reviews.[17] These assessments were then discussed in national and international conferences (i.e., boundary encounters). However, this was a challenging relationship. According to Wolfensohn in 2002, these groups were disproportionally focused on criticizing the past and not enough on making recommendations to the Bank as to how it could improve its practices. He simultaneously supported and contested the conclusions of CoPs he engaged with or established, making brokering a more complex process than one person advocating for change in a straightforward cycle.

> I wish some of them would change their tune and tell us that we haven't done enough on the next level of the things that we should be doing, rather than going back to things that were addressed five years ago and to which I think we have been particularly responsive.[18]

After the 1997 decentralization, boundary encounters with external communities became more frequent. Junior Bank managers were sent on six-week courses at Stanford or Harvard universities and then to a village in a Global South country for an additional week. The goal was to reinvigorate their sense of duty toward aid recipients. This novel exercise met with much internal resistance. Mark Malloch Brown, the Bank's external relations chief in the late 1990s, believed that sending people into villages was a ludicrous idea: "Mao and Pol Pot were the only people with similar ambitions, but even they thought reeducation would take more than a week."[19] A Bank consultant advocating for more community investment also contested this specific initiative, saying it sounded "ridiculous": "So you go in the field for one week and then you come back. What has changed really?"[20] He believed in the principle of inclusiveness but did not think that sending Bank managers to African rural communities for a week would be useful in rendering Bank projects more effective. Others, including senior country officers, reportedly "rolled their eyes" at the idea.[21]

Showing the constant fluctuation of practices, while some managers thought it was a very effective way to create familiarity with aid recipients, others contested these new practices.[22] The range of responses obtained on this initiative shows how contestation for and against change can be directed at new low-level mechanisms, concepts, or ideas, which are part of a broader set of practices. For example, while some managers disagreed with all types of inclusiveness, some Bank employees did not necessarily contest "inclusive practices" as a whole (which are, after all, only an analytical category), but contested the idea of sending people into the field for one week to be closer to people living in villages in countries of the Global South. Many other inclusive practices were likewise often contested, such as the participatory poverty assessments, the inclusion of NGOs in World Bank headquarters, or the PRSPs. Many components of this set of practices, like the broad consultations involved in preparing the PRSP, failed to be institutionalized and did not persist over time mainly because of internal resistance. However, this resistance is not an indicator that "change never happened" at the Bank.

Creating more boundary spaces between CoPs

As per boundary encounters with other organizations' CoPs, Wolfensohn was the first Bank president to have regular meetings in Jackson Hole, W.Y., with the secretary general of the United Nations, including Boutros Boutros-Ghali, as well as the IMF managing director, including Michel Camdessus.[23] He recalled how these meetings led to interesting conversations about the Bank's work. Wolfensohn and Camdessus were also regularly invited to the UN's biannual meetings, followed by a dinner at Boutros-Ghali's residence. This tradition continued with the next UN Secretary General Kofi Annan, making it an anchoring practice. These types of encounters were unprecedented in the history of both institutions. In 2000, Wolfensohn also became the first Bank president to deliver a speech to the UN Security Council; as Wolfensohn described it, "These social encounters built a trust that made all our efforts more effective."[24] While the Bank is historically closer to the IMF regarding policymaking practices, the late 1990s were marked by a rapprochement with the UN, as the Bank moved closer to the UN's position on the need to include and empower governments and populations.

His narrative shift, even if it did not closely follow the Bank's practices, participated in promoting an enabling environment for change. In his first address to the board of governors at the annual meeting of the Bank and the IMF in 1995, Wolfensohn stated that the Bank must be ready to listen to criticisms and to "learn from others." He also spoke of the need to "go beyond arrogance in the development business."[25] In a speech to senior employees one year after he took office, he declared the advent of "a new atmosphere of change": "We are open. We are flexible. We want to listen."[26] This speech shifted the narrative, which led communities inside the Bank to push for greater inclusion of aid-targeted populations and empowered communities outside the Bank to demand more institutional accountability.

Wolfensohn was not alone in brokering change at the boundaries between communities, internally and externally. In a speech at a conference in Germany in 1991 on the contribution of sociologists in development institutions, senior manager Michael Cernea mentioned that after 16 years of working at the Bank, the view of "in-house" sociologists by Bank employees has changed tremendously: "It changed from seeing them as the Bank's own luxury species, valued for its ranty but not really relevant to the daily struggle in the project trenches, to treating them as respected and desirable (although sometimes troublesome) professionals."[27] The evolution of the Bank's perspective regarding NGOs was similar.

Another example, in a speech at People's University in Beijing in 2001, Nicholas Stern, Bank chief economist, defined a two-pillar strategy for pro-poor growth: [1] good climate for investment and productivity growth and [2] empowerment.[28] This could have never been part of the official narrative of the Bank a decade prior. In what Stern called a new strategy for development, he emphasized that the goal of researchers at the Bank "should be to understand how people have succeeded in empowering themselves; it is not for us to instruct people on their own empowerment."[29] Stern stated that the new motto, to put "country in the driver's seat," was leading the Bank on the path toward "a major reappraisal and recasting of its relationship with client countries."[30] The main takeaway of Stern's speech was that the Bank had evolved and was still evolving toward a broader and deeper understanding of development. Stern and others' support of Wolfensohn's contestation claims and shift in narrative was paramount in accelerating the institutionalization of inclusive practices.

Between 1980 and 2010, and especially during his tenure from 1995 to 2005, Wolfensohn incorporated a growing number of new employees with backgrounds from the social sciences, community organizations, or civil society into the Bank. By doing so, he was accelerating boundary brokering for inclusive practices. This change in employees' background impacted the Bank's collective learning processes about the effectiveness of consulting with civil society organizations and NGOs. Except if they formed an *ad hoc* CoP, these new employees participated in brokering by bringing their resources and background knowledge into the Bank. They acted in the boundary space between their previous CoPs and their new CoPs in the Bank. Their competence was increasingly recognized as they moved to the center of their communities and gained institutional legitimacy.

After the Strategic Compact of 1997, the shift in employees and the amount of boundary brokering accelerated. From 1997 to 2002, more than 4,500 people left the Bank, and 3,800 were hired.[31] Many Bank employees noted that after having hired many economists in the 1980s, it became "normal" to have Indigenous specialists, sociologists, former NGO workers, or gender specialists in later years.[32] These boundary brokers, and the recomposition of existing communities of practice, are credited with setting examples of participatory methodologies and creating an "internal constituency" that would promote new policy tools for participation. A senior economist at the Bank explained that this movement of employees "sort of set the stage, more than anything else I can think of."[33] While the recognition of Wolfensohn's impact on inclusive practices is commonplace among Bank employees, how they define his impact often relies on its role in changing the composition of the Bank. Speaking only of Wolfensohn as enactor of change would be like speaking only of the butterfly's wings in a butterfly effect.

Coming from various external CoPs with expertise uncommon in the Bank at the time, new practitioners came with new background knowledge, routines, and resources to draw on. According to Michael Cernea, sociologists and anthropologists carried "a distinct professional knowledge about social organization, social structure, and social and cultural change."[34] These differences were not only based on professional training.[35] New employees had different background knowledge and tools developed in CoPs from different countries, sites, and fields, which were often unfamiliar to more senior Bank employees. They became involved in many CoPs inside the Bank (in-country teams, poverty assessment teams, evaluation teams) and they started to form their own CoP in various units and departments (e.g., the NGO Unit, Social Policy Division, Civil Society Team, Participation and Civic Engagement Team). Brokering happened primarily tacitly, in day-to-day practices, instead of being open and vocal. In teams with economists or in various country teams, sociologists and anthropologists influenced their new CoP toward considering social aspects of development and using consultative methodologies.

Boundary encounters like international or multipartite conferences between multiple CoPs also led Bank employees to learn faster about the effectiveness of including non-governmental actors. They would be presented with successes in projects where the relationship with those actors became a partnership. Collective learning in borrowing countries could then be scaled up through Bank-wide conferences and events. Anne Krueger, vice president for Economics and Research (1982–1987), calls this the spillover effect:

> [T]here is a lot of spillover back and forth, and certainly the lessons of experience were very important in terms of what we were researching and research results, finding out what worked and what didn't, and that was, I think, quite useful and used quite open in operations, as well as being disseminated through conferences and activities.[36]

Narrative shifts

A shift in the Bank management's narrative also contributed to the institutionalization of inclusive practices in Bank practices. While there is no straightforward "translation into practice" of texts or discourse,[37] new ways to talk about the purpose of the Bank gave the Bank's actions new intelligibility (i.e., how employees made sense of their work and what actions were considered most appropriate). An organization's narrative can be analytically reconstructed through three forms of discourse: coordinative discourse among senior officials, management, and employees; communicative discourse between the organization and the public; and stories told by employees about how their organization perceives itself and its mission. Therefore, if the narrative of an organization is most visible in official communications, it is also present in how managers and employees talk about the organization and its evolution. Methodologically, an international organization's narrative can thus be found in public speeches, official publications, and internal documents, as well as in how employees reconstruct their organization's narrative in interviews.

Bank presidents' discursive shifts contributed to the acceleration of initiatives already in motion in many Bank quarters. From the 1980s to the 2000s, higher management's narrative of the Bank evolved from a technocratic posture to one where they acknowledged ownership as more effective, desirable, and encouraged. Before this shift, the narrative was that Bank experts can help borrowing countries with technocratic solutions. In his 1983 address to the board of governors of the World Bank and the International Finance Corporation, then president Alden W. Clausen mentioned the need for "sharing [our] knowledge" to "help countries" and, by doing so, "touching the lives of hundreds of millions of people in the Third World."[38] The Bank's knowledge was to be shared, and only Bank's experts could "help countries." In 1986, his successor, Barber Conable, despite talking of "partnership" and "collaboration," stated in a speech to the board of governors that it is the Bank that "must deal with these problems with resolve and a clear sense of direction."[39] The "direction" that must be taken should, therefore, not be set by borrowing governments but by Bank experts.

As one columnist at the *Washington Post* states, Bank officials in the 1980s were more interested in projecting a particular image to Bank directors than to ministers in borrowing governments.[40] Brushing off criticisms concerning the one-size-fits-all or "cookbook" character of its policies, especially the policy framework paper, Bank officials would argue that similar problems required similar solutions. According to critics of the Bank, the uniformity in the Bank's poverty analysis should therefore not come as a surprise, given the posture of the Bank.[41]

Following Lewis T. Preston's sudden death in 1995, James Wolfensohn became the ninth president of the World Bank. The Australian banker wrote in his biography that, inspired by the presidency of Robert McNamara, he believed that the core of the World Bank's agenda should be the elimination of poverty, which led him early in his first tenure to adopt a new motto for the organization: "A World Free of Poverty."[42] Often ridiculed for his naïve optimism, his goals were called "magical unrealism" by external observers and long-time Bank employees alike.[43] Although described as very hierarchical in his dealings with Bank employees or managers, he often contested the Bank's existing top-down practices.

Because he was a banker who rarely had to deal with social issues, most of Wolfensohn's views on development, empowerment, and inclusion came from intuitions and experiences from his travels after being appointed president of the World Bank. For example, the first thing he did upon his appointment as president was to go to borrowing countries, and he traveled more than any other Bank president. While he was trained in similar fields as previous presidents, Wolfensohn was determined to get out of Washington and listen to borrowing governments. People already working at the Bank influenced his thinking on inclusivity issues. When he announced that he would go to Africa for his first official visit, Bank headquarters sent memos to field offices in the region to summon everyone to "make a case for inclusion on the presidential itinerary."[44]

In the end, his brokering had an indubitable impact on the Bank's openness to inclusion and ownership. He instituted a new discursive custom of talking about aid-targeted populations rather than solely their governments in public speeches. In 1997, his rethoric went even further.

> We must accept that the projects are not donor or World Bank projects – they are Costa Rican projects, Bangladeshi projects, or Chinese projects. And development projects and programs must be fully owned by local stakeholders if they are to succeed.[45]

A year later, at the 1998 annual meeting of the board of governors, he advocated for the participation of borrowing governments in policymaking, using arguments about the effectiveness of development projects:

> Participation matters, not only as a means of improving development effectiveness, as we know from our recent studies, but as the key to long-term sustainability and leverage. We must never stop reminding ourselves that it is up to the government and its people to decide what their priorities should be. We must never stop reminding ourselves that we cannot and should not impose development by fiat from above – or from abroad.[46]

Wolfensohn initiated a major discursive shift on the goal and purpose of the Bank, compared to his predecessors who never mentioned the involvement of all stakeholders as a factor for the success of Bank projects. In a 1999 discussion draft for the board of directors and World Bank staff entitled *A Proposal for a Comprehensive Development Framework*, he stated that ownership was essential: "Countries must be in the driver's seat and set the course. They must determine the goals and the phasing, timing and sequencing of programs."[47] He first pompously called the comprehensive development framework the *New Development Framework*. The framework encompassed four main elements: a holistic definition of development (based on more than economic stabilization and structural adjustment); ownership of reforms by borrowing governments; partnerships between all stakeholders (governments, multilateral agencies, civil societies, and the private sector); and results-based management of development programs. However, as noted by observers and Bank employees,[48] nothing was purely new in the comprehensive development framework, and it lacked a concrete plan to operationalize the recommendations.[49] A long-time employee at the Bank confirmed that the comprehensive development framework was "a lot of talking, not necessarily a lot of action."[50]

While the impact of this narrative shift should not be overemphasized, it enabled Bank employees in many quarters to implement participatory or consultative practices. Wolfensohn's capacity to be recognized as competent and thus generate epistemic power reinforced this narrative. This was also partially due to his positionality and social position in the hierarchy of the organization.

To underscore the importance of narratives, many Bank employees and officials interviewed for this research now use expressions publicly formulated by Wolfensohn to describe the Bank's trajectory during that period, such as the fact that he wanted to put borrowing governments "in the driver's seat."[51] This formulation was repeated in speeches and internal documents by other boundary brokers. From attributing the success of projects to the quality of the Bank's employees or the organization's capacity to cope with crises, Bank managers and employees started to attribute success to projects with governments "on board."[52] It is important to note the discrepancy, or the so-called hypocrisy, between the Bank talk and its practice, but the role of changes in the narrative of senior officials in practice also needs to be recognized.

A senior manager then formulated the probability of success of a project: "It depends on the context of ownership by the country. Some really good ones with lots and lots of ownership have helped countries absorb and used billions of dollars."[53] Ownership referred not only to the government but also to the entire population. As was clear to external activists for two decades by then, many Bank employees also believed that this official recognition of the need to tone down the arrogance was long overdue. One senior Bank official said that the Bank needed to remember that "the client is the country": The client is not the minister of finance, it's not just the government. It is the country." For him, this growing realization was a "pivotal moment" in the history of the Bank.[54]

The shift in Wolfensohn's discourse about the organization promoted new practices at the Bank and gave more epistemic power to boundary brokering. The epistemic impact of Wolfensohn's philosophy was often acknowledged in interviews for this research:

> Wow, I said: that comes from Wolfensohn, the president of the World Bank, a guy from Wall Street. He had such a deep belief in the agency of civil society in development that he was willing to push the Bank into new territory in terms of the imperative of increasing participatory approaches.[55]

However, as will be explored in the conclusion, Wolfensohn and other senior officials sometimes referred to a type of empowerment based on power-sharing that was never institutionalized; hence the narrative went in a direction that was not fully implemented in practice. As one NGO worker described it, what the Bank says is often "more plural" than what it does.[56] In his first term, Wolfensohn used buzzwords and phrases such as "public participation," "borrowing governments in the driver's seat," and "empowerment." By contrast, in his second term, Wolfensohn talked more often about scaling up best practices and learning from each other, a formulation that assumes that some best practices could be reproduced in multiple contexts instead of each community having a completely unique and truly "empowered" plan.[57]

From the mid-2000s to 2014, the narrative moved toward less politicized words like inclusion and consultation instead of empowerment. However, the 10th Bank president, Paul Wolfowitz, followed his predecessor in often mentioning civil societies and civil society organizations in most of his speeches: "In every country I have visited, civil society organizations offered a wealth of experience in learning, adapting, sharing knowledge, and contributing to growth in their local communities."[58] Speaking less of empowerment and participation, he emphasized "capacity building" and "consultation."[59]

His successor, Robert B. Zoellick, elected 11th president of the World Bank on July 1, 2007, always illustrated his speeches in boundary encounters with examples of people targeted by aid projects: "These are the human faces of the World Bank Group. They may be far from our capitals and conference halls, but they are at the heart of our mission to offer dignity and hope."[60] He emphasized that the Bank should listen more carefully to the voices of borrowing governments' officials and reflect better specific contexts.

> If developing countries are part of the solution, they must also be part of the conversation. The international system needs a World Bank Group that represents the international economic realities of the 21st century, recognizes the role and responsibility of growing stakeholders, and provides a larger voice for Africa.[61]

In sum, the narrative of the Bank, as told in official discourse and by employees, went from "old-fashioned thinking"[62] or a "traditional economic perspective"[63] toward being more open and "client-focused."[64] One senior official assured me that this rhetorical shift increased the perceived legitimacy of Bank teams in borrowing countries and that their daily language reflected this change:

> Some of it was even in our language. We would talk about going "on a mission." This is an interesting choice of words! Today, someone is actually sitting and working in Nairobi. The person goes to the Ministry of Finance, the Ministry of Trade, and the Central Bank. That's not really "a mission," that is just a person doing their job.[65]

The usefulness of examining the ontological narrative is not only to understand the evolution of the self-interpretation of Bank officials or to underline how it differs from one period to the next. The narrative is a set of discourses and understandings *about that evolution* or that historicity. The discourses were not only about the intrinsic effectiveness or lack thereof of including aid-borrowing governments in policymaking but also about the evolution of what is associated with effectiveness. Moreover, this shift in the narrative was not only top-down but also shared by mid-level managers. For example, Caroline Robb, one of the first IMF development specialists, said the following about the Bank's practices in the late 1990s:

> [M]any development practitioners and policymakers did not believe that including the poor in the policy dialogue was credible or even feasible. Since then, there has been a shift in the development thinking: the debate has moved from explaining why the poor *should* be included to *how* they *can* be included.[66]

As explained earlier, the relationship between practices and narratives is constitutive in that neither has ontological nor temporal precedence over the other. The shift in how Bank leaders, report writers, and employees talked about the Bank, its mission, and development corroborated with existing tendencies toward more inclusion of a multiplicity of actors in a repertoire of practices. Narratives and practices are related in three crucial ways. First, an evolving narrative enables new world intelligibility by opening spaces of possibilities for new practices. Second, the shift in narrative legitimized initiatives and practices already in motion and supported their multiplication. Third, it had a signaling effect on internal and external audiences that new practices could or should be implemented. On the one hand, the evolution of the Bank's narrative gave reasons for new practices to emerge and empowered individual Bank employees to establish new practices of participation and decentralization. On the other hand, the acceleration and institutionalization of inclusive practices stabilized and legitimized the shift in narrative toward a more country-focused stance. As one Bank manager put it, some people "think that the rhetoric runs ahead of the practice. That is not fair. Because in certain quarters, the practice ran ahead of the rhetoric."[67]

As one senior Bank official said, the official discourse about the Bank gave employees a "strong sense of what is correct, what is right" to do or not to do.[68] For another, when Wolfensohn said that "the country is the client and not the ministries" and that "civil society is probably the largest factor of development," he thought to himself: "Wow, this is a pivotal moment in the way the leadership of the Bank conceptualizes who the client is."[69] While this new narrative did not change practices overnight, it signaled to Bank employees that the organization's managers, and especially Wolfensohn, were "willing to push the Bank into new territory in terms of the imperative of increasing participatory approaches."[70]

Epistemic power in practice

Wolfensohn participated in many brokering processes of new practices, both by advocating for them and by contesting existing ones.[71] Alexander Shakow, former executive secretary for the development committee, believed that Wolfensohn's arrival changed the "interplay between people inside and outside" of the Bank regarding policy formulation.[72] NGOs dealing with the World Bank also recognize Wolfensohn as catalyzing the adoption of inclusive practices. In the mid-2000s, Justin Forsyth, an Oxfam official, recalled that no Bank managers would listen to his calls for debt relief before Wolfensohn became president.[73] Even though Wolfensohn was eventually criticized for not responding to all the concerns of NGOs, he still "broke the log jam" and advocated for change in management circles.[74] In his comprehensive development framework, Wolfensohn advocated for more partnerships with borrowing governments and more consultation with NGOs. His goal of embracing NGOs as partners, which was one of his new "commanding objectives," went against what the Bank was doing with the structural adjustment programs in the decades before his arrival.[75]

Wolfensohn had both the material means and the epistemic power to contest existing knowledge and to advocate for Bank practices to move in specific directions. Therefore, his contestation claims might have been more successful than those of other Bank practitioners, even senior managers. However, it would be unfair to picture Wolfensohn as the sole contester of the Bank's top-down policy-making practices. Far from being a lone wolf crying for change, he was part of an ongoing social process. His recognized competence and social position allowed him to accelerate the change's speed. Speaking about NGOs' and borrowing governments' calls for debt-relief practices without strict conditionalities, former vice president for Poverty Reduction and Economic Management, Masood Ahmed, argued that Wolfensohn "definitely accelerated the pace at which something was done. Without him, we would have dragged this out before we managed to confront it."[76] Both internal and external actors consider him to have had a strong influence in disrupting existing practices. According to a former Oxfam director of research, Wolfensohn's "political conviction, leadership, courage, and – at times – sheer bloody mindedness, were pivotal. . . . He really opened the door."[77] Wolfensohn strongly believed that to be successful, the Bank had to change the way it interacted with external stakeholders.

The CoP of senior Bank managers who were usually proponents of more inclusiveness, sometimes resisted change initiated by new members of their own community with more hierarchical power but less able to generate epistemic power in boundary brokering. For example, during a trip to Côte d'Ivoire after being elected Bank president, Wolfensohn was overtly critical of the Bank's work and suggested greater debt reduction to give borrowing governments more leeway to implement innovative development plans. Senior Bank officials resisted this suggestion; for former vice president for financial policy, Johannes Linn, it came from Wolfensohn's background as a banker and the fact that he saw the World Bank as a traditional Bank: "He [Wolfensohn] had the view that if you had a bad debt, you need to think about writing it off and taking a hit." Linn was receiving contestation from NGOs and the Bank's president. He added that the president came to that conclusion while visiting highly indebted countries and hearing complaints from NGOs.

> Mr. Wolfensohn kept pushing us, and so I remember that [we] were getting quite desperate. We recognized, on the one side, the hard financial view. . . . And on the other side, . . . [his] insistence that we needed to address this issue.[78]

Epitomizing the struggle between new and established ideas, a fight about debt reduction eventually erupted between Wolfensohn and the then vice president of the Africa Region, Edward Jaycox:

> When Wolfensohn yelled at Jaycox, Jaycox just yelled back: "Wake up, Jim. Wake up. That's the way it works. You may not like it, but that's the way it works," he screamed. . . . "I agree [that not giving debt relief] is pretty damn stupid." . . . "But that's the way it is around here. If I talked about debt relief, I'd have my balls cut off by Ernie Stern [then managing director], so I am not going to take this."[79]

Jaycox, who on other occasions was a strong advocate for inclusive practices, sometimes resisted change toward giving more power to borrowing governments on situations like this one. Thus, practical contestation is not always based on the value or appropriateness of a specific norm, idea, or practice – despite how norm contestation or the logic of arguing has been portrayed in IR. In day-to-day actions, contestation can be based on working conditions, personal feuds, or deep-seated anger against the organization promoting an idea. These less normative reasons for contesting are an important yet often unacknowledged part of how practices evolve in international organizations.

Contestation often arose not only from cognitive or normative disagreements over policies or projects, some believed to be futile or ineffective, but also from personal feelings of discomfort with a new practice or tool. Wolfensohn sometimes resisted Bank employees attempting changes toward inclusive practices, especially the Poverty Reduction Strategy Papers, which he believed were competing against his comprehensive development framework.[80] One Bank manager who worked on framing the poverty reduction strategy recalls that Wolfensohn "hated" the poverty reduction strategy, namely because he had the impression that it stole the thunder from his comprehensive development framework.[81] In the end, a working paper presented to the board of directors described the new poverty reduction strategy as a way to "operationalize" the comprehensive development framework, and the PRSP concept was eventually accepted in December 1999 by the board.[82]

While studying an individual leader's influence as a boundary broker (or norm entrepreneur) is analytically helpful to understand change, individuals—no matter how powerful—cannot control the complexity of bureaucratic practices and collective learning processes in CoPs. A senior Bank economist recalled that James Wolfensohn brought about many changes, but many others happened before his arrival: "It isn't that Wolfensohn said all of a sudden, 'Hey, you guys, you need to do some consultation once and for all.' There was social change happening."[83] Even the strongest leader will be unable to impose their priorities on a massive organization like the World Bank, and employees in such large bureaucracies have their own peer groups that have reasons to avoid strictly following top-down instructions.[84]

Hired by Wolfensohn in 1997, the former chief economist Joseph Stiglitz participated in contesting many of the Bank's top-down practices in boundary encounters. According to one senior Bank economist, Stiglitz was an "internal force" for change within the Bank.[85] An article in *The Economist* said he made "a great nuisance of himself" because of his harsh criticisms of top-down programs.[86] Among other things, he strongly contested one-size-fits-all policies and promoted democratic processes within the Bank. Again, showing how practices and allyship can fluctuate, while Wolfensohn was originally all ears to Stiglitz's complaints, Stiglitz became too vocal about his disagreements with the Bank's management community, and he was eventually forced to resign. Practice contestation should be understood as a two-way process that creates fluctuations instead of a teleological cycle or a trajectory of change.

Even if the competence of a contester is well recognized, as in the case of Stiglitz, their contestation claim may only be visible in the long term because they open new conceptual spaces for new practices or establish anchoring practices.[87] However, "unsuccessful contestation" is rarely acknowledged as significant in IR theory. A senior Bank economist remembered that because of Stiglitz's robust positions and expertise in economic theory, Stiglitz opened a space for others to criticize the one-size-fits-all and top-down market fundamentalist positions prevalent within the Bank: "Then he left and this kind of strong contestation became more moderate. But we never went back to the classic Washington Consensus."[88]

Stiglitz even talked of "radical changes in thinking about development policy, as compared with the ideas inherited from the 1980s".[89] While he is now far from being a World Bank advocate, having repeatedly criticized the institution, since his departure in 1999, he qualifies the early 2000s as a "new development paradigm." In the introduction to a book about the World Bank's structure and policies, he underscores the new emphasis on ownership and participation in the decision-making process and the fact that since changes in ways of thinking cannot be imposed, "successful development cannot be based on conditionality."[90]

Conclusion

As many Bank employees interviewed for this research explained, shifts in the official discourse by presidents and senior officials were crucial to "shaping the patterns" or "shifting the ethos," more than changing operational practices *per se*.[91] Many said that the shift in language at higher levels "created an atmosphere" of openness, which in turn created more internal debates about the organization's practice. As one manager explained, this new narrative made it "a lot easier to engage with critics of the Bank."[92] It became accepted and encouraged. As one senior manager explained, change was happening simultaneously in many quarters: "It isn't that the Bank thought all of a sudden, 'Hey, isn't consultation a good idea?' or that Mr. Wolfensohn said, 'Hey, you guys need to do some consultation once and for all!'"[93] Therefore, this narrative shift – promoted first at the top and adopted in many quarters of the Bank – did not *cause* a shift in practice but *contributed to* the multiplication of such practices and formal consultation tools, as well as their institutionalization.

This chapter aimed to show that the practice and narrative shift toward inclusivity did not happen smoothly or in perfect unison across the Bank. Even if a president like Wolfensohn, senior managers, official publications, and employees adopt a narrative that tends toward a specific set of ideals (e.g., real decentralization and empowerment), that may not mean a perfect application into practice. The mid-1990s saw increased mentions of empowerment, context-specific knowledge, and ownership in public speeches and publications. However, the requirement of broad-based participation for loans or debt reduction stopped with the end of the Highly Indebted Poor Countries initiative and the PRSP in 2014, and the narrative became less ambitious in the mid-2000s and the 2010s.

Notes

1 Wolfensohn, *A Global Life*, 259.
2 Interview 20, July 17, 2017.
3 (Ebrahim and Herz 2007, 19).
4 Wolfensohn, 337.
5 Nielson et al., "Bridging the Rationalist–Constructivist Divide," 116.
6 Wolfensohn, "The Challenge of Inclusion," 6.
7 Aycrigg, "Participation and the World Bank Success, Constraints, and Responses," 90.
8 Interview 31, November 6, 2017.
9 Interview 31, November 6, 2017.
10 Nielson et al., 123.
11 Nielson et al., 123.
12 Phillips, *Reforming the World Bank*, 283.
13 Interview OHP Mark Baird, May 5–6, 2010, 48.
14 Interview 33, November 7, 2017.
15 Sondarjee, "Coloniality of Epistemic Power in International Practices."
16 SAPRIN, "The Policy Roots of Economic Crisis and Poverty."
17 Aycrigg, 33.
18 Cited in Phillips, 124.
19 Mallaby, *The World's Banker*, 165.
20 Interview 36, November 10, 2017.
21 Interview 31, November 6, 2017.
22 Interview 31, November 6, 2017; Interview 35, November 9, 2017.
23 Wolfensohn, 349.
24 Wolfensohn, 349.
25 Wolfensohn, "New Directions and New Partnerships," 8.
26 Mallaby, 147.
27 Cernea, "Sociologists in a Development Agency," 28–29.
28 Stern, "A Strategy for Development," 1.
29 Stern, 18.
30 Stern, 19.
31 Phillips, 114.
32 Interview 6, May 27, 2017; Interview 9, June 9, 2017; Interview 21, July 19, 2017; Interview 24, July 21, 2017; Interview OHP Gloria Davis, June 28–29, 2004; Interview OHP Daniel Gross, April 30, 2008.
33 Interview 9, June 9, 2017.

34 Cernea, 28.
35 Sarfaty, "Doing Good Business or Just Doing Good: Competing Human Rights Frameworks at the World Bank."
36 Interview OHP Anne Krueger, January 29, 2010.
37 Bebbington et al., "Of Texts and Practices: Empowerment and Organisational Cultures in World Bank-Funded Rural Development Programmes," 614.
38 Clausen, "Progress and Innovation," 16–18.
39 Conable, "To the Board of Governors," 32–36.
40 Mallaby, 149.
41 Bajaj and Panchamukhi, "Aid in the 1990's with Special Reference to World Bank and IDA," 61.
42 Wolfensohn.
43 Mallaby, 5.
44 Mallaby, 92.
45 Wolfensohn, 6.
46 Wolfensohn, "The Other Crisis," 116.
47 Cited in Lie, "Developmentality," 726.
48 Interview 34, November 8, 2017.
49 World Bank, *1999 Annual Review of Development Effectiveness*, xii.; Mallaby.
50 World Bank, xii; Mallaby.
51 Wolfensohn, 116; Wolfensohn, "A Proposal for a Comprehensive Development Framework"; Stern, 19; Interview 20, July 17, 2017.
52 Interview 20, July 17, 2017.
53 Interview 31, November 6, 2017.
54 Interview 15, June 27, 2017.
55 Interview 15, June 27, 2017.
56 Interview 11, June 15, 2017.
57 Wolfensohn, "Scaling Up the Fight against Poverty"; Wolfensohn, "Securing the 21st Century, Protecting the Planet".
58 Wolfowitz, "Charting a Way Ahead – The Results Agenda," 3.
59 Wolfowitz, "Improving Governance and Fighting Corruption," 2.
60 Zoellick, "Opening Remarks," 2.
61 Zoellick, "The World Bank Group Beyond the Crisis," 9.
62 Interview 39, November 14, 2017.
63 Interview 41, November 21, 2017.
64 Interview 33, November 7, 2017.
65 Interview 33, November 7, 2017.
66 Robb, *Can the Poor Influence Policy?* xv.
67 Interview 14, June 26, 2017.
68 Interview 39, November 14, 2017.
69 Interview 15, July 16, 2017.
70 Interview 15, July 16, 2017.
71 Kagia, *Balancing the Development Agenda*; Mallaby; Bazbauers, "Leading the World Bank: The Wolfensohn, Wolfowitz, and Zoellick Presidencies."
72 Interview OHP Alexander Shakow, March 19–20, 2002, 6.
73 Mallaby, 60.
74 Mallaby, 60.
75 Interview OHP Thomas Blinkhorn, June 16–18, 2008.
76 Mallaby, 436.
77 Mallaby, 436.
78 Interview OHP Johannes Linn, April 6 and 13 2004, 37.
79 Mallaby, 105.
80 Mallaby, 236; Phillips, 133.

81 Interview 34, November 8, 2017.
82 Minutes World Bank Board of Governors, R99–214, December 10, 1999.
83 Interview 26, July 24, 2017.
84 Miller-Adams, *The World Bank*, 91.
85 Interview 21, July 19, 2017.
86 The Economist, "The Bumpy Ride of Joe Stiglitz."
87 Swidler, "What Anchors Cultural Practices"; Sending and Neumann, "Banking on Power: How Some Practices in an International Organization Anchor Others," 237.
88 Swidler; Sending and Neumann, 237.
89 Gilbert and Vines, *The World Bank*, 1.
90 Bajaj and Panchamukhi, 2.
91 Interview 31, November 6, 2017; Interview 41, November 21, 2017.
92 Interview 41, November 21, 2017.
93 Interview 26, July 24, 2017.

References

Aycrigg, Maria. "Participation and the World Bank Success, Constraints, and Responses." In *Draft for Discussion at the International Conference on Upscaling and Mainstreaming Participation: Lessons Learned and Ways Forward*. Washington, DC: The World Bank, 1998.

Bajaj, J. L., and V. R. Panchamukhi. *Aid in the 1990's with Special Reference to World Bank and IDA*. New Delhi, India: Research and Information System for the Non-Aligned and Other Developing Countries (RIS), 1990.

Bazbauers, Adrian Robert. "Leading the World Bank: The Wolfensohn, Wolfowitz, and Zoellick Presidencies." *International Journal of Economic Sciences* 1, no. 1 (2012): 2–18.

Bebbington, Anthony, David Lewis, Simon Batterbury, Elizabeth Olson, and M. Shameem Siddiqi. "Of Texts and Practices: Empowerment and Organisational Cultures in World Bank-Funded Rural Development Programmes." *The Journal of Development Studies* 43, no. 4 (May 2007): 597–621.

Cernea, Michael M. "Sociologists in a Development Agency." In *Workshop Proceedings*, 28–38. Eschbom, Germany: GTZ Germany, 1991.

Clausen, Alden. "Progress and Innovation." Address to the Board of Governors at the Annual Meetings of the World Bank and IMF, Washington, DC, September 27, 1983, 16–18.

Conable, Barber. "To the Board of Governors." Address to the Board of Governors at the Annual Meetings of the World Bank and IMF, Washington, DC, September 30, 1986, 32–36.

Ebrahim, Alnoor, and Steven Herz. *Accountability in Complex Organizations: World Bank Responses to Civil Society*. Cambridge, Harvard University: J.F.K. School of Government Faculty Research Working Paper Series, 2007.

Gilbert, Christopher L., and David Vines, eds. *The World Bank: Structure and Policies*. Digitally printed 1. paperback version. Global Economic Institutions. Cambridge: Cambridge University Press, 2006.

Kagia, Ruth, ed. *Balancing the Development Agenda: The Transformation of the World Bank under James D. Wolfensohn, 1995–2005*. Washington, DC: The World Bank, 2005.

Lie, Jon Harald Sande. "Developmentality: Indirect Governance in the World Bank–Uganda Partnership." *Third World Quarterly* 36, no. 4 (April 3, 2015): 723–40.

Mallaby, Sebastian. *The World's Banker: A Story of Failed States, Financial Crises, and the Wealth and Poverty of Nations*. London, UK: The Penguin Press, 2006.

Miller-Adams, Michelle. *The World Bank: New Agendas in a Changing World*. London: Routledge, 1999.

Nielson, Daniel L, Michael J Tierney, and Catherine E Weaver. "Bridging the Rationalist–Constructivist Divide: Re-Engineering the Culture of the World Bank." *Journal of International Relations and Development* 9, no. 2 (June 2006): 107–39.

Phillips, David A. *Reforming the World Bank: Twenty Years of Trial -- and Error*. New York: Cambridge University Press, 2009.

Robb, Caroline M. *Can the Poor Influence Policy? Participatory Poverty Assessments in the Developing World*. 2nd ed. Washington, DC: International Monetary Fund : World Bank, 2002.

SAPRIN. *The Policy Roots of Economic Crisis and Poverty*. Washington, DC: Structural Adjustment Participatory Review International Network (SAPRIN), 2002.

Sarfaty, Galit A. "Doing Good Business or Just Doing Good: Competing Human Rights Frameworks at the World Bank." In *The Intersection of Rights and Regulation: New Directions in Sociolegal Scholarship*, edited by Bronwen Morgan, 1st ed., 93–106. London and New York: Routledge, 2017. https://doi.org/10.4324/9781351146289.

Sending, Ole Jacob, and Iver B. Neumann. "Banking on Power: How Some Practices in an International Organization Anchor Others." In *International Practices*, edited by Emanuel Adler and Vincent Pouliot, 231–54. New York: Cambridge University Press, 2011.

Sondarjee, Maïka. "Coloniality of Epistemic Power in International Practices: NGO Inclusion in World Bank Policymaking." *Global Society* 38, no. 3 (2024): 328–50. https://doi.org/10.1080/13600826.2023.2236129.

Stern, Nicholas. "A Strategy for Development." Speech at People's University, Beijing, June 2001, 1.

Swidler, Ann. "What Anchors Cultural Practices." In *The Practice Turn in Contemporary Theory.*, edited by Karin Knorr Cetina, Theodore Richard Schatzki, and Eike Von Savigny. New York: Routledge, 2000.

Tenney, Sarah, and Anne C. M. Salda. *Historical Dictionary of the World Bank*. 2nd ed. Historical Dictionaries of International Organizations. Lanham: The Scarecrow Press, Inc., 2014.

The Economist. "The Bumpy Ride of Joe Stiglitz." *The Economist*, December 16, 1999, sec. Finance and economics.

Wolfensohn, James. "New Directions and New Partnerships." Address to the Board of Governors at the Annual Meetings of the World Bank and IMF, Washington, DC, October 10, 1995, 8.

Wolfensohn, James. "The Challenge of Inclusion." Address to the Board of Governors at the Annual Meetings of the World Bank and IMF, Washington, DC, September 23, 1997, 6.

Wolfensohn, James. "The Other Crisis." Address to the Board of Governors at the Annual Meetings of the World Bank and IMF, Washington, DC, October 6, 1998, 116.

Wolfensohn, James. "A Proposal for a Comprehensive Development Framework." Address to the Board of Governors at the Annual Meetings of the World Bank and IMF, Washington, DC, January 21, 1999.

Wolfensohn, James. "Scaling Up the Fight against Poverty." Opening Remarks at the Shanghai Conference on Scaling Up Poverty Reduction, Shanghai, May 26, 2004.

Wolfensohn, James. "Securing the 21st Century, Protecting the Planet." Address to the Board of Governors at the Annual Meetings of the World Bank and IMF, Washington, DC, October 3, 2004.

Wolfensohn, James. *A Global Life: My Journey among Rich and Poor, from Sydney to Wall Street to the World Bank*. 1st ed. New York: PublicAffairs, 2010.

Wolfowitz, Paul. "Charting a Way Ahead – The Results Agenda." Address to the Board of Governors at the Annual Meetings of the World Bank and IMF, Washington, DC, September 24, 2005, 3.

Wolfowitz, Paul. "Improving Governance and Fighting Corruption." Keynote Speech, International Conference on Improving Governance and Fighting Corruption, Brussels, March 14, 2007, 2.

World Bank. *1999 Annual Review of Development Effectiveness.* Washington, DC: The World Bank, 2002.
Zoellick, Robert. "Opening Remarks." Address to the Board of Governors at the Annual Meetings of the World Bank and IMF, Washington, DC, October 22, 2007, 2.
Zoellick, Robert. "The World Bank Group beyond the Crisis." Address to the Board of Governors at the Annual Meetings of the World Bank and IMF, Istanbul, October 6–7, 2009, 9.

7 Contestation in and of practices

Collective learning is only sometimes a smooth process of negotiating meaning at the boundaries of communities of practice. As in other international organizations, Bank employees interviewed for this research described conflict and contestation as defining features of their work in their communities of practice (CoPs). One senior manager stated that there is "plenty" of conflict among Bank employees, adding that there is contestation both regarding day-to-day practices and the Bank's overall approach: "Everybody questions everybody else. There is a lot of internal debate and criticism."[1] Another one said without hesitation,

> Yes, that's the entire job! You agree on some parameters, and then you find difficulties, and some people have some ideas about how to fix it, and some others have other ideas on ways to fix it. And you try to understand, and you agree somewhere in the middle.[2]

When asked if they often dealt with conflicts or opposition with colleagues, all Bank employees interviewed for this research answered in the affirmative: internal contestation is a defining feature of their day-to-day activities. This acknowledgment of constant debate about workplace dynamics challenges studies that portray the World Bank as monolithic or even as a coherent organization that states can manage with a clear sense of direction. In the 1990s, with the hiring of more sociologists and anthropologists, the institution made itself especially vulnerable to internal contestation. These new employees not only showed old-timers that inclusive practices were more successful through example-setting; they also contested top-down practices on a day-to-day basis. What became visible in conversations with Bank employees from various CoPs is that what is meant by "organizational actors" is often far more heterogeneous and conflictual than what is contained within organizational walls.

Collective learning can thus be linked to practical contestation, whether from individuals inside the organization or from outsiders. In addition to verbalized normative contestation, contesters also showed Bank employees in various CoPs that they could no longer continue to do business-as-usual if they wanted to remain relevant, through direct or indirect contestation in boundary encounters and brokering.

DOI: 10.4324/9781003529279-7

This process triggered a realization among many communities within the Bank that a purely expert-led mindset was no longer the most effective way to develop policies and projects. This chapter puts the focus on one domain of knowledge, the CoP of senior managers. It explores how contestation goes both ways: pushing for change and pushing against change, and is often multidirectional. In summary, practical contestation is multifaceted, constant, and processual.

Contesting for decentralization

During the 1980s and 1990s, the CoP of senior managers promoted decentralization and inclusiveness even before Wolfensohn's tenure. For example, the vice president of Africa from 1987 to 1996, Jaycox, used to say that the "motto of the Africa region" is "if you don't go, you don't know,"[3] so staying in the country you are working on became the norm. In 1995, he stated in an interview with Bank archivists that the African region aimed to achieve 100 percent "beneficiary participation" by the end of 1996.[4] This goal stayed unfulfilled, which proves how difficult it is to change an organization's practices drastically. Other managers did not always agree with Jaycox's contestation of centralized decision-making in Bank practices. He advocated that managers spend more time in borrowing countries instead of in their headquarters offices in Washington, D.C.:

> The one consistent theme I've gotten in my annual evaluation was that 'You travel too much, Jaycox. You are never here when we need you.' Whatever the hell that means. I don't think they need me around here at all. You really have to be out in the field. I get feedback from ministers, feedback from heads of state. A lot of this is inarticulate and problematic and self-serving from their point of view. But it is all extremely valuable feedback, from my point of view.[5]

Brokering against existing Bank practices was coupled with advocacy for greater country-based policymaking and ownership by brokers inside and outside the Bank. External critics, as well as many senior Bank employees, had been advocating for greater decentralization since the 1980s. In 1982, the director of Policy Planning and Program Review, Mahbub ul-Haq, who was also the chief economist of the Bank during the Robert McNamara era, was already suggesting a ten-year decentralization plan based on his previous experience in Pakistan:

> The Bank will have to decentralize. It has gone on for too long in a centralized fashion in a world which has been changing, where differences between countries are becoming more and more pronounced every day. . . . We are trying to do all this work in the headquarters, at the country desks, with a development strategy which is articulated centrally, with research work which is done centrally. I don't think that it is a viable structure. My suggestion would be that a real decentralization of the Bank would be thought through over a ten-year period. It can be brought about only in a graduated, step by step fashion.[6]

Demonstrating the constant fluctuation of practices and the bidirectionality of contestation, Haq's advocacy for decentralization was sometimes in the contestation of existing practices and sometimes in support of new ones. Haq contested the Bank's arrogance and centralized practices during his tenure. In 1982, he emphasized the need for nationally tailored plans and the hiring of more employees from Global South countries. This starkly contrasted with how most Bank CoPs interacted with the populations they worked with. Most Bank employees at the time came from creditor countries or were US-trained. Decentralization, Haq stated in an interview with Bank archivists, is the only way to "humanize" the Bank and avoid widespread criticisms of the Bank's "arrogance":

> The Bank has to shed its arrogance. I felt in the twelve years that I was here that the charge of arrogance against the Bank was a correct one. It's not that the top management of the Bank is arrogant. Most of them deal with the top people in the countries, at the Prime Minister or the Finance or Development Minister level and they are mature enough to deal very skillfully with policy issues. In fact, the charge of arrogance comes at the middle and young levels. I have seen this now from the other end, in Pakistan. It is the youngsters who have barely emerged from university, who are very aggressive at our top policy levels, and since I have known some of them here in Washington and know how much they count in policy making.[7]

Haq further suggested that the Bank should stop recruiting new employees from American universities and placing them in leadership positions where they must deal with Global South governments. Criticizing the top-down policymaking practices at the Bank, he advocated for decentralization of recruiting processes to hire employees directly from the countries the Bank worked with. He believed that "people who have lived in the country and know some of the bureaucratic niceties and delicacies and who have more sensitivity to what the structure of power or social status is in these countries" would render stakeholder relationships more effective.[8]

Finally, in 1987, with the support of the Bank's vice presidents who believed in the value of decentralized policymaking, the seventh Bank president, Barber Conable, and the then vice president for the East Africa region, Jaycox, implemented a broad reorganization of the Bank. Most of 1987 and the subsequent two years were thus devoted to implementing a broad reorganization of the Bank, largely to be more country-focused. In an interview shortly after the reorganization, Jaycox said that before 1987, most country knowledge was very abstract, and the paperwork was very hierarchical. The early 1980s, he added, were characterized as a "kind of chaos": "That's why we reorganized."[9] Previously divided into sector departments (e.g., education, transportation), the reorganization shifted the focus toward country departments, with department specialists (e.g., on health, population, transportation) integrated into each country or regional department. The Bank was reorganized into four vice presidencies: operations; finance; administration; and policy, planning, and research. Regions were reduced to four (Africa, Asia,

Europe, and the Middle East), and each included country departments, technical departments, and topic divisions on industries, agriculture, and various others.

Country managers also gained more financial and logistical resources to devise tools more attuned to each context.[10] This change increased the epistemic power in brokering at the country level for those interested in the social aspects of development or the social impacts of structural adjustment strategies. Bank employees working more closely with country-level advocates and officials also began to recognize the value of including them in consultations to gain more accurate country-specific knowledge. For example, one Bank employee who spent 14 years working in various management positions stated that after 1987, during country meetings, there would be the head of the department with a person from the division on transportation, another on agriculture, and someone in charge of developing health and education operations for this specific country. He concluded that this promoted better country-specific knowledge across a wide variety of issues.[11] Then Bank chief for population and human resources in Brazil, Nancy Birdsall, added that the new institutional structure allowed for differentiated country strategies to emerge, which were "much more attuned to (each) country."[12] This reorganization, partly triggered by contestation and boundary brokering in the senior managers' CoP, led to an acceleration of government ownership of multilaterally funded development policies.

Similar to Haq, who had background knowledge from previous domains of knowledge he subscribed to in Pakistan and elsewhere, internal brokers can be new employees from another CoP inside the Bank. After 1987, when country sector specialists were sent to country teams, the attention shifted from sector expertise to country expertise, which could be developed or strengthened by people originally from the countries in question. Recognizing the need to develop context-specific knowledge on many issues, top managers relocated Brazil's transportation specialists to the Brazil country team, East Africa health specialists to the East Africa team, etc. While Bank country offices were still primarily populated by Western experts, partly because of the coloniality of epistemic power, this decentralization reinforced the move from one-size-fits-all projects towards country-based ones. This reorganization eventually enabled more in-country hires instead of Washington-based employees. In addition, NGO specialists joined country teams, which promoted more consultation and openness toward civil society organizations.

Contesting for and against participation and consultation

Confronting someone from an external CoP who disagrees with the direction of a practice change can sometimes confirm your adoption of new mechanisms or tools. A senior Bank official recalled a joint travel with the IMF to Mongolia in the 1980s that reassured him of the value of consulting populations despite – or perhaps because of – contestation against it by his IMF counterparts. The IMF team intended to ask the Mongolian government to restructure its livestock and agriculture policies, and they had drafted an agreement to be signed by the minister of finance and the Central Bank. Upon their arrival, the Bank team was not planning on meeting with Mongolian populations. However, the spouse of one of the team members who had been tasked with wandering the city to find restaurants informed the team that he had seen herders camping on the outskirts of the city. The Bank delegation decided to meet informally and talk to farmers. Among other things, the Mongolians informed them that the proposed reforms to the geographic organization of herders' communities would hurt their well-being, thus impeding the acceptability of the national agriculture plan proposed by the IMF and approved by the Mongolian Central Bank. One team member was adamant about the need to take this new finding into account:

> So I went to the IMF mission leader's suite and knocked on her door. She was, of course, sitting with her end-of-the-day outfit reading a book. It was like 5:30 in the afternoon. I said:
>
> - I understand you are planning on asking for a restructuring of livestock policies.
> - Who told you that?
> - Well, who told you what you are basing this decision on?
> - Well, it's obvious to everyone.
> - Well, actually, the migrant herders are just at the outskirts of Ulaanbaatar, as three of us went to visit them today where they are camped. And had I known you were planning on making them do this, I would have asked what they thought about it. Because from talking to them, I can think of several reasons why that's not going to work. Because your assumption about how they actually herd, produce their cattle, and where they get the food is not right.
> - Well, that's what we're going to do, that's what the government agreed on.
> - Well, the problem is that I am not sure the government really agreed to it. I think the minister of livestock is pretty . . . have you met him yet? Oh, I am sure you will enjoy meeting him; we'll ask the Central Bank to bring him around and ask them whether they can do this. (She looked up from the book and glared at me.) I think the point is you are in a mission, which is a very good mission and I love you all, but your mission is not technically staffed to ask the government of Mongolia to do that. And while I didn't bring an agriculture specialist, three of us did go out to them to see where the herders were, because we heard they hung out in the summer in this particular spot outside Ulaanbaatar. I am doing what I can and I am sure your agriculture specialist will take careful note of what the minister says. Have a nice evening.[13]

Practitioners in various CoPs accross the development field contested changes in internal Bank CoPs' practices by writing and promoting epistemic boundary objects or by being vocal in boundary encounters, especially on the implementation of broad-based participation. Teams at the United Nations Development Program (UNDP), for example, did not overtly contest new consulting mechanisms but, in some contexts, resisted tacitly. A Bank economist working in Kampala, Uganda, remembered that in the mid-1990s, when the Bank's team in Uganda was helping the government to implement broad-based participation, the UNDP team "didn't like the project . . . I don't know what they did, but people came to me and said: 'did you know that the UN people are telling ministers that they shouldn't follow this thing?'"[14] A former UN official agreed that there is generally simultaneous cooperation and competition between UN and Bank managers, both about appropriate macroeconomic policies and specific tools. He added that while Bank employees would often get their way because of their financial resources, the UNDP ones often fought back with epistemic power:

> The Bank will always be suspected by the UNDP, and civil society organizations, to pursue a "neoliberal" view of development. There is a competition between the Bank and the UNDP for prestige and for the ear of governments. That always goes on. And the Bank has much more money. So when we disagreed with the Bank, we couldn't fight them in terms of money. We had to fight them on the terrain of ideas.[15]

Many borrowing governments' CoPs brokered for more inclusion of government actors but against participatory development and the consultation of civil society actors. For example, governments often contested consulting Indigenous populations targeted by resettlement plans. For a hydroelectricity project in Mexico that was initially approved in 1989, the Bank considered the levels of participation in preparing resettlement plans insufficient. The government of Mexico did not follow new Bank guidelines, which included a redefinition of who could be a "stakeholder" to include all those "affected by the outcome – negatively or positively – or those who can affect the outcome of a proposed intervention."[16] The negotiations with the Bank stopped when the Mexican administrators refused to follow the Bank's new policies regarding resettlement and consultation. Mexican officials tried to seek money from other institutions, but the government returned to the Bank seven months later to reinitiate the funding request and develop resettlement plans according to the Bank's new requirements.[17] How the Bank attempted to redefine its stakeholders was most visible in a 1994 internal report by the Operations Policy Department, where key stakeholders were defined as those "intended to be directly affected by a proposed intervention, those who expected to benefit or lose from Bank-supported operations."[18]

Contestation can be enacted by individual practitioners in domains of knowledge, but the process of contestation in brokering is always a social one. Many organizational sociologists and IR scholars studying international organizations have focused on how presidents or secretaries generally have individually promoted change.[19] This type of individual ontology shows only one side of the picture. Former director of the Social Development Department, Gloria Davis recalled that the contestation of expert-led practices and advocacy for the concentration of Bank lending at the lower level of government did not come only from Wolfensohn and Bank vice presidents but from various lower-level managers as well, such as then sector director for the Rural Development and Environment Department, Hans Binswanger:

> Hans Binswanger was instrumental in bringing that view. It wasn't his view initially, but he brought that view to Wolfensohn's attention, and Wolfensohn agreed that a significant portion of Bank lending should be directed to the community level. This led to, as it often does (not to be cynical), a lot of renaming of projects that weren't exactly community driven, but it also was a tremendous impetus to having a certain number of projects that were community driven. And the aggregate total of community-based projects is now very large, something around 6 billion dollars.[20]

Contestation against internalized knowledge is never an individual affair; contestation by brokering, in the use of boundary objects or in boundary encounters, is always enmeshed in relationality. An example of a boundary broker who needed the support of an internal constituency is Michael Cernea. He was a strong advocate of bringing non-economists into the Bank to humanize the organization and make it more responsive to the issues and criticisms raised by civil society actors. Cernea initiated a CoP, the "Sociology Group," which met to discuss social aspects of the Bank's work, invited outside guests to speak at Bank events, and organized various encounters with external communities of practice.[21] Cernea is also credited with developing a social methodology for rural participation in development projects. He wrote many influential reports, for example *Putting People First* and *The Building Blocks of Participation: Testing Bottom up Planning*.[22] These epistemic boundary objects were written and disseminated to contest existing top-down policymaking practices that many Bank managers employed.

In an interview with Bank archivists, the senior Bank anthropologist Daniel Gross underlined the role played by a group of Bank employees who helped Cernea claim more participatory resettlement projects – they were informally called "Cernea's Raiders." According to one Bank manager, the group of young Bank employees "went into the Bank's information system – the records were available, were accessible – and they would do things like comb through Bank hydropower projects and look for any evidence that there were resettlement problems."[23] One of Cernea's Raiders, Scott Guggenheim, later implemented community-driven development with his Bank country team in Indonesia. Cernea's impact on the emergence of inclusive practices thus cannot be considered alone but instead in combination with other internal boundary brokers; that is, as part of a social process of contestation. Practice contestation thus relies on a robust social ontology. Contesters should not be considered as individual actors but as part of a domain of knowledge that contributes to and sometimes helps reinforce their contestation claims for or against change.

Contesting from the grassroots

In 1990, 500 representatives of African grassroots organizations met in Arusha, Tanzania, for the International Conference on Popular Participation in the

Recovery and Development Process organized by the UN Economic Commission for Africa. As a transnational CoP, they adopted a charter that argued that the deteriorating economic and political conditions in many African countries during the 1980s were partly due to the lack of public participation in policymaking. The South Commission, established in 1987 and comprised of 29 advocates from Global South countries, also published a significant report in 1990 addressing issues of economic growth, good governance, and popular participation and recommending putting people back at the center of development concerns. Both became epistemic boundary objects, even if Bank employees interviewed for this research often dismissed the campaign or the methods of this external civil society CoP.

External CoPs exercised constant pressure for change in Bank practices through ongoing or occasional public campaigns and acting as watchdogs. Public campaigns were organized around specific themes or against specific Bank tools or actions. The year 1994 became notable in the history of the Bank with the launch of the "Fifty Years Is Enough" campaign, organized by a group of international NGOs. Demonstrations and street protests were held at the World Bank's headquarters and the annual meeting of the boards of directors of the Bank and IMF in Madrid.[24] The campaign, organized by CoPs outside the organizations, contested the existence of the World Bank and the IMF 50 years after their foundation. A significant confrontation happened at the Madrid meetings when protesters called for the dissolution of the Bretton Woods institutions. According to Martin Khor, director of the Third World Network in Malaysia and one of the instigators of the Fifty Years Is Enough campaign, structural adjustment programs had brought more misery than development, and the failure of the Washington Consensus was proof of the inefficacy of the World Bank and the IMF:

> Structural adjustment is a policy to continue colonial trade and economic patterns developed during the colonial period, but which the Northern powers want to continue in the post-colonial period. Economically speaking, we (countries of the Global South) are more dependent on the ex-colonial countries than we ever were. The World Bank and the IMF are playing the role that our ex-colonial masters used to play.[25]

It must be emphasized that collective learning through contestation often happens via practice rather than discourse. Marches and street protests were held at the World Bank headquarters from the mid-1990s onward and were associated with anti-globalization campaigns throughout the world. For example, in April 1998, 25 activists mobilized outside the spring meetings of the World Bank and the IMF. The following April, 25,000 protesters participated in mass, nonviolent civil disobedience against international financial institutions. Their main criticism was the imposition of a one-size-fits-all neoliberal program that impoverished countries of the Global South by increasing their indebtedness and "top-down globalization."[26] Even if these movements were often devalued by Bank macroeconomists, they pushed many CoPs to reflect on their policymaking practices.

These contestation movements culminated at the World Trade Organization meeting in Seattle in November and December 1999. Many "globalization discontents" marched against the institutions supporting economic integration and a series of riots and protests took place.[27] The protesters generally campaigned against international financial institutions, accusing them of promoting an unequal neoliberal globalization. These movements became known as the anti-globalization movement, which organized demonstrations and international citizens' meetings like the World Social Forum. International encounters of CoPs like the World Social Forums led to better organized campaigns and more effective contestation claims against the Bank. On May 19, 2001, the annual Bank conference on development economics was canceled due to such protests. The spokesperson for the Bank at the time, Caroline Anstey, expressed dismay that these groups could not join the debate in what she believed was a more constructive way. Their capacity as epistemic agents was devalued. Bank practitioners felt great uneasiness about the protests and contested this practice.

Boundary brokering and boundary encounters placed intense and continuous pressure for change on the organization and various country offices. According to many interviewees for this research, the collective actions of external CoPs greatly impacted the Bank employees' realization that the Bank was losing legitimacy. According to a former UN official, the Fifty Years Is Enough campaign made some Bank managers recognize that the NGO community hated them for their arrogant attitude toward borrowing populations.[28] Many Bank managers understood this contestation movement as a reaction to the Bank's lack of openness to other views and to borrowing governments and populations. While the criticisms of the neoliberal aspects of the Bank's policies did not trickle up to reach senior Bank officials, these external contestations were a great force for change toward more inclusiveness in World Bank practices. Senior Bank Manager Thomas Blinkhorn stated that this campaign propelled NGOs into development forums like never before: "There had been NGOs working here but never like this."[29]

More continuously, external CoPs like the Bank Information Center, the Bretton Woods Projects, the Green Alternative, or the Bankwatch Network were dedicated to regularly monitoring and contesting World Bank activities.[30] Organizations able to generate epistemic power include the Group of 24 (G-24), the proponents of the New International Economic Order, or the Group of 77 (G-77). Oxfam, ActionAid, and other NGOs also exerted constant pressure on the Bank, either on an ongoing basis or on specific projects. These organizations, activists, and social movements contested existing practices and often attempted change by critiquing them as rhetorical, inefficient, or more of the same.[31]

There was also continual contestation by civil society CoPs against specific projects or practices, which pushed CoPs within the Bank to modify their practice and devise new tools. Successful pressure by environmental NGOs is one of the most documented cases. After a series of environmental disasters linked to Bank projects in the 1980s, protests led by environmental NGOs and civil society groups erupted against the organization in the form of transnational environmental advocacy networks. Both through direct and indirect contestation aimed at member states' governments, these networks pressured Bank teams to change their practices to render their projects more environmentally sustainable. An example of an environmental campaign that also impacted inclusive practices is the contestation of relocation practices in the Sardar Sarovar projects on the Narmada River. Indian NGOs contested the Bank's irrigation projects in the region because they threatened the livelihoods of nearly 140,000 people living near the river. Eventually, they put so much pressure on the Bank that it abandoned the project altogether. In addition, these campaigns persuaded many Bank managers that they could no longer ignore civil society voices in developing projects if they wanted Bank projects to be effective.

Fluctuations of practice contestation

External contestation happens when individuals or communities outside the Bank contest Bank practices. Member states, through the CoP of the board of directors, for example, have the capacity to generate a lot of epistemic power to exert constant pressure on Bank management. The United States is often believed to hold a firm grip over the Bank's orientations and loans, either because they have always informally chosen the Bank's president (since the founding of the organization in 1944) or because it holds de facto veto power due to its share of votes on the board. Some go as far as portraying the World Bank as a tool of American imperialism.[32] Member states, especially the United States, do have power over the Bank's political orientations. However, in practice, the American executive director rarely blocks board decisions and barely ever micromanages Bank employees' practices. In fact, state representatives often admit their inability to influence the operational practices of such a bureaucracy.[33]

Donor states' influence is often limited to high levels of politics or specific foreign policy goals. However, board directors also make day-to-day contestations in board meetings and their interactions with Bank managers. For example, Scandinavian representatives at the Bank have strongly contested top-down approaches. They have been strong proponents of greater ownership of policies by borrowing governments, even if they hold only insignificant voting power. They have financed alternative initiatives and *ad hoc* learning groups to promote this change, such as the Learning Group on Participatory Development. The UK government has also often stated that Bank policies for particular countries should be based on context-specific criteria and objectives instead of top-down blueprints.[34] Therefore, while member states have a significant impact at the policy level, there is still a leeway for Bank employees working at the country level or in specific units to enact contestation and change.

However, member states CoPs can resist senior managers' attempts to modify existing practices. For example, board members fiercely contested the 1997 decentralization under the Strategic Compact. After a few weeks of discussion with Wolfensohn and other members of the CoP of senior managers, the board finally voted to adopt the Compact, although "nobody on the board liked it."[35] Executive directors have often been successful at muting American demands for change. In the mid-1990s,

> increased concern over the US attempts to tie aid contributions to conditions mandating that funds be used in part to hire US contractors led the European and Japanese governments to form an Interim Trust Fund within the International Development Association that would effectively deny US companies a chance to bid on development aid projects.[36]

In the 1980s, the American Congress sought to impose a rule at the Bank that no loans should be made to countries that violated congressional human rights' preferences. Despite pressure from the executive director of the American delegation to the Bank, the Bank disregarded this proposal because other representatives on the board disagreed, such as the representatives of Japan and the European Union. Thus, the United States' efforts to change the orientation of the Bank sometimes fail, despite their economic grip on the Bank. Like other actors in collective learning processes, the United States needs to mobilize epistemic power and use arguing skills, not only financial leverage. Member states' representatives also often contest attempted changes by the Bank management. For example, the board fiercely contested the 1997 decentralization under the Strategic Compact, but adopted it nonetheless when pressured by Bank administrators. After a few weeks of discussion with Wolfensohn and other senior managers, the board finally voted to adopt the Compact.

Contestation in boundary brokering, in encounters or through epistemic boundary objects, is enacted both for and against new practices. External communities not only contest existing practices, but they also sometimes resist attempts at change. Many IMF economists were incredibly uneasy at some of the Bank teams' new inclusive practices. They needed to understand the usefulness of changing how they interacted with governments in joint projects with the Bank. For example, in the mid-2000s, for example, the Bank's country team in Cameroon decided to ask the Cameroonian government to develop their framework for a poverty reduction strategy with the help of a set of new indicators developed by Bank economists. Upon approval of their plan, they would receive debt relief. A senior World Bank economist said that the IMF refused to endorse the plan, and there was a protracted conflict between the IMF and Bank representatives:

> First, [the IMF] said that they didn't have time to understand this new framework. Then, they said, "nonetheless, you have to present the result that comes out of our model." The Cameroonians said, "well, we thought this was the whole point of the PRSP, to have a conversation with your analysis and ours, and we compare where the differences are." And you know, it was kind of an ugly discussion. But the worst part of it was that the [IMF] mission chief sent an email to the minister of finance, basically saying, "unless you use our model, you will not get any debt relief."[37]

If involving borrowing countries was not easy for many Bank managers, it was even harder for the IMF's economists, leading to their often loud contestation of inclusive practices adopted at the Bank. This is mainly because the Bank historically has a more diverse workforce than the IMF, which is almost exclusively composed of macroeconomists. During the implementation of the poverty-reduction strategy, World Bank and IMF managers had to work together, and they clashed in many instances over their ability to cope with change in policymaking practices. As one senior Bank economist put it, the IMF teams usually had

> their own agenda. . . . They are really just interested in the macro part. At best, growth. It was more difficult for them to wrap their heads around new practices. I am not saying it was not difficult for the Bank, but we had to discipline the Fund because having the IMF involved was really important.[38]

Contestation against attempted practice change can also come from within a community of practice. Members of a CoP with the most internalized background knowledge and closer to the center of the community are the most likely to display such resistance. Bank CoPs often met attempts to implement inclusive practices with overt or tacit resistance from Bank managers, a resistance that tended to decrease over time but never vanished. Many managers trained as economists pushed back on openness and decentralization practices. One senior manager described new consultation processes as a "waste of time."[39] Many Bank managers became so accustomed to interacting as experts with borrowing governments and populations that they did not see the value of including aid-targeted populations differently in policymaking or project implementation. Then vice president of the Africa Region, Edward Jaycox, remembers how some of his close colleagues or superiors would challenge his attempts to engage with borrowing populations.[40]

Other boundary brokers, like advisory groups, could also enact practical contestation when they advised on the writing of reports, data collection, development projects, or day-to-day practices. For example, in the early 2000s, for the first time, an external advisory committee was set up by Bank employees Catherine Gwin and Alison Margaret Evans to help them write the International Development Association review: "Part of that was to say, okay, we're a team. Now we want an outside advisory committee to be a sounding board for us, to beat up on us if they think we're not doing a good job."[41] The committee, made up of researchers, NGOs, donors, and representatives of grant recipients, pushed the writers of the report to shift focus from donors' interests to those of all stakeholders. In an interview with Bank archivists, Gwin remembered the impact these brokers had on her team's review work:

> It wasn't so much standard practice at the time, and. . . . I saw the value in getting reactions to our work from expert representatives of different stakeholder groups: researchers, donor representatives, client representatives . . .

> NGOs. . . . We had various country consultations, and we held a couple of international workshops at both the design stage of the evaluation, and an international workshop when we had emerging findings, and we asked our advisory committee to be part of that . . . impacts I clearly remember were that they toughened our spine on what we were saying about [the International Development Association] shortfalls, particularly in regard to poverty and the role of donors, and the way in which donors tried to push the Bank around in their own interests.[42]

In sum, practice contestation is neither a one-way process nor does it relate to distinct moments in the history of a community. Contestation is constant in CoPs and does not impede the like-mindedness of its members. Contestation of practices happens internally and externally, as well as for and against change. It happens in various forms, and any member of a community can enact it, but with varying success depending on epistemic power. It is this generalized movement of contestation that enables broader learning processes and constant fluctuations in practices. Contestation happens simultaneously *and is reinforced* by the multiple interactions of a CoP at the boundaries with other CoPs. If contestation helps practitioners realize that their practices are not as effective as they had believed, interactions at the boundaries give them ideas about how to react to this failure. The volume of these processes can lead to the institutionalization of new practices, which requires a broad narrative change to give it institutional validity.

On the social character of contestation

Practical contestation in collective learning is rarely the result of one person or one organization's efforts. First, individuals, especially Bank presidents or directors of international NGOs and civil society networks, have previously been members of multiple communities and have learned from them. Other communities and individuals continue to influence them. Wolfensohn, for example, was deeply influenced by his first Bank field trip to Africa and his meetings with Bank employees in country offices. His unofficial biographer described how "his time in Uganda had confirmed his suspicion that the Bank's NGO critics could sometimes be correct, and that the Bank's own employees could be too arrogant to admit it."[43] Gloria Davis, the director of the Social Development Department from 1997 to 2000, also noted that Deepa Narayan's book, *Voices of the Poor*, had a significant impact on Wolfensohn's thinking: "It had a big influence on Wolfensohn . . . toward participation and the sort of change over time to being more empowering and getting people more involved in decisions."[44]

Second, the power of a contestation claim comes from the ability of contesters with less institutional power to find and mobilize facilitators for their claims. Senior managers (e.g., vice presidents) can enable, encourage, or discourage a range of possibilities for contestation at lower levels of management (e.g., country managers). In general, as part of a CoP, disrupters need other community members to support their claims. Former vice president of Strategy and Resource Management Mark Baird recalled that when Wolfensohn wanted to promote debt reduction and more partnerships with borrowing governments, the participation of Country Director Nawal Kamel was vital. She was tasked with writing a paper to defend the new idea of partnerships at a board meeting. Baird believed that she had a significant impact on practice change at the World Bank – that she promoted "a shift in the way the Bank was perceived, and the way the Bank worked. She was brilliant at taking ideas and putting them into practice."[45]

Third, a way for individual contesters to create a constituency for their contestation claim is to hire employees sympathetic to their ideas. Wolfensohn was able to initiate a significant turnover in employees in the late 1990s, hiring sociologists, gender specialists, and anthropologists.[46] In his biography, Wolfensohn noted that before this turnover, he faced much more contestation by well-established Bank managers:

> I was not coming through well to the staff, and as much as possible, I wanted to remedy that. I sought out younger and more junior people in particular, as I sensed in them more willingness to deviate from accepted practice. This was rare in the Bank's upper echelon, and often when I tried to bring the conversation with senior staff people around to the overwhelming priority we should give to the fight against poverty, most of my colleagues would look at me as if I were from another planet. Poverty reduction was already their objective, they would respond. They did not want me to review and change the well-established practices of the institution.[47]

Therefore, Wolfensohn appointed 24 out of 26 vice presidents and provoked a quarter of the Bank's 10,000 employee turnover between 1997 and 2000.[48] According to one observer, many older top managers who disagreed with him left the Bank or were fired, such as Ernest Stern (managing director), Gautam Kaji (managing director), Edward Jaycox (vice president of the Africa Region), Shahid Husain (vice president of Management and Personnel Services), and Rachel Lomax (vice president and chief of staff to the president).[49] In the late 1990s, Wolfensohn hired four managing directors with mindsets closer to his own: South African social activist Mamphela Ramphele, Jeffrey Goldstein from Bankers Trust, Peter Woicke from JP Morgan, and Shengman Zhang, who was previously China's minister of finance.[50]

Fourth, another social aspect of contestation is the feedback loops between external and internal communities. Often, an external contestation claim needs internal supporters to be successful, so outsiders will be more effective if they have allies inside the Bank. In the Sardar Sarovar projects on the Narmada River, for example, the NGO community would have been unable to trigger change through contestation without the involvement of internal supporters. It was only when internal Bank brokers for change sympathized with the cause of external environmental NGOs that an external evaluation was commissioned, which "opened up policy space for a significant learning process inside the Bank."[51]

The arrival of Wolfensohn at the head of the institution also helped outside lobbyists to ally with inside disrupters because they had better access to the institution. Oxfam, one of the most critical international NGOs toward the Bank, started to meet with Bank officials more often and participate in events. A senior economist was surprised to see this shift in the attitude of civil society leaders: "All of a sudden renowned social advocate Bono called Wolfensohn 'my Elvis.'"[52] The president started to invite NGO critics to have dinner with him[53] and organized a bit of a public relations operation to soften the image of the Bank.[54] Another example is when civil society actors allied with member states to pressure the Bank. In September 1987, a coalition of NGOs organized a press conference to advocate for a greater emphasis on poverty at the Bank, with a statement signed by 153 members of the US House of Representatives and 40 senators.[55] Despite their lack of resources, some NGOs managed to impact Bank practices. They were "frequently tiny but they were always fierce; they would swarm at big organizations such as the World Bank, like the mini-warriors of Lilliput who bound Gulliver and showered him with arrows."[56] After the Fifty Years Is Enough campaign shook off the organization, NGOs found in Wolfensohn, but even more so in former Bank chief economist Joseph Stiglitz, beneficial allies to their contestation claims.

Feedback loops between internal and external communities can also restrain change when there is internal resistance against external pressure for change. For example, the United Nations Children's Fund (UNICEF) report *Adjustment with a Human Face* promoted greater inclusiveness in the development process and encountered much resistance inside the Bank. A former UN official recalled that the Bank reaction was "UNICEF doesn't know what the f*** it is talking about. We deal with economics. You deal with children. We deal with *real* issues."[57] Senior Bank Manager Thomas Blinkhorn also remembered a lot of resistance among his colleagues when Wolfensohn was listening to external NGOs' contestation claims.

> A lot of people were saying, "Wait a minute!" This is just overdoing it there with these people. Because half of them are airy-fairy kind of people. They don't know what they're doing. They're do-gooders that don't do their homework.[58]

Talking about NGOs' criticisms of Bank projects in the northwest Amazon, Bank anthropologist Daniel Gross recounted that a colleague told him, "What the hell do they have to do with this? You know, this is not their business. It's not their country. And what legitimacy do they have to be criticizing us?"[59] The movement of disruption and resistance thus goes both ways, for and against change, and both levels (internal and external) interact in their contestation.

Conclusion

Contestation of the Bank's top-down policymaking practices in boundary encounters or in brokering processes pressured its employees to recognize the failures of top-down policymaking practices. Interactions at the boundaries offered them examples of other successful practices, such as consulting populations to collect data or including village representatives in project development. Collective learning happens intersubjectively and, as such, can be triggered by meaning negotiation with other practitioners, as well as through contestation of existing background knowledge. This case also demonstrates that the process of collective learning about the effectiveness of inclusive practices was bumpy and complex, and only some people needed to be on board for a change in practice to be institutionalized.

The inclusion of NGOs and civil society organizations, like the growing ownership of borrowing governments and the participation of aid-targeted populations, was a fluctuating, decentralized, and uneven process. The acceleration of this shift in the 1990s was due to the sheer quantity of boundary encounters, brokers, epistemic boundary objects, and through constant practice contestation. It did not happen overnight or without friction, nor was it solely the result of the leadership of influential individuals. The long, incremental process of the emergence and institutionalization of consultation mechanisms with NGOs and civil society organizations is an example of collective learning in and through CoPs. This social ordering of the knowledge domains interacting in and around the Bank was covered in detail in this chapter. Members of many CoPs inside the Bank, enmeshed in a web of intersubjective relations, started reflecting on their practices through (conflictual and harmonious) interactions with members of other communities.

Notes

1 Interview 15, June 26, 2017; Interview 36, November 10, 2017.
2 Interview 4, May 10, 2017.
3 Interview OHP Edward Jaycox, February 23 and May 24, 1995, 32.
4 Interview OHP Edward Jaycox, February 23 and May 24, 1995, 43.
5 Interview OHP Edward Jaycox, February 23 and May 24, 1995, 32–33.
6 Interview OHP Mahbub Ul Haq, December 3, 1982.
7 Interview OHP Mahbub ul Haq, December 3, 1982, 32–33.
8 Interview OHP Mahbub ul Haq, December 3, 1982, 33.
9 Interview OHP Edward V.K. Jaycox, April 5, 1991.
10 Interview 38, July 21, 2017; Interview OHP Yoshiaki Abe, March 16–17, 2005.
11 Interview 24, November 13, 2017.
12 Interview OHP Nancy Birdsall, September 23, 1992.
13 Interview 18, July 16, 2017.
14 Interview 39, November 14, 2017.
15 Interview 10, June 13, 2017.
16 World Bank, *The World Bank Participation Sourcebook*, 125.
17 World Bank, 125.
18 Operations Policy Department, "The World Bank and Participation," 2.
19 Kraske, *Bankers with a Mission*; Finnemore, "Redefining Development at the World Bank"; Kagia, *Balancing the Development Agenda*; Bazbauers, "Leading the World Bank: The Wolfensohn, Wolfowitz, and Zoellick Presidencies"; Bakvis, "Wolfensohn to Wolfowitz: What Does the Change at the Top of the World Bank Mean for Labour?".
20 Interview OHP, Gloria Davis, June 28–29, 2004, 22.
21 Vetterlein, "Seeing Like the World Bank on Poverty," 41.
22 Cernea, *Putting People First*; Cernea, *The Building Blocks of Participation.*

23 Interview OHP Daniel R. Gross, April 30, 2008, 17.
24 (Mallaby 2006, 60–62).
25 Cited in Danaher, *50 Years Is Enough*, 4.
26 Danaher, *Democratizing the Global Economy*, 9.
27 Stiglitz and Chemla, *La grande désillusion*; Stiglitz, "The World Bank at the Millennium."
28 Interview 10, June 13, 2017.
29 Interview OHP Thomas Blinkhorn, June 16–18, 2008, 60.
30 Stone and Wright, *The World Bank and Governance*, 5.
31 Bretton Woods Project, "PRSP Dangers Exposed Again"; Bretton Woods Project, "PRSPs: A Continuation of Structural Adjustment."
32 Kapur, "Do As I Say Not As I Do: A Critique of the G-7 Proposals on '"Reforming"' the World Bank"; Wade, "US Hegemony and the World Bank: The Fight Over People and Ideas"; Peet, *Unholy Trinity. The IMF, World Bank and WTO.*
33 Clegg, *Controlling the World Bank and IMF Shareholders, Stakeholders, and the Politics of Concessional Lending*, 2.
34 World Bank and IMF, "Heavily Indebted Poor Countries (HIPC) Initiative— Strengthening the Link between Debt Relief and Poverty Reduction," 22.
35 Mallaby, *The World's Banker*, 165.
36 US General Accounting Office 1995, cited in Weaver, "The World's Bank and the Bank's World," 500.
37 Interview 28, August 15, 2017.
38 Interview 34, November 8, 2017.
39 Interview 34, November 8, 2017.
40 Interview OHP Edward Jaycox, February 23 and May 24, 1995, 4.
41 Interview OHP Catherine Gwin, January 20, 2010, 11.
42 Interview OHP Catherine Gwin, January 20, 2010, 12.
43 Mallaby, 113.
44 Interview OHP Gloria Davis, June 28–29, 2004, 20–21.
45 Interview OHP Mark Baird, May 5–6, 2010, 45–46.
46 Interview 21, July 19, 2017.
47 Wolfensohn, *A Global Life*, 270.
48 (Fidler 2009, 1).
49 (Phillips 2009, 264–265).
50 Phillips, *Reforming the World Bank*, 265.
51 Vetterlein, "Change in International Organizations: Innovation or Adaptation? A Comparison of the World Bank and the International Monetary Fund," 137; Fox and Brown, *The Struggle for Accountability*.
52 Interview 31, November 6, 2017.
53 Mallaby, 145.
54 Clegg, 51.
55 Mallaby, 47.
56 Mallaby, 47.
57 Interview 10, June 13, 2017.
58 Interview OHP Thomas Blinkhorn, June 16–18, 2008, 60.
59 Interview OHP Daniel Gross, April 30, 2008, 50.

References

Bakvis, Peter. "Wolfensohn to Wolfowitz: What Does the Change at the Top of the World Bank Mean for Labour?" *Transfer* 4, no. 05 (2005): 633–38.

Barnett, Michael, and Martha Finnemore. *Rules for the World: International Organizations in Global Politics*. Ithaca and London: Cornell University Press, 2004.

Bazbauers, Adrian Robert. "Leading the World Bank: The Wolfensohn, Wolfowitz, and Zoellick Presidencies." *International Journal of Economic Sciences* 1, no. 1 (2012): 2–18.
Bretton Woods Project. "PRSP Dangers Exposed again." *Bretton Woods Project* 33 (April 1, 2003).
Bretton Woods Project. "PRSPs: A Continuation of Structural Adjustment." *Bretton Woods Project* 39 (April 5, 2004).
Cernea, Michael M., ed. *Putting People First: Sociological Variables in Rural Development.* New York: Published for the World Bank [by] Oxford University Press, 1991.
Cernea, Michael M. *The Building Blocks of Participation: Testing Bottom-up Planning.* World Bank Discussion Papers 166. Washington, DC: World Bank, 1992.
Clegg, Liam. *Controlling the World Bank and IMF Shareholders, Stakeholders, and the Politics of Concessional Lending.* London: Palgrave Macmillan, 2013.
Danaher, Kevin, ed. *50 Years Is Enough: The Case against the World Bank and the International Monetary Fund.* Boston, MA: South End Press, 1994.
Danaher, Kevin, ed. *Democratizing the Global Economy: The Battle against the World Bank and the International Monetary Fund.* A Global Exchange Book. Monroe, ME: Common Courage Press, 2001.
Fidler, Stephen. "Who's Minding the Bank?" *Foreign Policy* (2009): 40–50.
Finnemore, Martha. "Redefining Development at the World Bank." In *International Development and the Social Sciences: Essays on the History and Politics of Knowledge,* edited by Frederick Cooper and Randall M. Packard. Berkeley: University of California Press, 1997.
Fox, Jonathan, and L. David Brown, eds. *The Struggle for Accountability: The World Bank, NGOs, and Grassroots Movements.* Global Environmental Accord. Cambridge, MA: MIT Press, 1998.
Freire, Paulo. *The Pedagogy of the Oppressed.* New York: Continuum, 1970.
Kagia, Ruth, ed. *Balancing the Development Agenda: The Transformation of the World Bank under James D. Wolfensohn, 1995–2005.* Washington, DC: The World Bank, 2005.
Kapur, Devesh. "Do As I Say Not As I Do: A Critique of the G-7 Proposals on '"Reforming"' the World Bank." Working Paper. Center for Global Development, 2002.
Kraske, Jochen, ed. *Bankers with a Mission: The Presidents of the World Bank, 1946–91.* New York: Oxford University Press, 1996.
Mallaby, Sebastian. *The World's Banker: A Story of Failed States, Financial Crises, and the Wealth and Poverty of Nations.* A Council on Foreign Relations Book. London, UK: The Penguin Press, 2006.
Operations Policy Department. *The World Bank and Participation.* Washington, DC: The World Bank, 1994.
Peet, Richard. *Unholy Trinity. The IMF, World Bank and WTO.* New York: Zed Books, 2003.
Phillips, David A. *Reforming the World Bank: Twenty Years of Trial -- and Error.* New York: Cambridge University Press, 2009.
Stiglitz, Joseph E. "The World Bank at the Millennium." *The Economic Journal* 109, no. 459 (November 1999): 577–97. https://doi.org/10.1111/1468-0297.00473.
Stiglitz, Joseph E., and Paul Chemla. *La grande désillusion.* Paris: Fayard, 2002.
Stone, Diane, and Christopher Wright, eds. *The World Bank and Governance: A Decade of Reform and Reaction.* Routledge/Warwick Studies in Globalisation 14. London and New York: Routledge, 2007.
Vetterlein, Antje. "Change in International Organizations: Innovation or Adaptation? A Comparison of the World Bank and the International Monetary Fund." In *The World Bank and Governance: A Decade of Reform and Reaction,* edited by Diane Stone and Christopher Wright. Routledge/Warwick Studies in Globalisation 14. London and New York: Routledge, 2007.
Vetterlein, Antje. "Seeing Like the World Bank on Poverty." *New Political Economy* 17, no. 1 (2012): 35–58.

Wade, Robert. "US Hegemony and the World Bank: The Fight Over People and Ideas." *Review of International Political Economy* 9, no. 2 (2002): 215–43.
Weaver, Catherine. *Hypocrisy Trap: The World Bank and the Poverty of Reform*. Princeton: Princeton University Press, 2008.
Weaver, Catherine. "The World's Bank and the Bank's World." *Global Governance*, Poverty Alleviation and Human Development in the Twenty-First Century: The Role of the World Bank, 13, no. 4 (2007): 493–512.
Wolfensohn, James D. *A Global Life: My Journey among Rich and Poor, from Sydney to Wall Street to the World Bank*. 1st ed. New York: PublicAffairs, 2010.
World Bank, ed. *The World Bank Participation Sourcebook*. Washington, DC: The World Bank, 1996.
World Bank and IMF. *Heavily Indebted Poor Countries (HIPC) Initiative – Strengthening the Link between Debt Relief and Poverty Reduction*. Washington, DC: The World Bank and International Monetary Fund, 1999.

8 "Better practices" and the coloniality of epistemic power

Emanuel Adler believes that a community of practice (CoP) approach should help us determine which practices are better,[1] and Leonie Holthaus states that practice theories can improve our understanding of how international organizations (Western and non-Western) interact with civil society organizations, especially with regards to social structures of power, race, and gender dynamics.[2] Vincent Pouliot and Jean-Philippe Thérien add that to understand "who governs the globe,"[3] we must look at how practices (meaningful interactions) influence dynamics of inclusion and exclusion.[4] Therefore, how can a CoP approach help us determine if inclusive practices are "better" than top-down ones?[5] This chapter looks at social ordering and international workers' attempts to meaningfully integrate aid-targeted populations into policymaking in ways that challenge formal hierarchies.

On the one hand, global governance institutions have always been concerned with designing policies and practices to promote global common goods and do "what is right." Some scholars even defined international organizations as "palaces of hope" to design better practices.[6] Even if he does not argue that international activities always serve the betterment of humanity, Michael Zürn defines global governance as the exercise of authority across national borders, especially regarding common goods.[7] Global governance is often seen not only as a description of international relations but also as *a blueprint for what should be*[8]. The inclusion of civil society in global governance is often similarly perceived as a symbol of greater democracy for the voiceless.[9] Kal Raustiala, for example, studied how the collaboration between NGOs and international organizations can be mutually beneficial.[10]

However, in development and humanitarian aid, hierarchies persist between international (read, Western-led) organizations and Global South actors.[11] If international organizations used to justify themselves normatively in terms of their neutral expertise, they increasingly use the language of inclusion to legitimize their authority.[12] Inclusive practices in multilateral policymaking, especially the participation of NGOs in policymaking, project elaboration and service delivery, were supposed to challenge international hierarchies regarding who gets a seat at the table. To the most optimistics, aid-targeted populations were supposed to become the "drivers" of writing their own development programs[13] after decades of being told what to do.

DOI: 10.4324/9781003529279-8

On the other hand, some observers see the gradual opening of international organizations as a relegitimation strategy,[14] as limited in scope,[15] or as stabilizing the technocratic rationality of the Bank.[16] Terms like "participation" became empty buzzwords for some,[17] or worse, as Trojan horses hiding neoliberal policies.[18] Neo-Gramscians and neo-Marxists argue that these inclusive practices are either cooptation or social reproduction mechanisms for global capitalist forces.[19] Some critical political economy studies even define this shift as an attempt to control Global South populations or as neoliberal colonization.[20] In light of such a stark contrast in the literature, it is interesting to look away from intentionality and focus on *how* epistemic power *restructured* relationships through those attempts to include (sometimes despite the best of intentions). In the end, the democratization of international organizations remains one of the most profound changes in global governance.[21]

Better practices and common humanity

So, are inclusive practices better? Do they effectively challenge international hierarchies? IR practice-oriented scholars first aimed to distance themselves from norm-oriented IR constructivists by focusing on cognitive/background knowledge and practices as different from normativity, or appropriate standards of behavior. Thus, it can seem odd to look for "better" practices with a practice framework. By bracketing the "ought" of IR to focus on the "is," practice and CoP researchers have struggled to evaluate international practices on normative grounds, or the "oughtness" and "acceptability" of social practices.[22] However, the general avoidance of questions of normativity does not follow from original practice-oriented frameworks in social theory. Schatzki, for example, was careful not to associate practices only with cognitive knowledge but with a normative "teleoaffective structure."[23] Following a growing trend of scholars looking at the normativity of international practices[24] or normativity in practice,[25] this chapter is concerned with the question of what people think is appropriate, or what are "better" practices, and in what regards.

For Adler, a goal of practice theorists should be to explore "whether, how and why some practices become better than others."[26] As a "liberal humanist," he argues that better practices are linked to "less domination, less poverty, and less violence, atrocities, and war" and more "empathy" for one another.[27] Therefore, he associates values of common humanity with better practices by distinguishing between liberal and illiberal practices. He uses the case of the end of slavery as an example: anti-slavery (a better practice) became the norm because communities of enslavers and those who sustained slavery "learned in and through practice and political processes to endow all individuals with a common humanity status – to exempt individuals' statuses and functions from domination."[28] However, despite policies to end slavery, previously enslaved people were not suddenly endowed with common humanity status. On the contrary, the persistence of exploitation, mass imprisonment, and devaluation of epistemic value tends to point to an ongoing lack of recognition of their common humanity.[29] As will become apparent in this chapter, even in liberal practices like inclusive processes of consultation or participation, there can subsist remnants of dehumanization through epistemic power, the power to attribute cognitive agency, and, therefore, humanity.

I argue that despite "better" (read, liberal) practices, which give access to previously excluded agents to spaces of policymaking, the negotiation of meaning in these spaces remains influenced by the coloniality of epistemic power, defined as racial stratifications in meaning-making processes. While exploring what constitutes better practices should be associated with this idea of common humanity, "better" liberal practices do not necessarily lead to full participation as epistemic agents (ergo, humans) in collective learning processes. Common humanity should be understood through racial and colonial mechanisms of dehumanization, which are linked to the devaluation of epistemic capacities[30]. There is something more than the distinction between liberal and illiberal ideals to evaluate better practices: colonial dehumanization sometimes persists even within more liberal practices. Intersectional scholars and activists remind us that the capacity to be recognized as competent or an effective speaker is linked to systemic lines of differences such as race or gender.[31]

Colonial epistemic devaluation comes from what Frantz Fanon called the zone of being (*zone de l'être*) versus the zone of non-being (*zone du non-être*),[32] a racial hierarchy also called coloniality of power.[33] This logic of racialization and dehumanization led to the colonial subject being defined with ontological weight compared to the colonized subject, who is devoid of that essence of humanity. This ontological devaluation initially enabled looting, apartheid, rape, killing, enslavement, and modern-day mass imprisonment and later led to what Maldonado Torres called the "coloniality of being," the fact that Western agents assumed that Others "did not think" or "did not think properly," therefore did not exist as human beings.[34] Because the Western experience became the universal "human experience" and Western knowledge became the master epistemic template, the knowledge produced by Global South communities is not only undervalued but also considered non-existent.[35] Surprisingly, when scholars write about logistical problems in consultations or participation processes at the Bank,[36] or about inclusion/exclusion in global governance,[37] they rarely delve into the colonial undertones of those issues. However, relationships between international organizations and so-called "local populations" (which are ironically only present in the Global South) can be problematic not only because they are akin to colonial encounters but *specifically* because of the colonial social positions they come from.[38]

For example, Pouliot and Thérien studied the dynamics of inclusion (giving a voice to more actors, flatter forms of cooperation, and enhanced accountability) and exclusion (arbitrary selection criteria, reproduction of existing inequalities, and marginalization of certain viewpoints) in global governance.[39] They conclude that new exclusions have emerged despite increased inclusiveness in current global governance practices like multistakeholder partnerships or NGO accreditation. This book complements their argument by examining at how coloniality and epistemic power support these dynamics. By building more critically on scholarship on the coloniality of knowledge and beings in conjunction with practice theories, exclusion mechanisms become at least partly linked to the colonial attribution/

rejection of common humanity. In short, despite institutionalized access to spheres of power for Global South NGOs, the coloniality of power has reinvented itself more subtly in meaning-making processes. By building on Global South research, this chapter goes beyond the idea that better practices equate having more empathy with people beyond one's national, religious, or ethnic social group.[40] It seeks to understand more profoundly the rejection of humanity as linked to epistemic value and worth as a human being.

Coloniality of epistemic power in CoPs

Power at the Bank, or the capacity to achieve something whether by influence, force, or control, is often studied to analyze how the United States directs political orientations[41] or the power to reinforce a neoliberal ideology.[42] In the CoP literature, power (in its epistemic form) is linked to the authority to validate, confirm, or formulate new knowledge and to construct subjectivities and social facts.[43] In short, not everyone has the same ability to negotiate meaning effectively in a field of knowledge or in a desired direction; power mediates the acquisition, maintenance, and transformation of meaning to the extent that it influences what is deemed legitimate and valid. It refers to the capacity to influence epistemes effectively, which is influenced by coloniality of power (including gendered and class-based devaluation processes).[44] Because it happens in practice, this type of power is "emergent" through "the generation and deployment of endogenous resources—social skills and competence."[45] Epistemic power thus refers to the negotiation of competence and the attribution of the authority to define what is and is not competent, that is, the competence of whom it is presumed.[46] The perceived competence of practitioners arranged in communities of practice is based on race, class, colonialism, and gendered systemic lines of differences.[47] Who gets to define competence criteria and access to meaning-making spaces is based on the coloniality of epistemic power, that is, racial hierarchies perduring since colonization.[48]

Competence politics

The most obvious way epistemic power is visible through inclusive practices is in the selection of which NGOs get to be included by Bank CoPs. Bank employees did not attribute all NGOs the same consideration and equal access to the spaces of meaning negotiation. For obvious reasons, large, Western, and well-funded organizations have been included differently than localized sector-specific ones. This is partly explained by the fact that organizations in Western countries usually have larger budgets, more connections with governments, foundations, and international media, and structures more akin to functioning bureaucracies.[49] How the location of headquarters influences the activities of NGOs has been studied extensively without necessarily mentioning that these choices were influenced by colonial lines of difference.[50]

Bank practitioners have developed mechanisms for funding NGOs within Bank-sponsored projects, but financing has historically gone to larger organizations with the capacity to answer calls for applicants. One former NGO practitioner told me that "the local NGOs are sometimes jealous of the attention and funding that the big international NGOs get like Oxfam, Care International, etc."[51] NGOs acting only in one country (often in the Global South) will also be included less often than transnational ones.[52]. The case of inclusion of NGOs at the IMF showed similar trends: they were "skewed toward urban, professional, propertied, male, and culturally Western circles."[53] In short, international organizations will interact differently with NGOs with symbolic or scientific capital,[54] which is influenced by epistemic power. If Global South NGOs have sometimes been included in consultations to render projects more "effective,"[55] what Spivak called the "subaltern"[56] has not been included in a way that could have challenged epistemically the orientation of policies: "the broader lesson could be that global governance 'outreach' to civil society is not a panacea for inclusion; indeed, if conducted in certain ways, the activity can actually deepen exclusion."[57]

As I argued elsewhere, the Bank also prioritizes NGO CoPs with similar technocratic and neoliberal orientations.[58] In addition to their country of origin, the style of advocacy or criticism is an essential factor in being discredited epistemically. As specified by many Bank employees interviewed for this research, there are some NGOs that you "can or cannot work with."[59] Peter Woicke, a former executive vice president of the Bank, mentioned how when they started to consult non-state actors, he was "shocked, disappointed," and "frustrated" by some NGOs' unwillingness to work cooperatively with the Bank."[60] The North/South cleavage in NGO inclusion is very apparent, as well as the dynamics of cooptation of moderate organizations or self-marginalization of more radical ones.[61] The often-unstated obligation for NGOs to align their motivations with the Bank's own objectives makes a de facto selection.[62] For some Bank managers, "it took time" to "start differentiating between NGOs,"[63] and they eventually started to dismiss the ones who were too confrontational in favor of better-funded Western organizations like Amnesty International or the World Wildlife Fund. Organizations that disagreed too openly with borrowing governments or donors, or were too critical of their policies, such as some labor unions, were often sidelined from consultations.[64] This divide followed the lines between the "reformers" (who could be included) and the "rejectionists" (who could not).[65] Through this selection process, institutions "fragmented critique" and created hierarchies between organizations.[66]

In the 1980s, there was also an asymmetry between the amount of (Western) academic formation between Bank practitioners and NGO workers (and Global South government representatives, for that matter), which tainted their epistemic relationship. Today, the "technical firepower" is better distributed, but Bank practitioners will favor NGOs practitioners trained in Western institutions. For example, one international practitioner interviewed for this research remembered a meeting between the Uganda delegation and a World Bank team:

> I was a member of the Ugandan government delegation. There were three of us. Moreover, the World Bank sent a commission on social protection. We faced this group of about 20 Bank staffers with PhDs from top universities

and MBAs from top business schools. Trapped on one side of the table was the Ugandan delegation, two people from the Ugandan Ministry of Economic Planning and Development, and me, from UNICEF. (laughs). A total of five university degrees between the three of us. Total asymmetry of technical firepower.[67]

Including NGOs with the right data

Bank practitioners often explain the selection of members of civil society CoPs with references to the amount of "evidence" they bring to the table. They underline that the size of the organization does not matter as much as the "evidence" they use to support their claims.[68]The Bank CoPs, many employees told me, "respond to data" and "don't want to answer to anecdotal criticism."[69] However, claims to competence are not only linked to professional standards or the amount of "data" an NGO brings to the table. What data is needed and valued depends on ethical judgment. The evaluation of competence is based on normative values on what is considered competent at a certain point in time.[70] Someone who worked for decades at the Bank linked NGOs who had less to offer in terms of evidence with their political orientations:

> There are a lot of organizations on the ground that are often doing outstanding work. But they often do not have the empirical evidence in support of what they are doing. They may way that they do not have the resources to do that kind of additional investigative work. But on the other hand, the result is sometimes that they are not listened to because they do not seem to be. . . . They seem to be standing in a whole set of values but not with always a lot of evidence into what an investment in that program is going to do and whether what the group is doing could be taken to scale.[71]

Especially in the rare instances when macroeconomic or fiscal issues were discussed for the poverty reduction strategy paper (PRSP), only handpicked NGO CoPs, selected according to a strict set of criteria, were allowed to participate. In Malawi, for example, after repeated criticisms by civil society CoP, the government created a working group on macroeconomic and poverty targets, but only two civil society representatives were invited, arguably the less critical ones.[72] Sarah Lister and Warren Nyamugasira believe that in Uganda, groups known to disagree fundamentally with the government or with donors, such as labor unions, were rarely invited to comment on policymaking.[73]

Furthermore, if Global South CoPs still lacked the training Bank teams deemed appropriate, the organization would finance Western training for them. Bank managers would spot and "cherry-pick" mid-level civil society leaders or employees in government offices, and "they would take them off for an all-expenses paid trip for six weeks to Washington, D.C."[74] One interviewee mentioned that the goal of this was to create a "cluster of right-minded individuals in Global South countries . . . so they would end up having people [in the country] that would basically go along with their views."[75] Throughout my discussions with officials and macro-economists at the Bank, I noticed that the "lack of capacity" in many Global South countries, while real, was often equated with a lack of training in the United States.[76] Many interviewees working in NGOs criticized the "hegemony of American economics training" around the world for having silenced dissenting views.[77]

This sort of epistemic selection resulted in the fact that the macroeconomic analysis supporting Bank projects and policies in the 2010s are not fundamentally different from the ones developed in the 1990s. However, NGO workers and other Global South stakeholders more readily agree with them: "these days, the client is more willing, the client job is much more willing because they are starting from a *better base* anyway."[78]

To "train people" was often a way to convince Global South representatives to change their mindset and accept the Bank's orientations, as described by this Bank economist:

> Getting people to move out of that way of thinking, . . . that was the most difficult run of all. And we are still not there in many of these countries. Now that those attitudes have changed just because the old guys have retired and have been replaced by younger people with a different type of training, which is much more market-oriented, it's much easier to communicate to that.[79]

Bank CoPs also eventually saw the value added of contextual knowledge for the success of implementing various projects. Getting context-specific knowledge from aid-targeted communities was cited as probably the "single best reason" for developing participatory projects.[80] NGOs from the Global South have been recognized to have a deeper knowledge of each context than larger ones[81] and NGOs, in general, to be able to offer assistance and expertise to international organizations.[82] For example, Jan Aart Scholte explains how listening to farmers could palliate an urban bias in development policies.[83]

Additionally, if NGOs were selected based on whether they could be instrumental to the effectiveness of Bank projects, delivery NGOs were notably more involved in Bank activities than advocacy ones, which would have had a lot to contribute in terms of establishing priorities. This selection is not neutral but based on including organizations that can serve a specific Western and technocratic idea of a development project or economic success.[84] This focus on effectiveness led to some instrumentalist interpretations of participation:

> Basically, our [community logic] in water projects was that villagers are cheaper than public servants or private contractors. So if we can get free labor from the community to think about or maintain the water tanks, it will increase efficiency. . . . Because villagers' work doesn't really count, it's not in the GDP, they will not get paid for it. It was a very economistic . . . approach to cost. And [WB practitioners] viewed participation in projects

like rural infrastructure, in sanitation, in healthcare, as just a way to get cheap labor. To reduce the cost.[85]

Controlling the process in informal practices

Epistemic power is enacted not only through interactions in a domain of knowledge but also through who controls the process.[86] If controlling the process can reproduce more formal or material hierarchies, it is also tainted by the coloniality of power. First, the preliminary diagnosis of what policies to adopt is often still made by the Bank. A senior manager who worked at the Bank for 15 years explained that he often conducted diagnostics in advance of consultations: "In any negotiations about what to do, the Bank says giving our analysis, this is what we think is feasible."[87] Then, the parameters of what is feasible fall into what the Bank has laid out. One former vice president for the Africa region adds that when a stakeholder is not on board with a project or a decision, the Bank's job is to convince them with their groundwork:

> Hopefully you convince them if you have the arguments. That's why technical work is important. That's why analytical work is important. That's where it comes to me. My office in the region, the whole is to generate that analytical work, to disseminate it, and to use it to inform the design of our operations.[88]

Second, how the Bank regulates the accreditation of NGOS is very politicized and flows from who is defined as a competent participant in policymaking. The definition of competence in practice is not only based on professional evaluations but is at least partly based on racial and gendered structures of differentiation.[89] Giving the coloniality of epistemic power, the Bank sets out criteria for admission in advance: "Organizations that have general consultative status . . . may contribute in a discussion, whereas roster consultative status enable participation by invitation only (i.e., when and where member states deem it relevant)."[90] These criteria follow formal hierarchies (who can include/exclude NGOs from formal negotiations) and informal rules in practice (who is mentioned in the invitation list, whom organizers know, etc.). In the ECOSOC NGO committee, for example, states often try to regulate NGOs access based on their former political positions.[91] Leon Gordenker and Thomas Weiss describe this process as a "mixture of conflict, competition, cooperation, and cooptation."[92]

An economist working at the Bank since 1996 added that the "coordination" between stakeholders and consulted parties also remains in the hands of Bank CoPs because otherwise it "wouldn't make sense."[93] Therefore, Bank teams often keep control of the logistical aspects leading to meaning-negotiation processes, which establishes informally Western consultation practices. However, more decentralized processes and more informality in coordinating would not necessarily equate to greater participation. While ensuring more flexibility, the informality of participation rules can also open the door to arbitrariness, self-mandating, and exclusion in the participation process.[94]

The recording of consultative meetings with NGOs is likewise under the control of Bank practitioners. African researchers who participated in consultations criticized this routine, especially regarding the inclusion of African scholars and advocacy NGO in World Bank policies. While being invited to the table (formal inclusion), the recording of their thoughts differed from their Western counterparts (informal rules). If they were pressuring the Bank to integrate cultural and socio-political aspects of development, they noticed that the Bank only retained concepts such as "good governance" and only within countries rather than good governance between countries.[95] These inequalities are based not only on formal power to control the process but also on whose points Bank organizers deemed valid to register in official recordings. The Bank would still inscribe on a given report that so and so were consulted, but African NGOs had the impression that their participation could have been more meaningful. One Bank senior manager who worked at the Bank for over 40 years underlined the importance of the control of the recording of meetings:

> The question you must ask is the extent to which the summary of what happened is accurate if you read the minutes of these meetings. Remember, it's the Bank summary of what happened: does that summary capture the full texture, the mood of the meeting? Does it capture all the suggestions, including the ones the Bank did not seem to [like]. You have to ask who had the final say on the final draft. There was one meeting I attended, I read the summary and I called the officer and I said: "Hm, was I at the same meeting"? I was sort of there, but I don't remember most of this happening. . . . I am not sure I would call this a summary of the discussion. Because this is not, in my opinion, an accurate description of either the balance or the mood.'[96]

This expression of the coloniality of epistemic power created resentment among NGOs who participated in meetings and consultative processes under the PRSP. A manager working at the Bank since 1998 said that, in his opinion, the development agenda is not about "figuring out what we need to do but about implementing, measuring and ensuring compliance with what has already been agreed to do." He explained the bitterness felt by some organizations with which he worked with:

> They still express great concern about community consultation. Participation is often described as 'be invited to a meeting to discuss the plan, the poverty reduction plan for a country and be asked for their opinion'. And often that ends there. So people are increasingly reluctant to take part in consultative processes of that nature because the result is even if they disagreed: it will be described as "we had a consultation with communities with this or this part of Kenya for instance, and those kinds of things." You know: inviting people to respond to a plan is really different from a community-based planning. The civil society groups that I keep contact with a number of countries are still

very skeptical about how they classify inaction as being participatory and going to meetings that are not, in the end, participatory.[97]

Conclusion

Even if the experience of the PRSP ended in 2014 with the end of the Highly Indebted Poor Countries initiative, many observers and a majority of people I spoke to at the Bank still consider the PRSP as a "tipping point" in multilateral development policy.[98] Even without radical power-sharing and the persistence of the coloniality of epitsemic power, the Bank's practices have evolved. The PRSP, and especially the tenure of James Wolfensohn, participated in "breaking the ice" with NGOs.[99] In other words, PRSPs acted as an anchoring practice: they rendered other practices possible as they accelerated the adoption of consultative mechanisms, tools, and concepts that endured beyond 2014.[100]

However, many Bank employees today recognize that inclusion does not mean "empowerment" in terms of "power-sharing":

> When you ask the difference between the structural adjustment programs and the PRSP, your starting point is that we are not going to level the playfield so everybody will be equal. Because they are not equal: they do not have equal power. I am still not convinced that the Bank has a concept of empowerment that refers to power sharing.[101]

Without depoliticizing the term "to decolonize,"[102] IR scholars still need to address the impact of the coloniality of power ontologically (in the world) and epistemologically (in our discipline). This will give us not only a better understanding of world politics but also a glimpse of epistemic freedom: "the right to think, to rise, interpret the world, develop own methodologies and write from where one is located and unencumbered by Eurocentrism."[103]

Notes

1 Adler, *World Ordering. A Social Theory of Cognitive Evolution*, chapter 10.
2 Holthaus, "Practice Theory and the Opening Up of International Organizations."
3 Avant et al., *Who Governs the Globe?*
4 Pouliot and Thérien, "The Politics of Inclusion: Changing Patterns in the Governance of International Security."
5 This chapter builds on Sondarjee, "Coloniality of Epistemic Power in International Practices," 328–50.
6 Niezen and Sapignoli, *Palaces of Hope: The Anthropology of Global Organizations.*
7 Zürn, "Contested Global Governance," 138.
8 Steffek, "Explaining Cooperation between IGOs and NGOs – Push Factors, Pull Factors, and the Policy Cycle," 999; Rosenau and Czempiel, *Governance without Government: Order and Change in World Politics*; Dingwerth et al., "The Rise of Democratic Legitimation."

9 Falk, *On Humane Governance: Toward a New Global Politics*; Edwards and Gaventa, *Global Citizen Action*; Mackenzie, *Democratizing Global Governance: Ten Years of Case Studies and Reflections by Civil Society Activists*; Kumar, "Global Civil Society: Emergent Forms of Cosmopolitan Democracy and Justice."
10 Raustiala, "States, NGOs, and International Environmental Institutions."
11 Autesserre, *Peaceland: Conflict Resolution and the Everyday Politics Of International Intervention*; Pingeot, "International Peacebuilding as a Case of Structural Injustice"; Sondarjee, "Practice Contestation in and between Communities of Practice."
12 Dingwerth et al., 715.
13 Wolfensohn, *A Global Life*.
14 Tallberg et al., "NGO Influence in International Organizations: Information, Access and Exchange."
15 Woods and Narlikar, "Governance and the Limits of Accountability," 569–83.
16 Sondarjee.
17 Cornwall, "Buzzwords and Fuzzwords: Deconstructing Development Discourse"; Momani, "IMF Rhetoric on Reducing Poverty and Inequality."
18 Lapeyre, "Objectifs Du Millénaire Pour Le Développement : Outils de Développement Ou Cheval de Troie Des Politiques Néolibérales ?"
19 Rahnema, "Participatory Action Research: The Last Temptation of Saint Development"; Amoore and Langley, "Ambiguities of Global Civil Society"; Germain and Kenny, *The Idea of Global Civil Society*; Ruckert, "Producing Neoliberal Hegemony? A Neo-Gramscian Analysis of the PRSP in Nicaragua."
20 Lie, "Developmentality," 13; Dutta and Rastogi, "Deconstructing PRSP Measurement: Participation as Neoliberal Colonization"; Weber, "A Political Analysis of the PRSP Initiative: Social Struggles and the Organization of Persistent Relations of Inequality."
21 Tallberg et al.; Cromm and Volk, "A Partnership of Convenience? Transnational Civil Society, International Organisations and Practices of Global Order."
22 Hofius, "Practice Approaches in International Political Theory," 91.
23 Schatzki, *The Site of the Social: A Philosophical Account of the Constitution of Social Life and Change*, 80.
24 Brown, "The 'Practice Turn', Phronesis and Classical Realism: Towards a Phronetic International Political Theory?"; Frost and Lechner, "Understanding International Practices from the Internal Point of View"; Ralph and Gifkins, "The Purpose of United Nations Security Council Practice: Contesting Competence Claims in the Normative Context Created by the Responsibility to Protect"; Pratt, "From Norms to Normative Configurations"; Hofius, "Practice Approaches in International Political Theory"; Chessé and Sondarjee, "A Feminist Critique of International Practices."
25 Wiener, *Contestation and Constitution of Norms in Global International Relations*.
26 Adler, 268.
27 Adler, 267.
28 Adler, 270.
29 Fanon, *Les Damnés de La Terre*; Mills, *The Racial Contract*; Davis, *Are Prisons Obsolete?*
30 Maldonado-Torres, "On the Coloniality of Being: Contributions to the Development of a Concept."
31 Niemann et al., *Presumed Incompetent*; Chessé and Sondarjee, "A Feminist Critique of International Practices."
32 Fanon, *Les Damnés de La Terre*.
33 Quijano, "Colonialidad y Modernidad/Racionalidad."
34 Maldonado-Torres, 252.
35 Van Milders and Toros, "Violent International Relations," 123.
36 Aycrigg, "Participation and the World Bank Success, Constraints, and Responses"; Mansuri and Rao, *Localizing Development*; O'Meally, "The Contradictions of Pro-Poor Participation and Empowerment: The World Bank in East Africa."

37 Autesserre, *Peaceland: Conflict Resolution and the Everyday Politics of International Intervention*; Pouliot and Thérien.
38 Pingeot; Pampinella, "'The Way of Progress and Civilization': Racial Hierarchy and US State Building in Haiti and the Dominican Republic (1915–1922)."
39 Pouliot and Thérien.
40 Crawford, "Toward a Theory of Progress in International Relations," 456–58.
41 Wade, "US Hegemony and the World Bank: The Fight over People and Ideas"; Peet, *Unholy Trinity. The IMF, World Bank and WTO*; Andersen et al., "US Politics and World Bank IDA-Lending."
42 Haslam, "The Firm Rules: Multinational Corporations, Policy Space and Neoliberalism"; Ruckert; McGoey et al., "Le Philanthrocapitalisme et Les « crimes Des Dominants »"; Sondarjee.
43 Adler and Bernstein, "Knowledge in Power: The Epistemic Construction of Global Governance."
44 Lugones, "Toward a Decolonial Feminism"; Tamale, *Decolonization and Afro-Feminism*.
45 Adler-Nissen and Pouliot, "Power in Practice: Negotiating the International Intervention in Libya," 889.
46 Niemann et al.; Adler-Nissen and Pouliot, "Power in Practice: Negotiating the International Intervention in Libya."
47 Chessé and Sondarjee, "A Feminist Critique of International Practices."
48 Quijano.
49 Elliot, "Some Aspects of Relations between the North and South in the NGO Sector"; Salm, "Coping with Globalization: A Profile of the Northern NGO Sector."
50 Eccleston, "Does North-South Collaboration Enhance NGO Influence on Deforestation Policies in Malaysia and Indonesia?"; Mawdsley et al., "Trust, Accountability, and Face-to-Face Interaction in North-South NGO Relations."
51 Interview 10, June 13, 2017.
52 Alger, "The Emerging Role for NGOs in the UN System: From Article 71 to a People's Millennium Assembly."
53 Scholte, "A More Inclusive Global Governance? The IMF and Civil Society in Africa," 187.
54 Eagleton-Pierce, "Professionalizing Protest."
55 Sondarjee, "Collective Learning at the Boundaries of Communities of Practice."
56 Spivak, "Can the Subaltern Speak?"
57 Scholte, 187.
58 Sondarjee.
59 Interview 14, June 26, 2017.
60 Interview, OHP Peter Woicke, March 7, 2005.
61 Pouliot and Thérien, 168; Anderl, *Broken Solidarities*.
62 Willetts, "What Is a Non-Governmental Organization? UNESCO Encyclopedia of Life Support Systems."
63 Interview OHP Peter Woicke, March 7, 2005.
64 Lister and Nyamugasira, "Design Contradictions in the 'New Architecture of Aid'?" 99; Anderl et al., "Keeping Your Enemies Close? The Variety of Social Movements' Reactions to International Organizations' Opening Up."
65 (Scholte 2004).
66 Anderl, *Broken Solidarities*, 7.
67 Interview 10, June 13, 2017.
68 Interview 5, May 25, 2017.
69 Interview 15, June 27, 2017.
70 Frost, *Global Ethics*; Gross Stein, "Background Knowledge in the Foreground: Conversations about Competent Practices in 'Sacred Space'," 90; Hofius, "Practice Approaches in International Political Theory," 92.
71 Interview 5, May 25, 2017.

72 International Confederation of Free Trade Unions, Submission to IMF/World Bank Review on the PRSP Process, Washington DC, November 13, 2001, cited in Rowden and Irama 2004.
73 Lister and Nyamugasira, "Design Contradictions in the 'New Architecture of Aid'?" 99.
74 Interview 11, June 15, 2017.
75 Interview 11, June 15, 2017; Interview 26, July 24, 2017.
76 Interview 26, July 24, 2017.
77 Interview 11, June 15, 2017.
78 Interview 26, July 24, 2017, *emphasis added.*
79 Interview 26, July 24, 2017.
80 Interview 9, June 9, 2017.
81 Elliot.
82 Steffek, "Explaining Cooperation between IGOs and NGOs – Push Factors, Pull Factors, and the Policy Cycle," 1004–5; Albin, "Can NGOs Enhance the Effectiveness of International Negotiation?"; Charnovitz, "Two Centuries of Participation: NGOs and International Governance."
83 Scholte, 186.
84 Sondarjee.
85 Interview 10, June 13, 2017.
86 Pouliot and Thérien, 168.
87 Interview 4, May 10, 2017.
88 Interview 20, July 17, 2017.
89 Chessé and Sondarjee, "A Feminist Critique of International Practices"; Nair, "Sociability in International Politics."
90 Pouliot and Thérien, 168.
91 Martens, *NGOs and the United Nations: Institutionalization, Professionalization and Adaptation*, 132.
92 Gordenker and Weiss, "NGO Participation in the International Policy Process," 551.
93 Interview 7, May 29, 2017.
94 Bexell and Mörth, "Introduction: Partnerships, Democracy, and Governance," 171.
95 Mkandawire, "'Good Governance': The Itinerary of an Idea," 680; Pierre, "The Racial Vernaculars of Development: A View from West Africa."
96 Interview 18, July 16, 2017.
97 Interview 5, May 25, 2017.
98 Christiansen and Hovland, "The PRSP Initiative."
99 Interview 32, November 6, 2017.
100 Swidler, "What Anchors Cultural Practices"; Sending and Neumann, "Banking on Power: How Some Practices in an International Organization Anchor Others," 237.
101 Interview 5, May 25, 2017.
102 Sondarjee and Andrews, "Decolonizing International Relations and Development Studies"; Moosavi, "The Decolonial Bandwagon and the Dangers of Intellectual Decolonisation."
103 Ndlovu-Gatsheni, *Epistemic Freedom in Africa*, 3.

References

Adler, Emanuel. *World Ordering. A Social Theory of Cognitive Evolution*. Cambridge: Cambridge University Press, 2019.

Adler, Emanuel, and Steven Bernstein. "Knowledge in Power: The Epistemic Construction of Global Governance." In *Power in Global Governance*, 294–318. Cambridge: Cambridge University Press, 2005.

Adler-Nissen, Rebecca, and Vincent Pouliot. "Power in Practice: Negotiating the International Intervention in Libya." *European Journal of International Relations* 20, no. 4 (2014): 889–911.

Albin, Cecilia. "Can NGOs Enhance the Effectiveness of International Negotiation?" *International Negotiation* 4, no. 3 (1999): 371–87.

Alger, C. "The Emerging Role for NGOs in the UN System: From Article 71 to a People's Millennium Assembly." *Global Governance* 8, no. 1 (2002): 93–117.

Amoore, L., and P. Langley. "Ambiguities of Global Civil Society." *Review of International Studies* 30, no. 1 (2004): 89–110.

Anderl, Felix. *Broken Solidarities: How Open Global Governance Divides and Rules*. Bristol: Bristol University Press, 2022.

Anderl, Felix, P. Daphi, and Nicole Deitelhoff. "Keeping Your Enemies Close? The Variety of Social Movements' Reactions to International Organizations' Opening Up." *International Studies Review* 23, no. 4 (2021): 1273–99.

Andersen, Thomas Barnebeck, Henrik Hansen, and Thomas Markussen. "US Politics and World Bank IDA-Lending." *The Journal of Development Studies* 42, no. 5 (July 2006): 772–94.

Autesserre, Séverine. *Peaceland: Conflict Resolution and the Everyday Politics of International Intervention*. Cambridge: Cambridge University Press, 2014.

Avant, Deborah D., Martha Finnemore, and Susan K. Sell, eds. *Who Governs the Globe?* Cambridge Studies in International Relations 114. Cambridge, UK and New York: Cambridge University Press, 2010.

Aycrigg, Maria. "Participation and the World Bank Success, Constraints, and Responses." In *Draft for Discussion at the International Conference on Upscaling and Mainstreaming Participation: Lessons Learned and Ways Forward*. Washington, DC: The World Bank, 1998.

Best, Jacqueline. "Technocratic Exceptionalism: Monetary Policy and the Fear of Democracy." *International Political Sociology* 12, no. 4 (December 1, 2018): 328–45.

Bexell, M., and U. Mörth. "Introduction: Partnerships, Democracy, and Governance." In *Democracy and Public–Private Partnerships in Global Governance.*, 3–23. Basingstoke: Palgrave Macmillan, 2010.

Brown, Chris. "The 'Practice Turn', Phronesis and Classical Realism: Towards a Phronetic International Political Theory?" *Millennium – Journal of International Studies* 40, no. 3 (2012): 439–56.

Charnovitz, Steve. "Two Centuries of Participation: NGOs and International Governance." *Michigan Journal of International Law* 18, no. 1 (1997): 183–286.

Chessé, Alice, and Maïka Sondarjee. "A Feminist Critique of International Practices." *International Studies Quarterly* 68, no. 2 (2024): 1–10.

Christiansen, Karin, and Ingie Hovland. *The PRSP Initiative: Multilateral Policy Change and the Role of Research*. London: Overseas Development Institute, 2003.

Cornwall, Andrea. "Buzzwords and Fuzzwords: Deconstructing Development Discourse." *Development in Practice* 17, no. 4/5 (2007): 471–84.

Crawford, Beverly. "Toward a Theory of Progress in International Relations." In *Progress in Postwar International Relations*, edited by Emanuel Adler and Beverly Crawford. New York: Columbia University Press, 1991.

Cromm, Christiane, and Christian Volk. "A Partnership of Convenience? Transnational Civil Society, International Organisations and Practices of Global Order." *Global Society* 38, no. 3 (2024): 317–27.

Davis, Angela Y. *Are Prisons Obsolete?* Open Media Book. New York: Seven Stories Press, 2003.

Dingwerth, Klaus, Henning Schmidtke, and Tobias Weise. "The Rise of Democratic Legitimation: Why International Organizations Speak the Language of Democracy." *European Journal of International Relations* 26, no. 3 (September 2020): 714–41.

Dutta, Mohan, and Rahul Rastogi. "Deconstructing PRSP Measurement: Participation as Neoliberal Colonization." *Journal of Creative Communications* 11, no. 3 (2016): 211–26.

Eagleton-Pierce, Matthew. "Professionalizing Protest: Scientific Capital and Advocacy in Trade Politics." *International Political Sociology* 12, no. 3 (September 1, 2018): 233–55. https://doi.org/10.1093/ips/oly011.

Eccleston, Bernard. "Does North-South Collaboration Enhance NGO Influence on Deforestation Policies in Malaysia and Indonesia?" *Commonwealth & Comparative Politics* 34, no. 1 (1996): 66–89.
Edwards, M., and J. Gaventa. *Global Citizen Action*. Boulder, CO: Lynne Rienner Publishers, 2001.
Elliot, Charles. "Some Aspects of Relations between the North and South in the NGO Sector." *World Development* 15, no. 1 (1987): 57–68.
Falk, R. *On Humane Governance: Toward a New Global Politics*. Cambridge: Polity Press, 1995.
Fanon, Frantz. *Les Damnés de La Terre*. Paris: Maspéro, 1961.
Frost, Mervyn. *Global Ethics: Anarchy, Freedom and International Relations*. Critical Issues in Global Politics. London and New York: Routledge, 2009.
Frost, Mervyn, and Silviya Lechner. "Understanding International Practices from the Internal Point of View." *Journal of International Political Theory* (2015): 1–21.
Germain, R. D., and M. Kenny. *The Idea of Global Civil Society*. London: Routledge, 2005.
Gordenker, Leon, and Thomas G. Weiss. "NGO Participation in the International Policy Process." *Third World Quarterly* 16, no. 3 (1995): 543–56.
Gross Stein, Janice. "Background Knowledge in the Foreground: Conversations about Competent Practices in 'Sacred Space'." In *International Practices*, edited by Emanuel Adler and Vincent Pouliot, 87–107. Cambridge: Cambridge University Press, 2011.
Haslam, Paul Alexander. "The Firm Rules: Multinational Corporations, Policy Space and Neoliberalism." *Third World Quarterly* 28, no. 6 (September 2007): 1167–83.
Hofius, Maren. "Practice Approaches in International Political Theory." In *Perspectives on International Political Theory in Europe*, edited by Vassilios Paipais, 87–106. Cham: Springer International Publishing, 2021. https://doi.org/10.1007/978-3-030-77274-1_6.
Holthaus, Leonie. "Practice Theory and the Opening Up of International Organizations." *Global Studies Quarterly* 1, no. 3 (September 14, 2021): 1–5.
Kumar, A. "Global Civil Society: Emergent Forms of Cosmopolitan Democracy and Justice." In *Power Shifts and Global Governance: Challenges from South and North* (, edited by A. Kumar and D. Messner. London: Anthem, 2010.
Lapeyre, Frédéric. "Objectifs Du Millénaire Pour Le Développement: Outils de Développement Ou Cheval de Troie Des Politiques Néolibérales ?" *Institut d'études Du Développement de l'Université Catholique de Louvain* (2006). https://www.cetri.be/Objectifs-du-millenaire-pour-le-82.
Lie, Jon Harald Sande. "Developmentality: Indirect Governance in the World Bank–Uganda Partnership." *Third World Quarterly* 36, no. 4 (April 3, 2015): 723–40.
Lister, Sarah, and Warren Nyamugasira. "Design Contradictions in the 'New Architecture of Aid'? Reflections from Uganda on the Roles of Civil Society Organisations." *Development Policy Review* 21, no. 1 (January 2003): 93–106.
Lugones, Marìa. "Toward a Decolonial Feminism." *Hypatia* 25, no. 4 (2010): 742–59.
Mackenzie, H., ed. *Democratizing Global Governance: Ten Years of Case Studies and Reflections by Civil Society Activists*. New Delhi: Mosaic, 2009.
Maldonado-Torres, Nelson. "On the Coloniality of Being: Contributions to the Development of a Concept." *Cultural Studies* 21, no. 2–3 (2007): 240–70.
Mansuri, Ghazala, and Vijayendra Rao. *Localizing Development: Does Participation Work?* Washington, DC: The World Bank, 2013.
Martens, Kerstin. *NGOs and the United Nations: Institutionalization, Professionalization and Adaptation*. Basingstoke: Palgrave Macmillan, 2005.
Mawdsley, Emma, Janet G. Townsend, and Gina Porter. "Trust, Accountability, and Face-to-Face Interaction in North-South NGO Relations." *Development in Practice* 15, no. 1 (2005): 77–82.
McGoey, Linsey, Thiel Darren, and Robin West. "Le Philanthrocapitalisme et Les 'crimes Des Dominants '." *Politix* 121 (2018): 29–54.

McIntosh, Mary, Anni Poikolainen, Kimberly Hewitt, Tara Lubin, Kathlen Knoll, Elizabeth McGaha, and Jean D'Amico. *The Global Poll: Multinational Survey of Opinion Leaders 2002*. Washington, DC: Princeton Survey Research Associates for the World Bank., 2003.
Mills, Charles W. *The Racial Contract*. Ithaca: Cornell University Press, 1997.
Mkandawire, Thandike. "'Good Governance': The Itinerary of an Idea." *Development in Practice* 17, no. 4/5 (2007): 679–81.
Momani, Bessma. "IMF Rhetoric on Reducing Poverty and Inequality." In *Global Governance, Poverty and Inequality*, Jennifer Clapp and Rorden Wilkinson, 71–90. New York: Routledge, 2010.
Moosavi, Leon. "The Decolonial Bandwagon and the Dangers of Intellectual Decolonisation." *International Review of Sociology* 30, no. 2 (May 3, 2020): 332–54.
Nair, Deepak. "Sociability in International Politics: Golf and ASEAN's Cold War Diplomacy." *International Political Sociology* 14, no. 2 (June 1, 2020): 196–214. https://doi.org/10.1093/ips/olz024.
Ndlovu-Gatsheni, Sabelo J. *Epistemic Freedom in Africa: Deprovincialization and Decolonization*. Rethinking Development. London and New York: Routledge, Taylor & Francis Group, 2018.
Niemann, Yolanda Flores, Gabriella Gutiérrez y Muhs, and Carmen G. Gonzáles, eds. *Presumed Incompetent: The Intersections of Race and Class for Women in Academia*. Boulder, CO: University Press of Colorado, 2012.
Niezen, Ronald, and Maria Sapignoli, eds. *Palaces of Hope: The Anthropology of Global Organizations*. Cambridge: Cambridge University Press, 2017.
O'Meally, Simon. "The Contradictions of Pro-Poor Participation and Empowerment: The World Bank in East Africa." *Development and Change* 45, no. 6 (2014): 1248–83.
Pampinella, Stephen. "'The Way of Progress and Civilization': Racial Hierarchy and US State Building in Haiti and the Dominican Republic (1915–1922)." *Journal of Global Security Studies* 6, no. 3 (March 1, 2021): 1–17.
Peet, Richard. *Unholy Trinity. The IMF, World Bank and WTO*. New York: Zed Books, 2003.
Pierre, Jemima. "The Racial Vernaculars of Development: A View from West Africa." *American Anthropologist* 122, no. 1 (March 2020): 86–98.
Pingeot, Lou. "International Peacebuilding as a Case of Structural Injustice." *International Peacekeeping* 27, no. 2 (March 14, 2020): 263–88.
Pouliot, Vincent, and Jean-Philippe Thérien. "The Politics of Inclusion: Changing Patterns in the Governance of International Security." *Review of International Studies*, no. 41 (2015): 211–37.
Pratt, Simon Frankel. "From Norms to Normative Configurations: A Pragmatist and Relational Approach to Theorizing Normativity in IR." *International Theory* 12, no. 1 (March 2020): 59–82.
Quijano, Aníbal. "Colonialidad y Modernidad/Racionalidad." *Peru Indigena* 13, no. 29 (1991): 11–29.
Rahnema, Majid. "Participatory Action Research: The Last Temptation of Saint Development." *Alternatives* 15 (1990): 199–226.
Ralph, Jason, and Jess Gifkins. "The Purpose of United Nations Security Council Practice: Contesting Competence Claims in the Normative Context Created by the Responsibility to Protect." *European Journal of International Relations* 23, no. 3 (2017): 630–53.
Raustiala, Kal. "States, NGOs, and International Environmental Institutions." *International Studies Quarterly* 41, no. 4 (1997): 719–40.
Rosenau, James N., and Ernst-Otto Czempiel. *Governance without Government: Order and Change in World Politics*. Cambridge: Cambridge University Press, 1992.
Ruckert, Arne. "Producing Neoliberal Hegemony? A Neo-Gramscian Analysis of the PRSP in Nicaragua." *Studies in Political Economy* 79 (2007): 91–118.
Salm, Janet. "Coping with Globalization: A Profile of the Northern NGO Sector." *Nonprofit and Voluntary Sector Quarterly* 28, no. 1_suppl (1999): 87–103.

Schatzki, Theodore Richard. *The Site of the Social: A Philosophical Account of the Constitution of Social Life and Change*. University Park: The Pennsylvania State University Press, 2002.
Scholte, Jan Aart. "Civil Society and Democratically Accountable Global Governance." *Government and Opposition* 39, no. 2 (2004): 211–33.
Scholte, Jan Aart. "A More Inclusive Global Governance? The IMF and Civil Society in Africa." *Global Governance: A Review of Multilateralism and International Organizations* 18, no. 2 (August 12, 2012): 185–206.
Sending, Ole Jacob, and Iver B. Neumann. "Banking on Power: How Some Practices in an International Organization Anchor Others." In *International Practices*, edited by Emanuel Adler and Vincent Pouliot, 231–54. New York: Cambridge University Press, 2011.
Sondarjee, Maïka. "Change and Stability at the World Bank: Inclusive Practices and Neoliberal Technocratic Rationality." *Third World Quarterly* 42, no. 2 (2021): 348–65.
Sondarjee, Maïka. "Collective Learning at the Boundaries of Communities of Practice: Inclusive Policymaking at the World Bank." *Global Society* 35, no. 3 (2021): 307–26.
Sondarjee, Maïka. "Coloniality of Epistemic Power in International Practices: NGO Inclusion in World Bank Policymaking." *Global Society* 38, no. 3 (2024): 328–50. https://doi.org/10.1080/13600826.2023.2236129.
Sondarjee, Maïka. "Practice Contestation in and between Communities of Practice: From Top-Down to Inclusive Policymaking at the World Bank." *Global Studies Quarterly* 4, no. 1 (January 27, 2024): 1. https://doi.org/10.1093/isagsq/ksad071.
Sondarjee, Maïka, and Nathan Andrews. "Decolonizing International Relations and Development Studies: What's in a Buzzword?" *International Journal: Canada's Journal of Global Policy Analysis* 77, no. 4 (2023): 551–71. https://doi.org/10.1177/00207020231166588.
Spivak, Gayatri Chakravorty. "Can the Subaltern Speak?" In *Marxism and the Interpretation of Culture*, edited by C. Nelson and L. Grossberg, 271–313. Basingstoke: Macmillan, 1988.
Steffek, Jens. "Explaining Cooperation between IGOs and NGOs – Push Factors, Pull Factors, and the Policy Cycle." *Review of International Studies* 39, no. 4 (October 2013): 993–1013.
Swidler, Ann. "What Anchors Cultural Practices." In *The Practice Turn in Contemporary Theory.*, edited by Karin Knorr Cetina, Theodore Richard Schatzki, and Eike Von Savigny. New York: Routledge, 2000.
Tallberg, Jonas, Lisa M. Dellmuth, Hans Agné, and Andreas Duit. "NGO Influence in International Organizations: Information, Access and Exchange." *British Journal of Political Science* 48, no. 1 (January 2018): 213–38.
Tamale, Sylvia. *Decolonization and Afro-Feminism*. Ottawa: Daraja Press, 2020.
Van Milders, Lucas, and Harmonie Toros. "Violent International Relations." *European Journal of International Relations* 26, no. 1_suppl (September 2020): 116–39.
Wade, Robert. "US Hegemony and the World Bank: The Fight over People and Ideas." *Review of International Political Economy* 9, no. 2 (2002): 215–43.
Weber, Heloise. "A Political Analysis of the PRSP Initiative: Social Struggles and the Organization of Persistent Relations of Inequality." *Globalizations* 3, no. 2 (2006): 187–206.
Wiener, Antje. *Contestation and Constitution of Norms in Global International Relations*. Cambridge: Cambridge University Press, 2018. https://doi.org/10.1017/9781316718599.
Willetts, Peter. "What Is a Non-Governmental Organization? UNESCO Encyclopedia of Life Support Systems." 2002. www.sta.city.ac.uk/p.willetts/CS-NTWKS/NGO-ART.HTM.
Wolfensohn, James D. *A Global Life: My Journey among Rich and Poor, from Sydney to Wall Street to the World Bank*. 1st ed. New York: PublicAffairs, 2010.
Woods, Ngaire, and Amrita Narlikar. " 'Governance and the Limits of Accountability: The WTO, the IMF and the World Bank." *International Social Science Journal* 53, no. 170 (2001): 569–83.
Zürn, Michael. "Contested Global Governance." *Global Policy* 9, no. 1 (February 2018): 138–45. https://doi.org/10.1111/1758-5899.12521.

9 Conclusion

Implications for multilateral development policymaking

This book presented a story of social ordering through communities of practice in world politics. From 1980 to 2014, World Bank employees, organized in domains of knowledge, increasingly adopted inclusive practices because they learned that it improved the effectiveness of projects and policies. Effectiveness was conceived in terms of social acceptability, access to more comprehensive data, and better results. If the goal remained to devise effective technical solutions to problems, Bank communities of practice (CoPs) redefined the procedures to get there. While including borrowing governments, populations, or civil society organizations was considered a waste of time or an undue burden during the early 1980s, it was reconceived as a necessary step to effectiveness by the mid-2010s. This growing perception of the value of inclusive practices is connected to a changing relationship between the Bank and aid-targeted populations. To uncover collective learning processes, this book disaggregated the Bank into a collective of communities, and the focus was put on the interactions between CoPs inside and outside the formal walls of the organization. Collective learning has been described as a relational and processual unfolding of social interactions that occur at the boundaries between CoPs on a day-to-day basis. Finally, inclusive practices were analyzed in terms of coloniality of epistemic power or racial stratifications in meaning-making processes.

While there is no "scientific" way to measure precisely *when* a change of practice happened in the social world, the volume of contestation and interactions at the boundaries between CoPs is a good indicator. This is why manuals and how-to books in management emphasize the creation of CoPs for employees to learn.[1] These processes around the value of inclusion amounted to critical mass of practice institutionalization in the 2000s. The amount of new inclusive tools and mechanisms eventually weighed so much that we may analytically assert that we witnessed the institutionalization of inclusive practices. Many other attempted changes never reached such a tipping point. In this case, the shift occurred because of the number of interactions at the boundary (including smooth and conflictual ones). Methodologically, because this book was an effort at theory building, the goal was not to catalogue all instances of boundary encounters, boundary brokering, and the use of epistemic boundary objects or to focus on only one CoP, like others did.[2] The goal was to demonstrate an extensive collective learning process within an organization as a whole and the interactions between multiple CoPs.

DOI: 10.4324/9781003529279-9

In the end, a collective learning framework tells a commonsensical but rarely told story – arguably a useful story to understand reality better. Everyone agrees that people learn, but seldom are those who investigated those processes in IR. Like Kenneth Waltz stated more than 40 years ago, the aim is not to construct an all-encompassing law-like theory but to "construct a theory of international politics that remedies the defects of present theories."[3] Wrongly associated with positivist epistemological approaches, Waltz, instead, was not attempting to test a theory on reality or develop a true depiction of reality, but to design "a picture, mentally formed, of a bounded realm or domain of activity."[4] After carefully looking at the World Bank and inclusive practices for years and reading what a multitude of scholars have written about it, this book is an attempt to form a helpful picture to understand the emergence and institutionalization of inclusive practices.

Change and stability

> The Bank should be making a claim that it is not just more of the same – more of the past – that we are a new paradigm. We're behaving in a new way. . . . It doesn't mean we were wrong (in the past). For example, if you go to a doctor to get a treatment today, it would be very different from the same disease you got 25 years ago. Doesn't mean the doctor was a quack 25 years ago. It means that our knowledge and our science has progressed. It would be a disaster if it didn't![5]

> To what extent do Bank policies and practices represent something qualitatively different than was done in the past? I see very little evidence that they represent something that is qualitatively different than the things that they have done in the past.[6]

As these quotes suggest, opinions diverge greatly about the extent of the change the Bank went through since the 1980s. Many observers criticize the ideological stability of the Bank, while others (including most Bank officials and employees interviewed for this research) claim that despite stability in macroeconomic prescriptions, the procedural practices of the organization changed a great deal because of a modification in attitude and procedures. A collective learning framework shows how both can be true. Change and stability in social ordering are not only simultaneous processes but self-reinforcing ones. I explored more in-depth elsewhere how the process of translation of new practices in CoPs not only fitted but also reinforced an existing political rationality: new knowledge is mediated through an organization's predispositions and often reinforces them.[7] Knowledge is not transferred but transformed through translation. Inclusive practices were institutionalized either because they fitted the Bank's political, neoliberal, and technocratic rationality or because they were easily translatable into a neoliberal, technocratic version. In other words, a certain ethos of the Bank was reinforced precisely because it modified its procedural practices. This follows studies that look at how international organizations translate potentially transformative ideas into technocratic objects, such as toning down macroprudential agendas at the IMF;[8] the development of measurable poverty indicators at the World Bank;[9] the economization of climate change;[10] and more generally, how the Bank has made countries of the Global South legible by providing one-size-fits-all developmental responses.[11]

Bank employees institutionalized inclusion practices without contradicting their technocratic and neoliberal ethos. When we learn, it is less challenging to our consciousness to translate new knowledge, tools, and practices through our political rationality to make them fit our existing predispositions. Change thus happened at the tactical level (the effectiveness of development projects and policies) rather than through a redefinition of the goals that should be pursued (development and growth through technical solutions). While substantively significant and meaningful, the emergence and institutionalization of inclusive practices stabilized the Bank's technocratic and neoliberal political rationality.[12] In other words, Bank employees did not adopt new practices in opposition to the Bank's political rationality, but translated them *through it.*

While the emergence of inclusive practices impacted the relationship of the Bank to Global South communities and officials by making it in principle more democratic – or at least less paternalistic – Bank employees translated radical ideas of empowerment and ownership into technocratic consultative practices. By doing so, they not only reinforced their technocratic political rationality but also spread this vision of development to other stakeholders. Collective learning is a conceptual apparatus that has the potential to explain change and stability, points to the relationship between levels of analysis, and highlights factors that induce fluctuations of practices, which are not only linked to organizational culture or normative structures.

This book argues that Bank employees genuinely adopted inclusive practices, which simultaneously served to stabilize the overall ethos of the organization. If institutions often "create the fragmentation of critique through its disorientation,"[13] the process of integration of critique sometimes happens through the translation of radical ideas to make them fit institutions' existing mode of thought. Even if some inclusive mechanisms were too radical to be scaled up, most were malleable enough to be translated into versions that fit the Bank's political rationality, which reinforced it. New knowledge in a community of practice is always circumscribed by existing predispositions.

In the case of the Bank, their technocratic vision is closely linked to a neoliberal one. Neoliberalism is neither a set of economic prescriptions (e.g., liberalization, privatization, macroeconomic stability) nor a bourgeois ideology imposed by capitalist elites. Neoliberalism is first and foremost a form of power that dictates a set of standards of action for our subjectivity – what Uma Kothari calls the "neoliberal development imaginaries."[14] In this sense, as French philosophers Pierre Dardot and Christian Laval define it, a neoliberal rationality includes discourse, techniques, tools, and practices that homogenize our *rationality* in a form of managerial effectiveness.[15] Neoliberalism as a mode of thought is not an external constraint like the neoliberal economic policies of the structural adjustment programs in the 1980s, nor is it only a form of government in which laws or tactics are imposed on borrowing populations to arrange things in such a way that a dominant actor's goals can be achieved.[16] The neoliberal political rationality affects how we think we should act in the economic sphere, as well as how we should act in all situations, in the most intimate corners of our subjectivity.[17] While neoliberalism as macroeconomic policy prescriptions may have been relaxed since the heyday of the structural adjustment period, it is more appropriate to see neoliberalism today as a socially diffuse system of norms that operates in the form of imperatives of managerial effectiveness. It is through this rationality that Bank employees understand and adopt new practices.

Neo-Gramscian and Marxist scholars have argued that the Bank's inclusive practices serve to co-opt and control subaltern forces;[18] are a tactic employed to hide neoliberal policies;[19] are part of a coherent strategy to build a capitalist hegemony;[20] or aim to support capitalist elites.[21] In critical development approaches, in general, there is often an assumption of malevolence by Bank employees. For example, using a developmentality framework, Jon Sande Lie argues that donors implemented inclusive practices in an attempt to control or "govern" aid-targeted populations in what he calls an "orchestrated shift."[22] However, describing changes at the Bank as intentionally instigated to dominate Global South communities or to impose an economic framework comes from a misunderstanding of how practices evolve in bureaucracies and often does not acknowledge aid-targeted communities' agency.

Such critiques also tend to give an analytical priority to stability, as if because the Bank's ethos appears similar over time, it *did not change*, or it changed *in order to stay the same.* This attribution of intentionality or inherent stability leads to strong but flawed criticisms of development institutions. To accurately criticize Bank actions in the Global South and their impact on development knowledge – a crucial task for development scholars – we need to refine our understanding of what Bank employees do and why. The argument here is that significant and genuine change toward more inclusive policymaking processes *reinforced* World Bank employees' neoliberal, technocratic rationality. Consequently, in adopting inclusive practices, Bank employees maintained and transmitted a vision of development as a technical problem that can be solved through reproducible, effective solutions. This study thus goes one step further than scholars who study how Bank employees adopt technocratic tools, discourse, or knowledge to look at the *evolution* of radical practices into technocratic ones. While they learned about inclusive practices, Bank CoPs translated radical tools and mechanisms associated with empowerment and participation through their political rationality into specific technocratic and neoliberal versions. This rationality led them to adopt what they defined as "non-ideological" solutions to development problems that were theoretically replicable in other contexts.[23] It also led to a sustained effort to quantify, standardize, and formalize problems and solutions to reduce ambiguity in an unpredictable world.[24]

The translation of radical practices through Bank employees' neoliberal rationality explains why inclusive practices faded away from their radical roots, such as supporting bottom-up social movements, initiating citizen-led projects or financing grassroots organizations. This neoliberal rationality prevented the adoption of more radical practices by Bank CoPs and translated them into versions that fit into the overall ethos of the organization. It also explains why other more radical practices were never adopted in the first place, as they would have contradicted the Bank's rationality. Examples of practices that were not adopted include radically redistributing voting rights at the Bank, considering Indigenous knowledge in infrastructure projects, or supporting union struggles.

This idea of translation through a political rationality sheds light on issues of intentionality and might be useful for social activists' advocacy claims or criticisms of international institutions. World Bank practitioners did not participate in spreading a neoliberal technocratic rationality because of a cost-benefit calculation and a rational desire to either integrate Global South countries into global capitalism or to better control their populations. Many CoPs within the Bank participated in promoting inclusive practices because they *genuinely believed* that they would improve development projects and policies. Bringing to light these intentions is important for our understanding (and our criticism) of international practices in general.

A discussion of intentionality is meant to answer critics of the emergence of inclusive practices at the Bank who have used terminologies such as a "strategy of appropriation" and "successful cooptation,"[25] a hidden "true agenda,"[26] or a "conscious strategy" of co-optation and social control.[27] The deployment of the neoliberal technocratic rationality goes beyond the mere mechanical imposition on unrepentant individuals and societies; it is integrated into subjectivities in such a way that subjects are encouraged to perform effectively in a given setting without stripping them of their agency.[28] To understand the forms of resistance that the Bank encounters (or the lack thereof), we need to understand neoliberal technocracy as a rationality, that is, as operating through the agency of active subjects, not despite it.

Looking forward

Many political implications flow from this book. First, it showed that it is now difficult to wholeheartedly criticize the Bank without acknowledging the presence of many individuals within the organization who, while making mistakes, aim to democratize their practices. While some Bank employees only aspire to co-opt dissenting voices by including them in the policymaking process or to disaggregate criticisms, many of those who adopted inclusive tools and mechanisms did so as a genuine response to criticisms and to render their projects more effective. As shown empirically, Bank employees now see aid-targeted populations differently, include them in the process of policymaking, and have more respect for their knowledge. Many observers have proved the outdatedness of the vision of development experts who design one-size-fits-all technical projects in Washington, D.C., without having enough context-specific knowledge. The Bank has learned to do things differently, albeit still in a technocratic manner.

One political implication that extends beyond the limits of this book is that we must criticize what is lost in translation. There are many limits of technocratic approaches to solve so-called development problems and recognize that the Bank promotes a certain political vision of effectiveness. The cost of transforming potentially radical practices of inclusion into technical tools to improve effectiveness narrows the potential for Global South populations to achieve emancipation and autonomy. Development workers should thus develop critical awareness of the process of translating radical practices into technocratic ones. Observers and development workers who participate in consultations and participatory practices also need to be critical of their technocratic mindset or their white gaze when they work with so-called partners in the Global South. Such critical awareness should enjoin them to question their assumptions about their work and search for alternatives to existing development models. By doing so, development workers should weave in political action, collective mobilization, *as well as* more technical tools. Poverty should be better captured qualitatively and locally, and solutions should equally be context-based.

Another implication concerns the pressing need to repoliticize the development process. A technocratic rationality leads most organizations to depoliticize development projects and solve the symptoms instead of the deep-seated causes of global inequalities and poverty. International self-identified experts too often consider development as a technical issue and global power relations and market inequalities as given, as well as ignoring village or city feuds. There is already a global movement to bring national histories back, to understand each context differently, and to avoid one-size-fits-all solutions. This would lead to the adoption of locally tailored solutions led by Global South actors without necessarily rejecting support from international organizations, which can act as powerful actors in dismantling inequalities. Re-politicization also means that there is a need to understand extra-national factors such as unequal trade relationships, neo-colonial interactions, and the growing power of multinationals and foreign direct investment in Global South communities – elements that are currently largely ignored by liberal development organizations. Understanding the relationship between the Bank discursive claims and its actions has political implications for how activists wish to target the organization and push it toward new practices.[29]

That being said, inclusive practices, even if technocratic, can offer pockets for emancipation. An interesting parallel case is Elisabeth Prügl's study of the neoliberalization of feminism, which has entailed the translation of feminist ideas into mainstream (neoliberal) ideas, including the commodification of non-market values and the casting of women as individualized economic agents. Under the pretense of "corporate social responsibility," multinational companies such as Levi Strauss and Co. or Unilever's Shakti Project seek "to empower them within a neoliberal rationality of government."[30] While critical of corporate social responsibility, Prügl argues that this process is not only a matter of co-opting women to already defined plans: neoliberal inclusive practices sometimes have the potential to open a space for mobilization and collective emancipation. Activists and advocates against the World Bank must be aware of these potential spaces for influence.

A group of researchers also analyzed the impact of a participatory forest management project in India and concluded that, despite many challenges, the project generated political strength, enabling villagers to mobilize from the bottom up. During the project, villagers were able to successfully rally against a polluting mine and managed to secure the construction of a new road. After the project, the power imbalances with respect to forest resources between some village groups were righted. If these outcomes were not caused by the participatory project per se, they were the effect of "villagers taking the project and using it to create their own futures."[31] The project, in that sense, opened up a novel political space for villagers, one that might have been absent otherwise.

Finally, consulting Global South populations or so-called partners should mean being ready to challenge one's assumptions, and aid workers should aim for a greater qualitative depth and breadth when they develop inclusive tools. They should demonstrate a willingness to challenge their own points of view. This has been identified as perhaps the most fundamental demonstration of procedural fairness and legitimacy in the deliberative process.[32] Participation should be a "multi-way set of interactions" between citizens, governments, external actors, and other stakeholders to produce the desired outcome.[33] This is often the goal in so-called localization processes. This will require work but is necessary if development workers and institutions want to address development challenges in the Global South in a truly democratic manner.

Additionally, inclusion should be more gender-sensitive and consider racial privilege. The international cooperation sector in Western countries is now realizing its often implicit racial and colonial biases and is currently searching ways to establish more equal relationships with non-Western partners and to deconstruct the colonial biases of development policies.[34] Yet, the white savior industrial complex is still an overarching structure in world politics. It is a double-edged sword where companies and Western governments exploit, dispossess and oppress from one hand and offer palliative sectoral solutions from the other, making them feel good in the process.[35] Inclusive development, or new trends of localization, should especially be understood in intersectional and decolonial terms. Development organizations and bilateral actors can do better in their attempt to redistribute wealth while establishing equal relationships with aid-targeted populations.

One avenue for future research would be including more systematically systemic racism and colonial variables in our understanding of inclusion and participation. Inclusion as a liberal endeavor might be a better way to devise practices, projects, and policies in world politics, but remnants of colonial power and thinking might hinder such processes. To understand resistance to Western organizations and unwillingness to work within the confines of Western liberalism, we need to better grasp the coloniality of power and the resistance movements against it. This is something that IR practice-oriented research and communities of practice literature have not fully grappled with.

In the end, this book is neither fully optimistic nor fully pessimistic. The change toward more inclusive policymaking practices is encouraging. Adding people to the table, even if the table is not flipped over, is still "better" than not doing so. Even if this process is supported by the coloniality of epistemic power, real utopias must start somewhere.[36] This book does not contend that a technocratic approach to development led by experts is "the worst of all worlds."[37] Even though inclusion has not challenged colonial hierarchies, even if it has stabilized a rationality that ignores the roots of inequality, it has opened space for discussions with actors that were previously ignored. It is undeniable that until everyone can participate equally in world politics, more inclusive practices have had real impacts on real people, making them "better practices," at least in a liberal sense.

Notes

1 Wenger et al., *Cultivating Communities of Practice*; Handley et al., "Within and beyond Communities of Practice: Making Sense of Learning Through Participation, Identity and Practice"; Probst and Borzillo, "Why Communities of Practice Succeed and Why They Fail."
2 Mosse, "Is Good Policy Unimplementable? Reflections on the Ethnography of Aid Policy and Practice"; Sarfaty, "Doing Good Business or Just Doing Good: Competing Human Rights Frameworks at the World Bank."
3 Waltz, *Theory of International Politics*, 1.
4 Waltz, 8; LaRoche and Pratt, "Kenneth Waltz Is Not a Neorealist (and Why That Matters)," 167.
5 Interview OHP Ismail Serageldin, October 25–26 2000, emphasis added.
6 Interview 18, July 16, 2017.
7 Sondarjee, "Change and Stability at the World Bank: Inclusive Practices and Neoliberal Technocratic Rationality."
8 Kranke and Yarrow, "The Global Governance of Systemic Risk."
9 Freistein, "Effects of Indicator Use."
10 Skovgaard, *The Economisation of Climate Change*.
11 Vetterlein, "Seeing Like the World Bank on Poverty."
12 Dardot and Laval, *La nouvelle raison du monde*; Dardot and Laval, "Néolibéralisme et subjectivation capitaliste."
13 Anderl, *Broken Solidarities*, 7.
14 Kothari, "Authority and Expertise," 427.
15 Dardot and Laval, 21.
16 Foucault, "Governmentality."
17 Dardot and Laval.
18 Ruckert, "Producing Neoliberal Hegemony? A Neo-Gramscian Analysis of the PRSP in Nicaragua."
19 Rahnema, "Participatory Action Research: The Last Temptation of Saint Development."
20 Cammack, "What the World Bank Means by Poverty Reduction and Why It Matters."
21 Boas and McNeill, *Global Institutions and Development: Framing the World?*; Goldman, *Imperial Nature*; Moore, *The World Bank: Development, Poverty, Hegemony*.
22 Lie, "Developmentality," 723, 724, 736.
23 Ferguson, *The Anti-Politics Machine*.
24 Best, "Bureaucratic Ambiguity."
25 Kothari, 425.
26 Jackson, *The Globalizers*, 3.
27 Ruckert.
28 Dardot and Laval, 433.
29 Bebbington et al., "Of Texts and Practices: Empowerment and Organisational Cultures in World Bank-Funded Rural Development Programmes," 597–98.
30 Prügl, "Neoliberalising Feminism," 614.
31 Hildyard et al., "Pluralism, Participation and Power: Joint Forest Management in India," 68.

32 Barisione, "Framing a Deliberation. Deliberative Democracy and the Challenge of Framing Processes."
33 Pateman, "APSA Presidential Address: Participatory Democracy Revisited," 421.
34 Peace Direct et al., "Time to Decolonise Aid, Insight and Lessons from a Global Consultation"; Anti-Racist Cooperation, "Emerging Anti-Racist Practice for Canadian International Cooperation"; Khan et al., *White Saviorism in International Development*.
35 Sondarjee, *Perdre Le Sud. Décoloniser La Solidarité Internationale*; Khan et al.; Cole, "The White-Savior Industrial Complex."
36 Wright, *Utopies réelles*.
37 Easterly, *The Tyranny of Experts*, 254.

References

Anderl, Felix. *Broken Solidarities: How Open Global Governance Divides and Rules*. Bristol: Bristol University Press, 2022.

Anti-Racist Cooperation. *Emerging Anti-Racist Practice for Canadian International Cooperation*. Ottawa, Canada: Cooperation Canada et al., 2021.

Barisione, Mauro. "Framing a Deliberation. Deliberative Democracy and the Challenge of Framing Processes." *Journal of Public Deliberation* 8, no. 1 (2012): 1–22.

Bebbington, Anthony, David Lewis, Simon Batterbury, Elizabeth Olson, and M. Shameem Siddiqi. "Of Texts and Practices: Empowerment and Organisational Cultures in World Bank-Funded Rural Development Programmes." *The Journal of Development Studies* 43, no. 4 (May 2007): 597–621.

Best, Jacqueline. "Bureaucratic Ambiguity." *Economy and Society* 41, no. 1 (February 2012): 84–106.

Boas, Morten, and Desmond McNeill, eds. *Global Institutions and Development: Framing the World?* London: Routledge, 2004.

Bonal, Xavier. "Plus Ça Change . . . The World Bank Global Education Policy and the Post-Washington Consensus." *International Studies in Sociology of Education* 12, no. 1 (2002): 3–21.

Cammack, Paul. "What the World Bank Means by Poverty Reduction and Why It Matters." *New Political Economy* 9, no. 2 (2004): 189–211.

Cole, Teju. "The White-Savior Industrial Complex." *The Atlantic* (2012).

Dardot, Pierre, and Christian Laval. *La nouvelle raison du monde: essai sur la société néolibérale*. La decouverte poche 325. Paris: Éd. La Découverte, 2009.

Dardot, Pierre, and Christian Laval. "Néolibéralisme et subjectivation capitaliste." *Cités* 41, no. 1 (2010): 35.

Easterly, William. *The Tyranny of Experts: Economists, Dictators, and the Forgotten Rights of the Poor*. New York: Basic Books, Inc., 2014.

Ferguson, James. *The Anti-Politics Machine: "Development," Depoliticization, and Bureaucratic Power in Lesotho*. Cambridge [England] and New York: Cambridge University Press, 1990.

Foucault, Michel. "Governmentality." In *The Foucault Effect: Studies in Governmentality: With Two Lectures by and an Interview with Michel Foucault*, edited by Graham Burchell, Colin Gordon, and Peter Miller. Chicago: University of Chicago Press, 1978.

Freistein, Katja. "Effects of Indicator Use: A Comparison of Poverty Measuring Instruments at the World Bank." *Journal of Comparative Policy Analysis: Research and Practice* 18, no. 4 (August 7, 2016): 366–81.

Goldman, Michael. *Imperial Nature: The World Bank and Struggles for Social Justice in the Age of Globalization*. Yale Agrarian Studies Series. New Haven, CT and London: Yale University Press, 2005.

Handley, Karen, Andrew Sturdy, Robin Fincham, and Timothy Clark. "Within and beyond Communities of Practice: Making Sense of Learning through Participation, Identity and Practice." *Journal of Management Studies* 43, no. 3 (2006): 641–54.

Hildyard, N., P. Hegde, P. Wolvekamp, and S. Reddy. "Pluralism, Participation and Power: Joint Forest Management in India." In *Participation: The New Tyranny?* edited by Bill Cooke and Uma Kothari. London and New York: Zed Books, 2001.

Jackson, Jeffrey T. *The Globalizers: Development Workers in Action*. Johns Hopkins Studies in Globalization. Baltimore: Johns Hopkins University Press, 2005.

Khan, Themrise, Kanakulya Dickson, and Maïka Sondarjee, eds. *White Saviorism in International Development: Theories, Practices and Lived Experiences*. Cantley, Quebec: Daraja Press, 2023.

Kothari, Uma. "Authority and Expertise: The Professionalisation of International Development and the Ordering of Dissent." *Antipode* 37, no. 3 (June 2005): 425–46.

Kranke, Matthias, and David Yarrow. "The Global Governance of Systemic Risk: How Measurement Practices Tame Macroprudential Politics." *New Political Economy* 24, no. 6 (November 2, 2019): 816–32. https://doi.org/10.1080/13563467.2018.1545754.

LaRoche, Christopher David, and Simon Frankel Pratt. "Kenneth Waltz Is Not a Neorealist (and Why That Matters)." *European Journal of International Relations* 24, no. 1 (March 2018): 153–76. https://doi.org/10.1177/1354066117696561.

Lie, Jon Harald Sande. "Developmentality: Indirect Governance in the World Bank–Uganda Partnership." *Third World Quarterly* 36, no. 4 (April 3, 2015): 723–40.

Moore, David, ed. *The World Bank: Development, Poverty, Hegemony*. Scottsville, South Africa: University of KwaZulu-Natal Press, 2007.

Mosse, David. "Is Good Policy Unimplementable? Reflections on the Ethnography of Aid Policy and Practice." *Development and Change* 35, no. 4 (2004): 639–71.

Pateman, Carole. "APSA Presidential Address: Participatory Democracy Revisited." *Perspectives on Politics* 10, no. 1 (2012): 7–19.

Paul, Elizabeth. "Le Document de Strategie de Réduction de La Pauvreté (DSRP): Du Neuf à l'Horizon de l'Aide Au Développement?" In *Pauvreté et Hénémonismes: Les Sociétés Civiles Africaines Face Aux Ajustements Structurels de Type Nouveau*, edited by Jacques Habib, 221–64. Dakar: Aid Transparency/Oxfam America, 2002.

PeaceDirect, Adeso, Alliance for Peacebuilding, and WCAPS. *Time to Decolonise Aid, Insight and Lessons from a Global Consultation*. London: Peace Direct, 2021.

Probst, Gilbert, and Stefano Borzillo. "Why Communities of Practice Succeed and Why They Fail." *European Management Journal* 26, no. 5 (2008): 335–47.

Prügl, Elisabeth. "Neoliberalising Feminism." *New Political Economy* 20, no. 4 (2015): 614–31.

Rahnema, Majid. "Participatory Action Research: The Last Temptation of Saint Development." *Alternatives* 15 (1990): 199–226.

Roberts, Joanne. "Limits to Communities of Practice." *Journal of Management Studies* 43, no. 3 (2006): 623–39.

Ruckert, Arne. "Producing Neoliberal Hegemony? A Neo-Gramscian Analysis of the PRSP in Nicaragua." *Studies in Political Economy* 79 (2007): 91–118.

Sarfaty, Galit A. "Doing Good Business or Just Doing Good: Competing Human Rights Frameworks at the World Bank." In *The Intersection of Rights and Regulation: New Directions in Sociolegal Scholarship*, edited by Bronwen Morgan, 1st ed., 93–106. London and New York: Routledge, 2017. https://doi.org/10.4324/9781351146289.

Skovgaard, Jakob. *The Economisation of Climate Change: How the G20, the OECD and the IMF Address Fossil Fuel Subsidies and Climate Finance*. 1st ed. Cambridge University Press, 2021.

Sondarjee, Maïka. *Perdre Le Sud. Décoloniser La Solidarité Internationale*. Montréal: Écosociété, 2020.

Sondarjee, Maïka. "Change and Stability at the World Bank: Inclusive Practices and Neoliberal Technocratic Rationality." *Third World Quarterly* 42, no. 2 (2021): 348–65.

Vetterlein, Antje. "Seeing Like the World Bank on Poverty." *New Political Economy* 17, no. 1 (2012): 35–58.

Waltz, Kenneth N. *Theory of International Politics*. 1st ed. Boston, MA: McGraw-Hill, 1979.

Wenger, Etienne, Richard A. McDermott, and William Snyder. *Cultivating Communities of Practice: A Guide to Managing Knowledge*. Boston, MA: Harvard Business School Press, 2002.

Wright, Erik Olin. *Utopies réelles*. Paris: La Découverte, 2017.

Zack-Williams, Tunde, and Giles Mohan. "Editorial: Africa from SAPs to PRSP: Plus Ca Change Plus C'est La Meme Chose." *Review of African Political Economy* 32, no. 106 (2005): 501–3.

Index

Note: Page numbers in *italic* indicate a figure and page numbers in **bold** indicate a table on the corresponding page.

For Product Safety Concerns and Information please contact our EU representative GPSR@taylorandfrancis.com
Taylor & Francis Verlag GmbH, Kaufingerstraße 24, 80331 München, Germany

www.ingramcontent.com/pod-product-compliance
Ingram Content Group UK Ltd.
Pitfield, Milton Keynes, MK11 3LW, UK
UKHW022043061126
477531UK00009B/506
* 9 7 8 1 0 3 2 8 6 8 0 4 2 *